# DEBUTANTES

***When Glamour Was Born***

# DEBUT

RIZZOLI
NEW YORK
New York · Paris · London · Milan

# A N T E S

## *When Glamour Was Born*

DIANA OSWALD

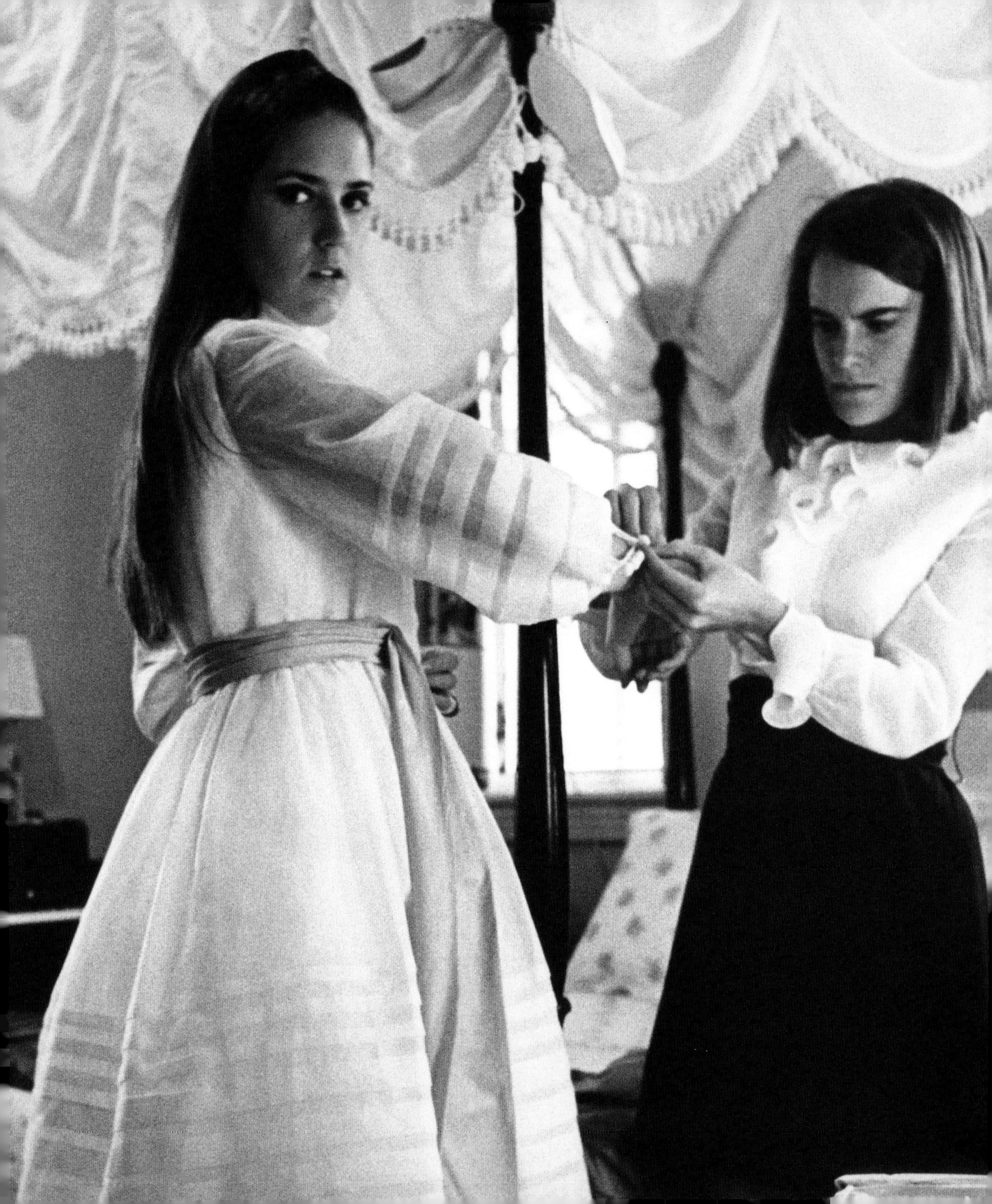

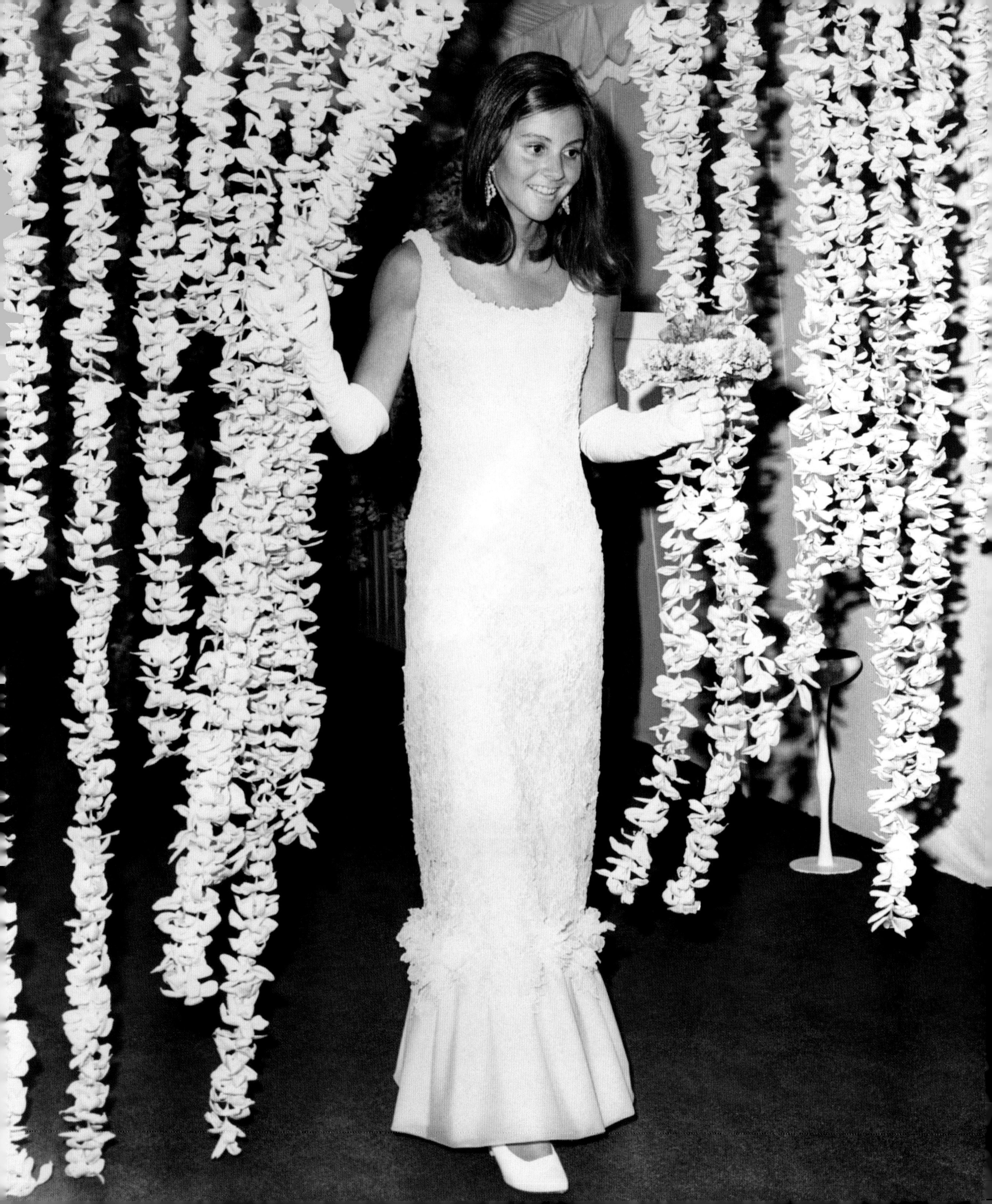

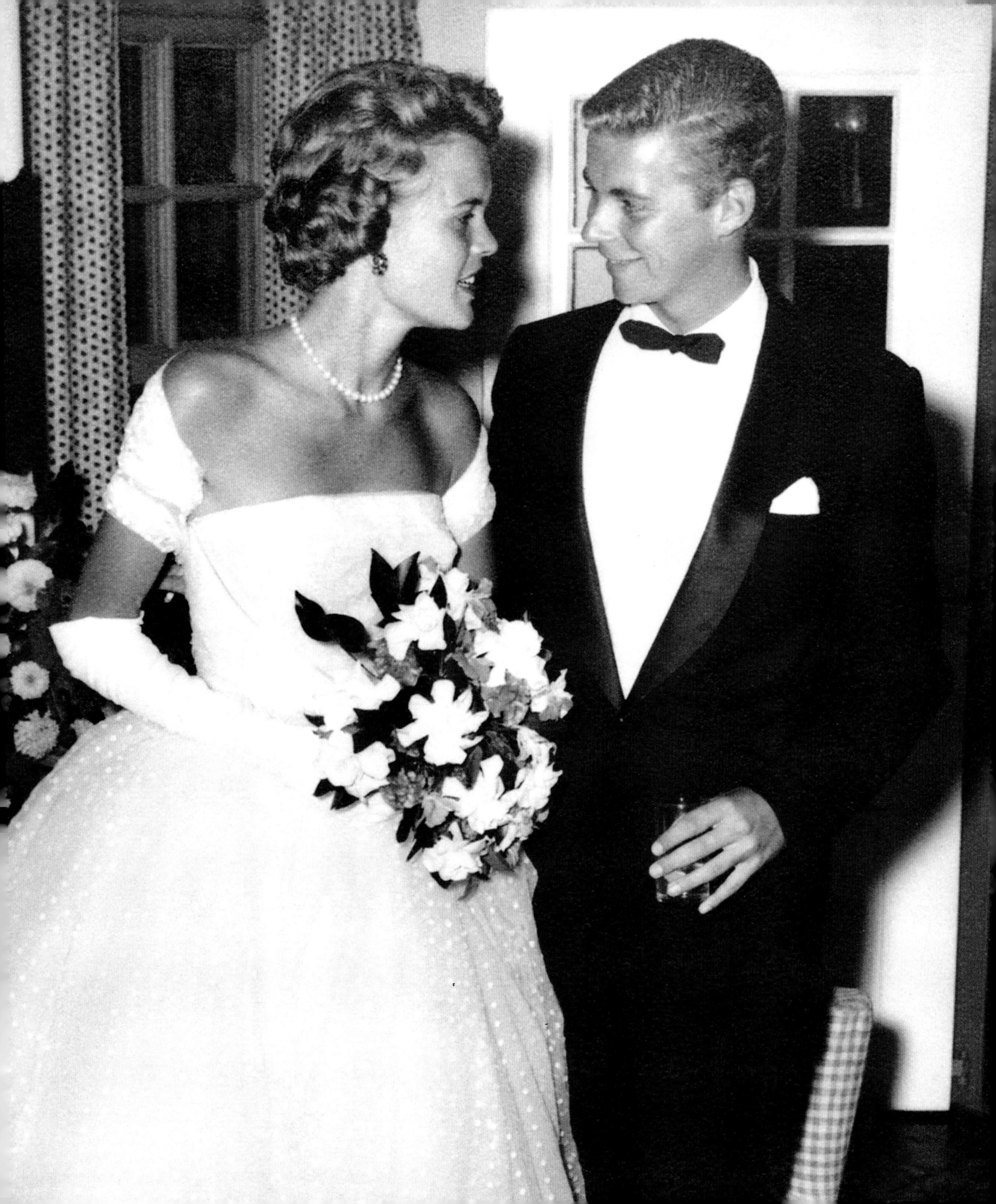

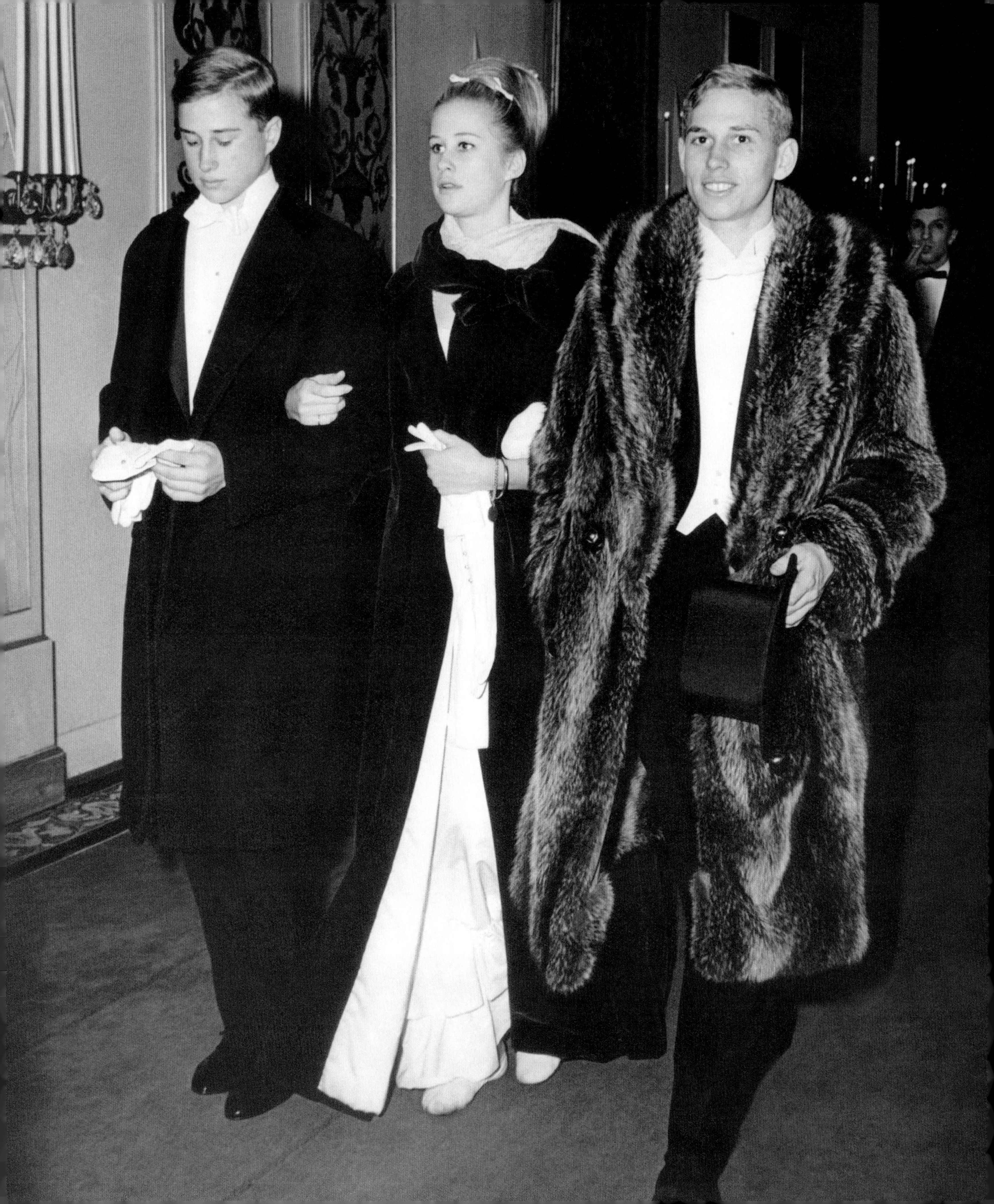

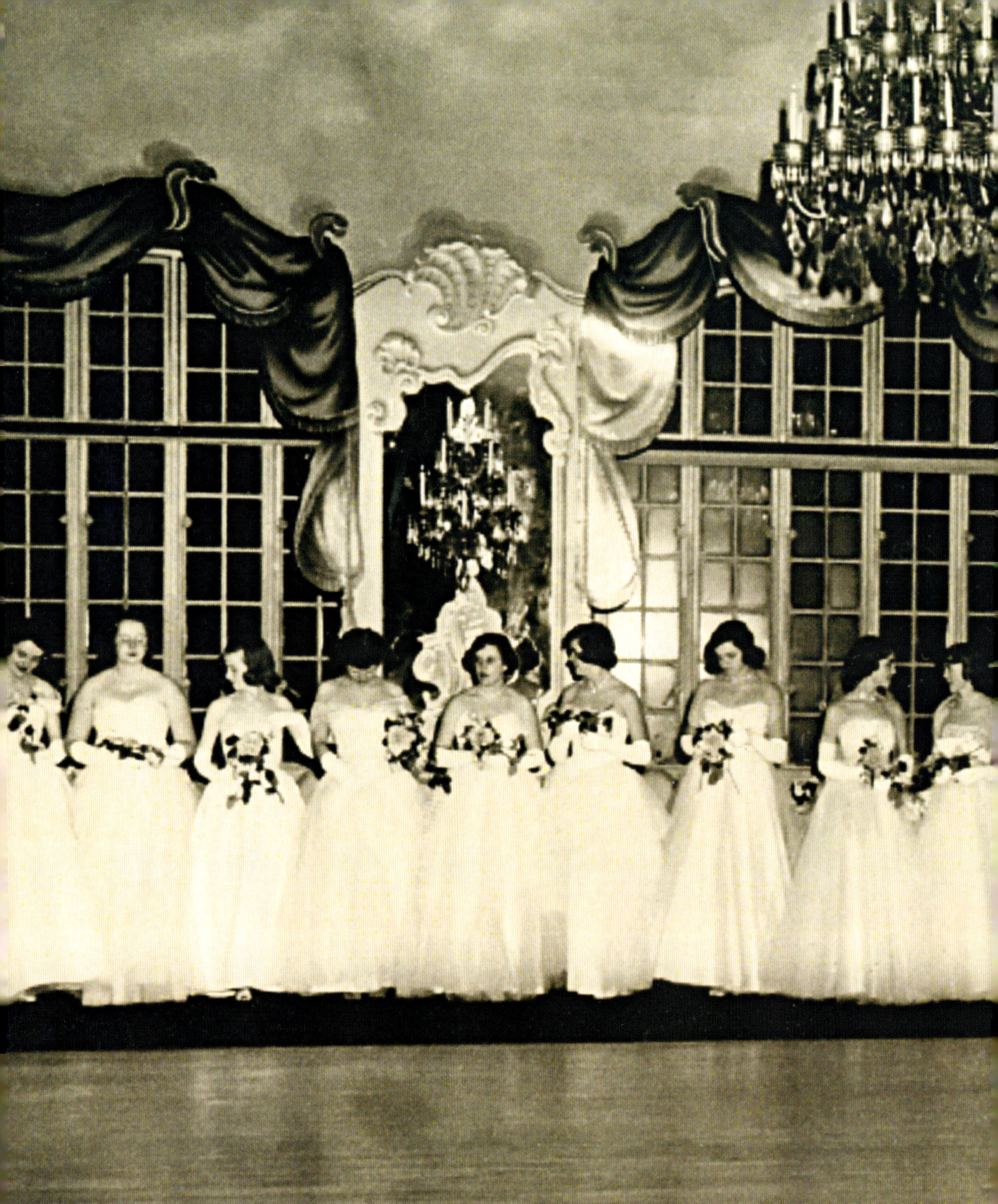

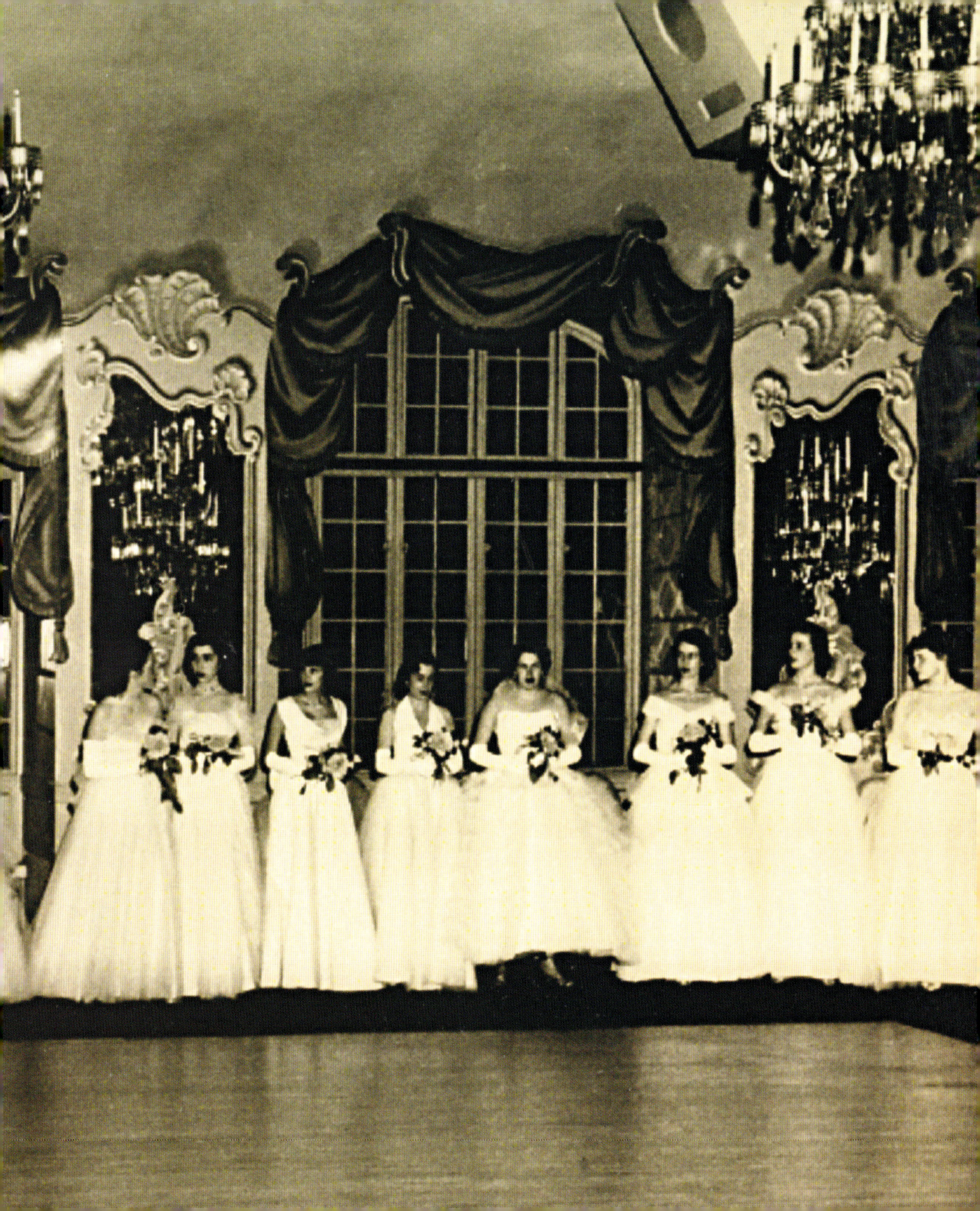

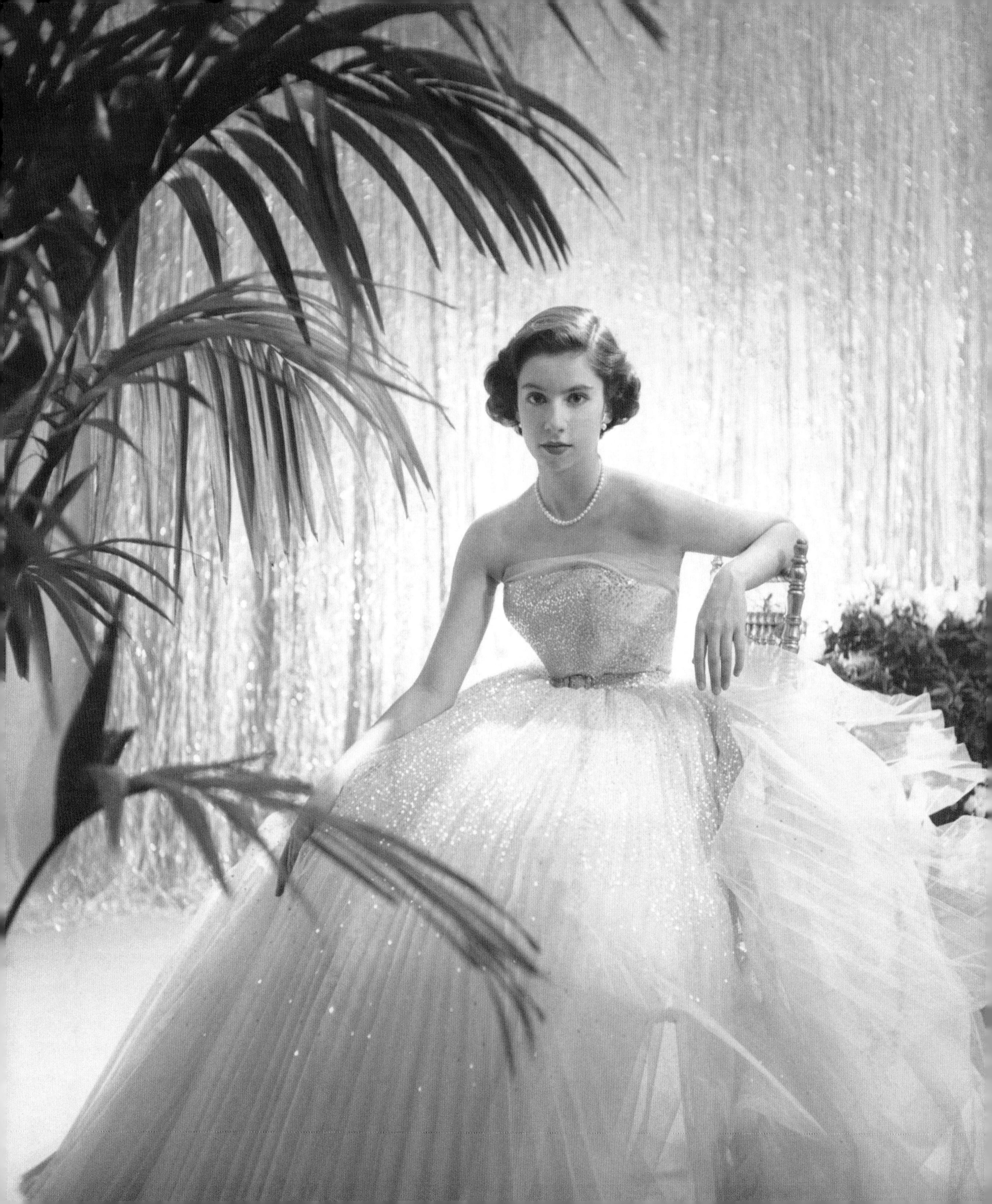

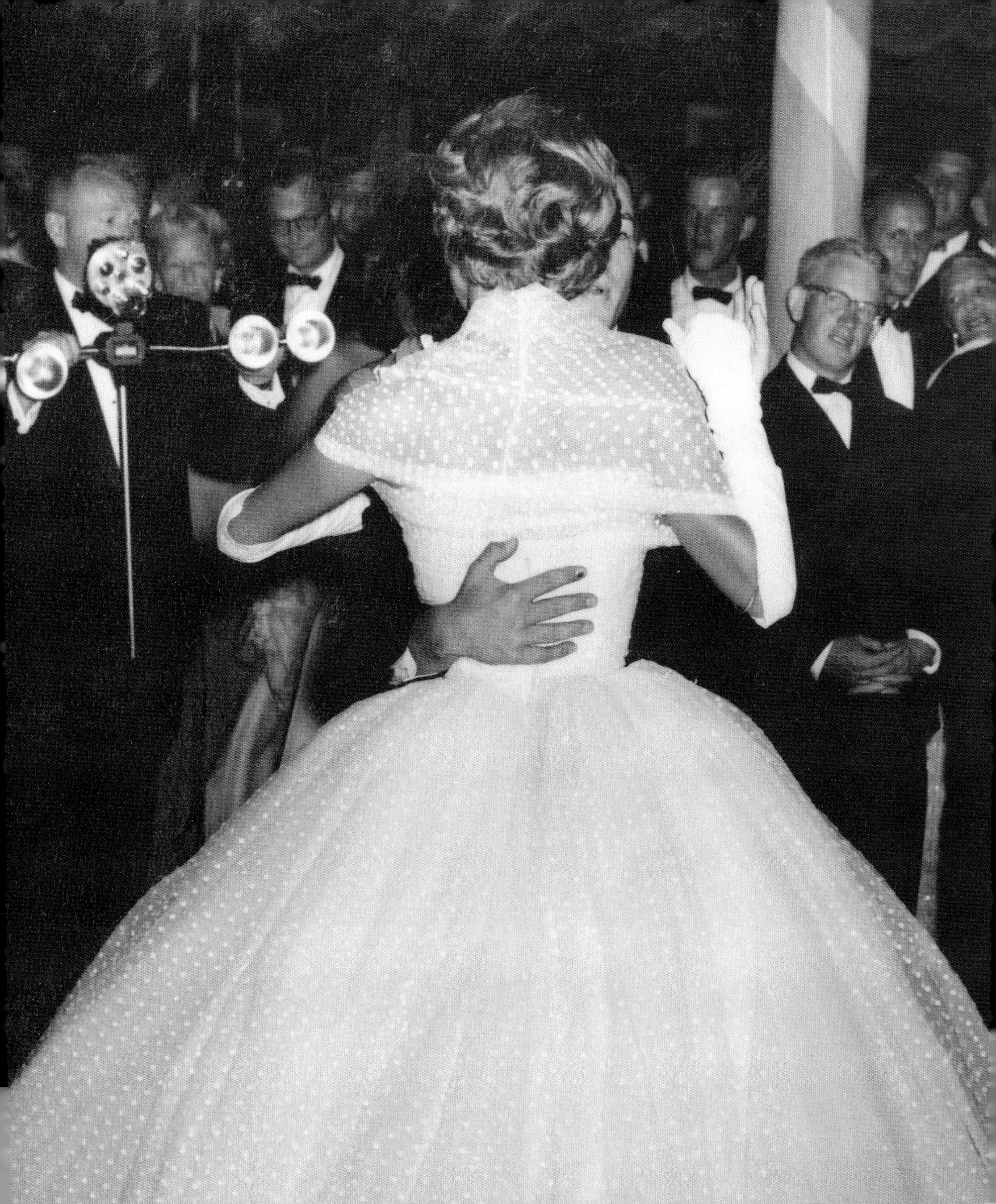

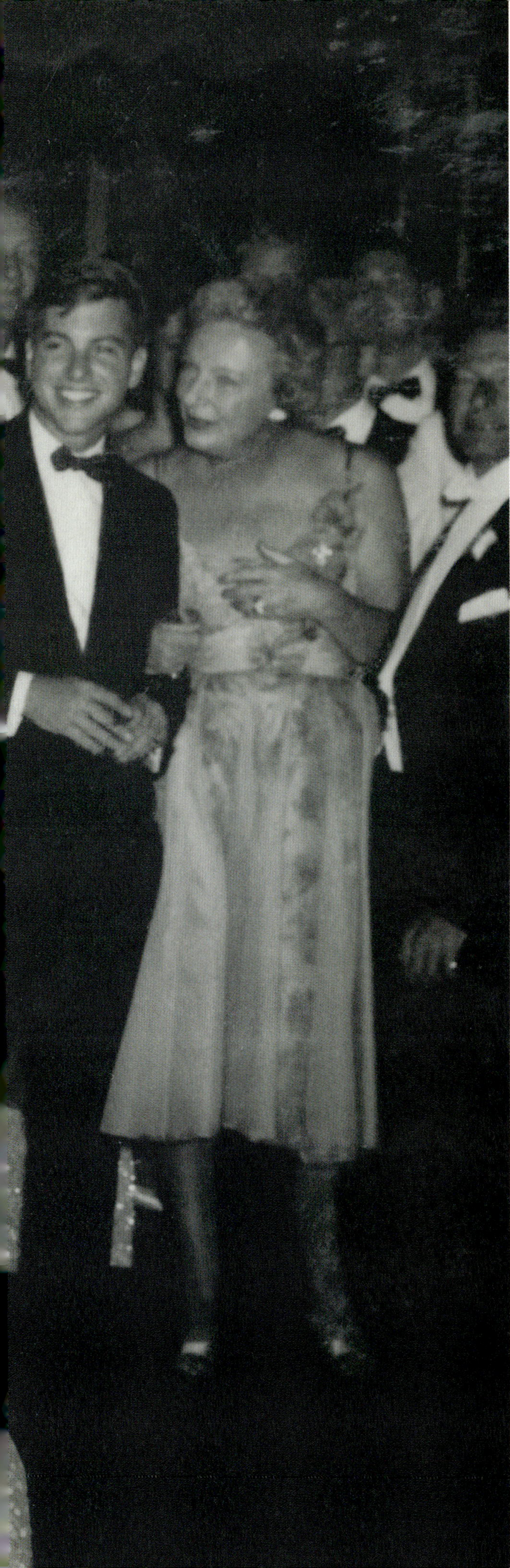

# CONTENTS

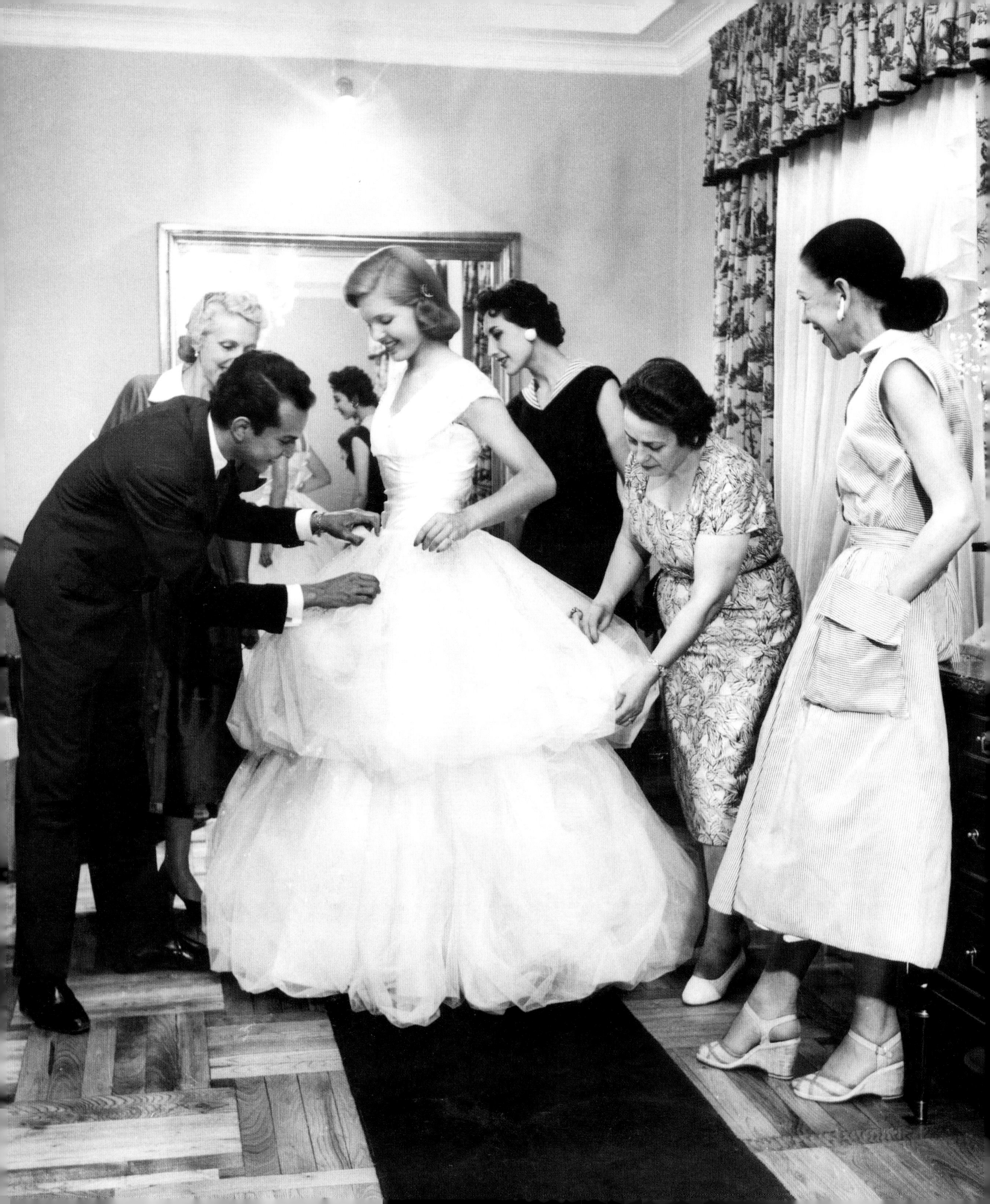

# FOREWORD

*Oscar de la Renta*

IN 1956, I DESIGNED A DRESS FOR the debut of Beatrice Lodge, the daughter of John A. Henry Cabot Lodge, a diplomat from one America's oldest families, who was at the time a U.S. Ambassador to Spain. I had made a dress that caught the eye of the Ambassador's wife Francesca, who asked if I would design something for her daughter Beatrice's coming out party at the American embassy in Madrid.

At the time, Spain was emerging into international acceptance under Francisco Franco. The significance of the moment was so resonant that a photo of Beatrice Lodge appeared on the cover of *Life* magazine in the white tulle double-tiered bubble dress I made for her. It was my first cover, and my big break in America. I was twenty-four; that cover changed the course of my life.

For over forty years I have had the incredibly good fortune of dressing women from all corners of life; society, Hollywood, politics—even royalty. Whether they are presented as a debutante to a daunting crowd of suitors, or have landed a role in the biggest film of the year, or are simply going to the theater, women want to feel beautiful when all eyes are upon them. Confidence can be difficult to come by and is by no means a guaranteed attribute. If somehow I've made that entrance into a room, or that walk down an aisle or even that short stroll to the front table at a restaurant a memorable one, then I suspect I have done my job.

Women have changed in unbelievable ways since I made the dress for Ms. Lodge. To "debut" then meant that a young woman was eligible to marry; the purpose of her coming out was to present her to young men and their families. Today women are much more in control of their destinies. They know that their femininity is a tremendous asset. The modern debutante is more concerned with the perfect dress than the perfect suitor. As a designer, there has never been a more exciting time to fulfill her dreams and aspirations.

PREVIOUS PAGES

Nicole du Pont. Wilmington Delaware, 1959.

OPPOSITE

Baroness Aino Bodisco (right) looks on as Beatrice Lodge (center) is fitted in a debutante gown by fashion designer Oscar De La Renta. 1956.

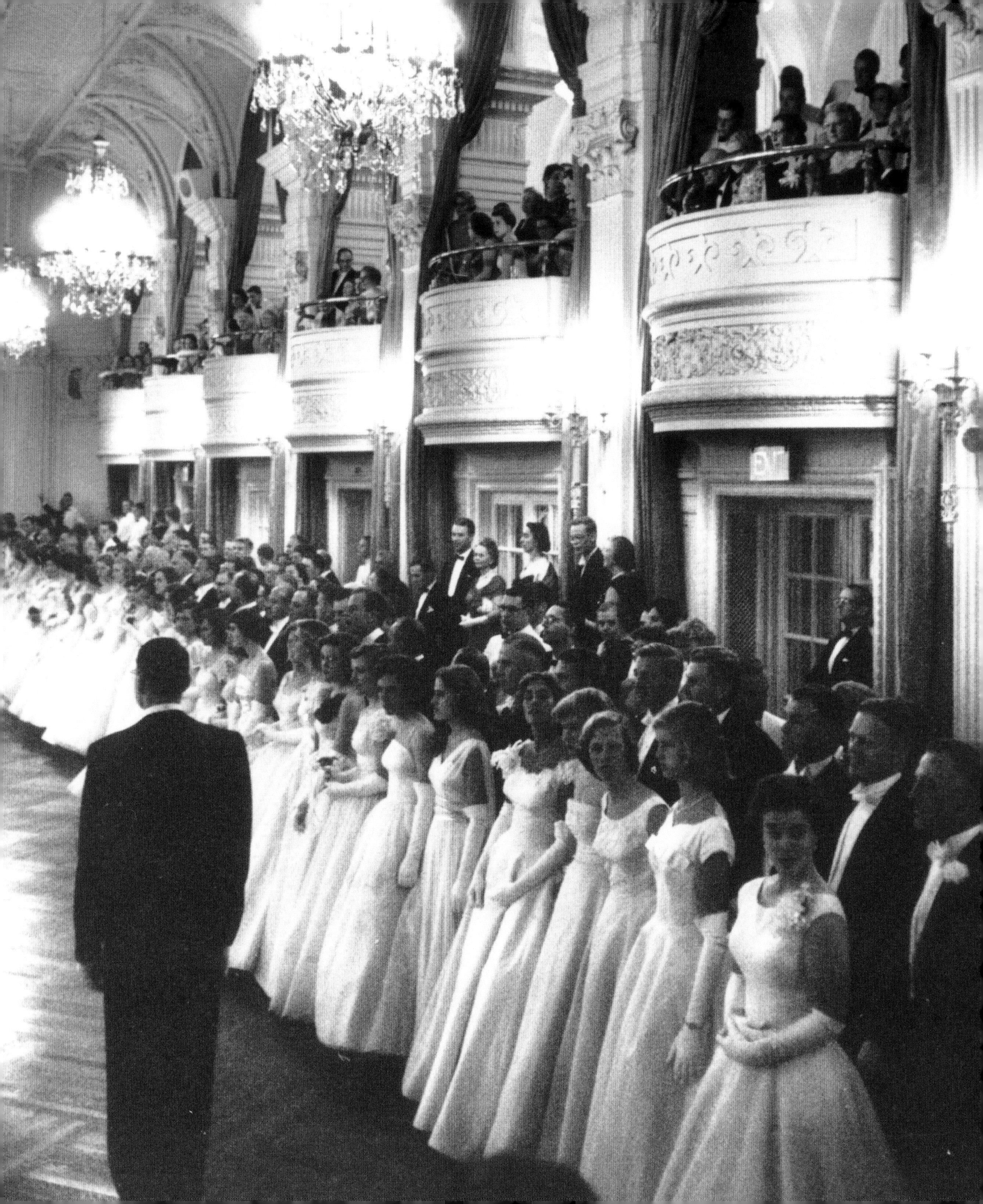

# A LITTLE HISTORY *of the* DEBUTANTE

*David Patrick Columbia*

IF YOU WERE BORN ANY TIME in the last century, it was easy to see debutantes as rich girls in their late teens got up in glamorous gowns and being given a big parties once a year, very often around the Christmas vacation or school holiday time. Photographed and written about in the daily papers—escorted in what looked like marching formation by young men wearing white tie and tails, sometimes one of those girls got so much press that she became a celebrity. Sometimes she even became a fairy-tale princess, like Cinderella. And sometimes her fairy tale was about a wayward heiress.

The tradition of the debutante is not a twentieth-century phenomenon in the West. It is an ancient and tribal custom, dating back further than the fourteen-year-old Cleopatra being prepared to take the throne of Egypt. It was a rite of passage, a ritual with a specific and practical use—finding husbands—and it had a lot riding on it. Those who didn't succeed often became governesses or nuns. Or spinsters.

The objective has always been the same: matchmaking. By the late seventeenth and early eighteenth centuries, the rich Europeans "civilized" the process by presenting the young lady to "society" in a decorous fashion that nonetheless was as clearly intended as if she were put on a sales block and sold to the highest bidder.

Debutantes, accompanied by their fathers, present themselves to the awaiting patronesses. The fathers bow and the daughters curtsey, representing their acceptance into society. The main ballroom of the Copley Plaza. Boston, 1958. Photo by Slim Aarons.

The French gave us the word, first applying it to the male—*debutant*, a boy coming of age and making his "debut" in some adult capacity, usually business, or the official confirmation of his place as a man in his society. For the female, they added the *e*—*debutante*—and a lot more work.

As recently as a century ago, girls in the upper classes did not go into business or any profession. Opportunity came only with a suitable husband. "Suitable" meant two things: money and virility to carry on the family name. Lacking the latter, the man could still be suitable if he had the financials. "Suitable" for a woman, however, meant fertility, a family name, *and* the money. Lacking fertility, the woman would be *not* suitable. Unless of course, she was an heiress.

Before this matchmaking process began in a girl's life, she was shielded and protected from opportunities to get to know or even meet members of the opposite sex who might eventually be considered suitable when she came of age. She was never alone in any social situation involving the opposite sex.

These matters were considered seriously and with due diligence (yes, *that* due diligence). The age of majority for the young lady was eighteen—the year a girl who was "eligible" would "come out," and be "introduced" to society. The process was completed in a final grand gesture—at the ball, like Cinderella—where she would make her splash, cast her impression; cut her groove, in today's parlance.

This was not an easy task for any girl to accomplish, although as it is in life, some girls had more of a knack for it than others. Nor was it available to just anyone. Besides the prerequisites of background and money, she also had to be acceptable in the eyes of the men and women who vetted the "eligibles." This put great pressure on her to succeed according to the wishes of others—such as social-climbing mothers or financially conscious fathers or grandfathers.

For young women of wealth and social stature in Europe in these earlier centuries, the ultimate "coming out" was a girl's presentation to the monarch. This was the final seal of approval. After that, a young girl's future was up to the gods (i.e., the bankers, the lawyers, and those dowagers who gave all those dinners and balls where young women could meet eligible young men).

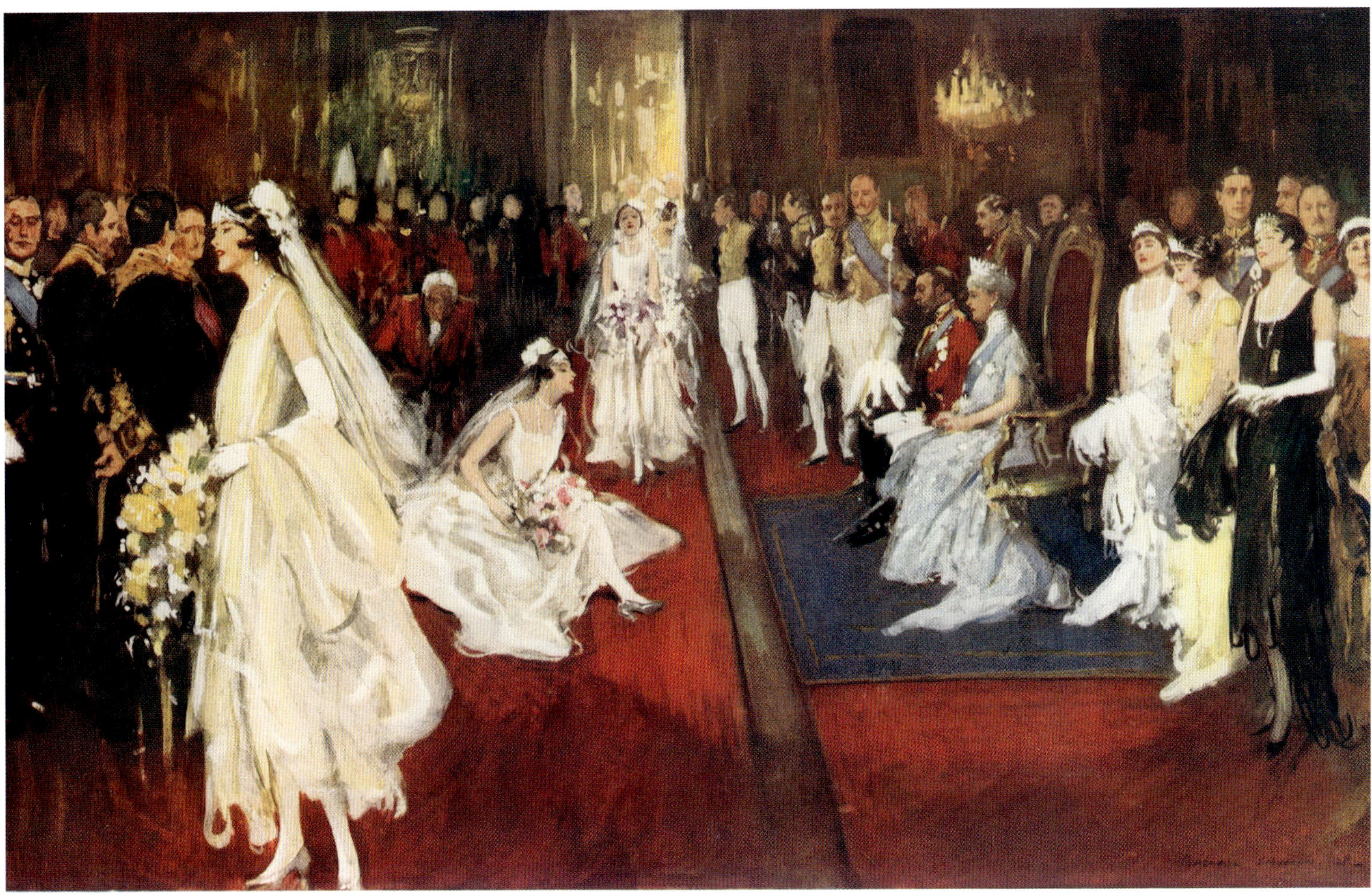

Debutantes clad in their finery curtsey to King George V and Queen Mary during a court presentation. London, 1928.

By the mid-nineteenth century, the Americans, having acquired substantial wealth and subsequent social power, began adapting the traditions of the Europeans and especially the British when it came to "presenting" a girl to society.

Conscious of their newness as a young country and a new society, the Americans were very strict about a young woman's conduct in polite society. Everyone followed the rules—at least on the surface. For women, there were no exceptions. Even when a woman brought property and assets to the marriage, everything she possessed, including herself, became the estate of the husband.

In America, everything changed after the Civil War ended. With the expansion of the railroads and the opening of the West, New York became the cultural and financial center. Although women were also becoming educated,

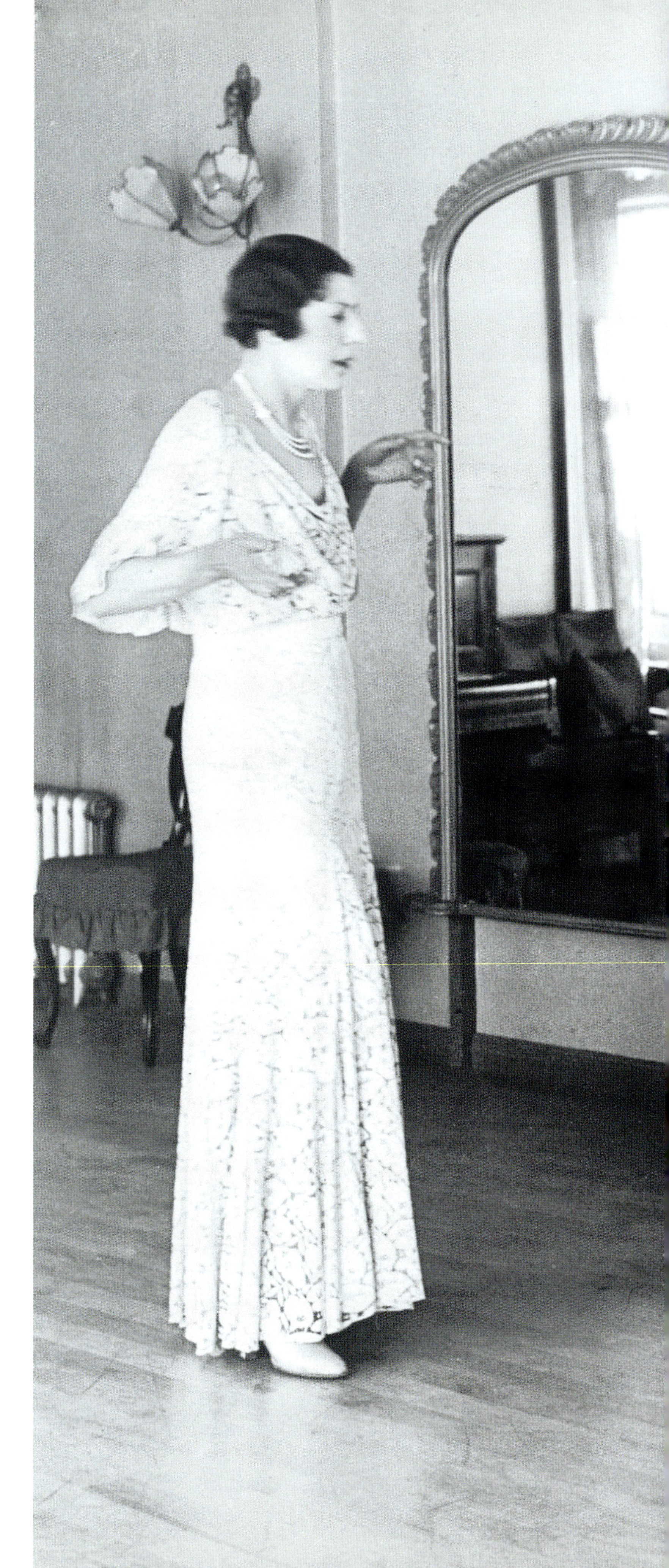

Pupils at Muriel Simmons School of Dancing receive instruction in order to perfect the stately bow of the debutante. London, 1933.

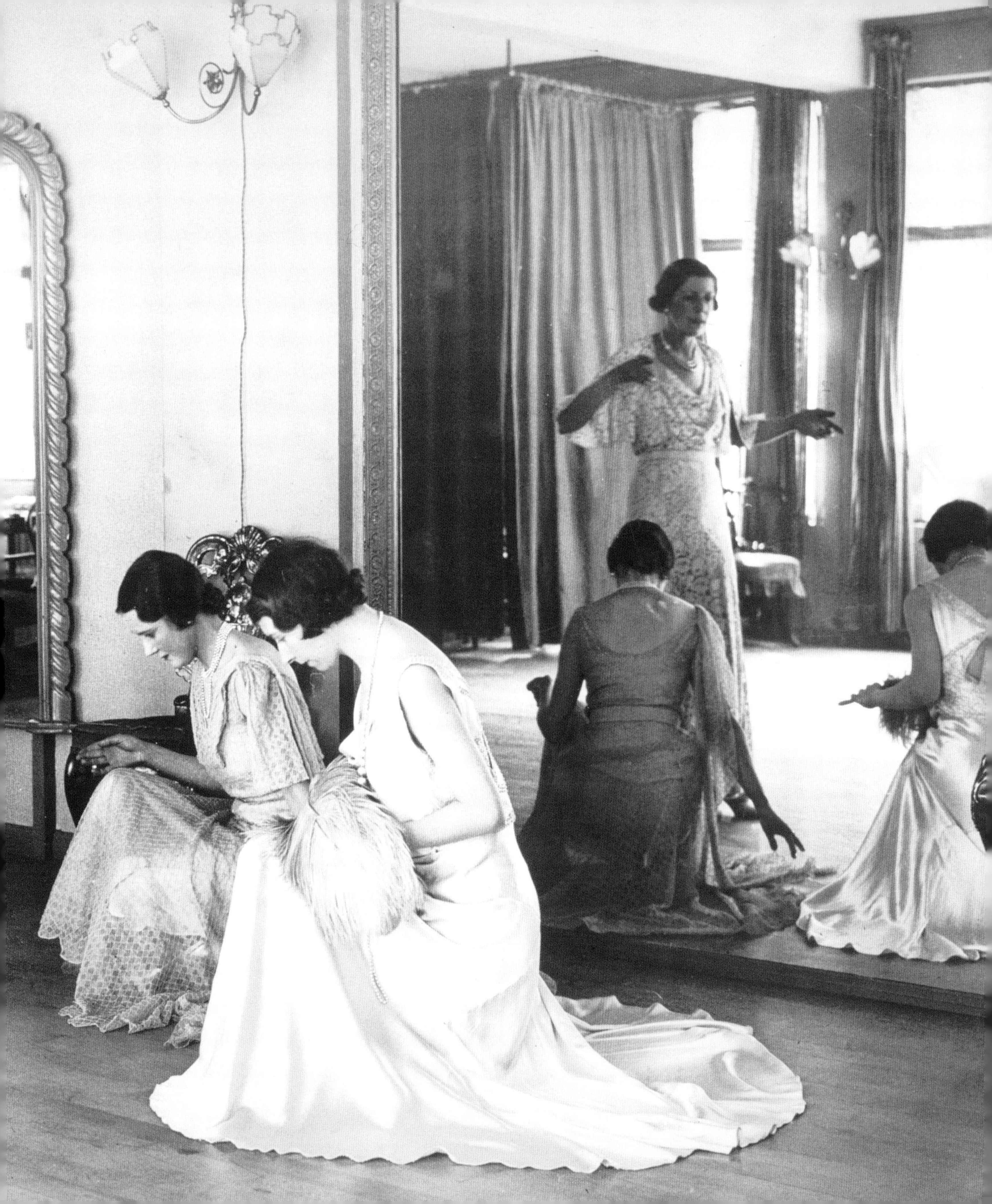

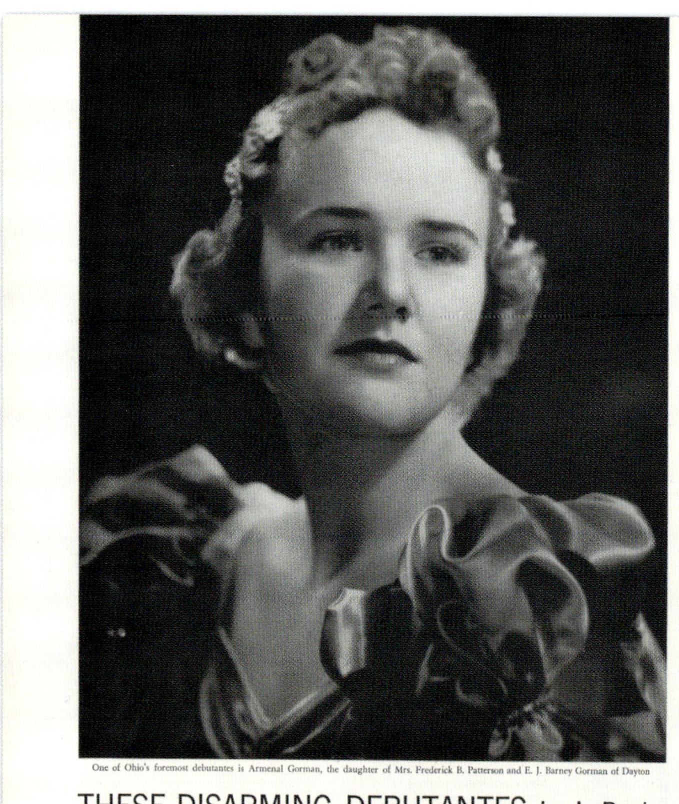

One of Ohio's foremost debutantes is Armenal Gorman, the daughter of Mrs. Frederick B. Patterson and E. J. Barney Gorman of Dayton

THESE DISARMING DEBUTANTES by LaRoche

REPORTS FROM OUT-OF-TOWN

POLLY UIHLEIN of Milwaukee knows more about the taste in jewelry, gents, and junkets displayed by Mary Robins of Buffalo than she does about a last season's debutante who happens to live next door. A kind of cosmopolitan camaraderie binds together a season's debutantes no matter how far apart they live. During their coming-out year they see each other at proms and football games, across the handle bars at Bermuda (their pet resort), and in dressing-rooms during rounds of parties. They exchange ideas and beaux, and learn so much about each other it isn't funny.

A popular, energetic girl who has gone to Farmington, Westover, or Foxcroft can garner enough invitations to make a grand tour of the major debutante festivities from Lake Minnetonka to Beacon Street.

But not to miss a trick her first season, a girl must take in the "Big Three" of the debutante calendar. These are not Harvard, Yale, and Princeton, but St. Louis' Veiled Prophet's Ball, Baltimore's Bachelors' Cotillon, and Charleston's St. Cecilia Ball, conveniently date-lined for October, December, and January.

The Veiled Prophet's Ball is the climax of Veiled Prophet's Week, which was started in 1878 by some St. Louis businessmen as a sort of Mardi Gras promotion scheme. It is a colossal affair, staged in the Auditorium with plenty of hocus-pocus.

68

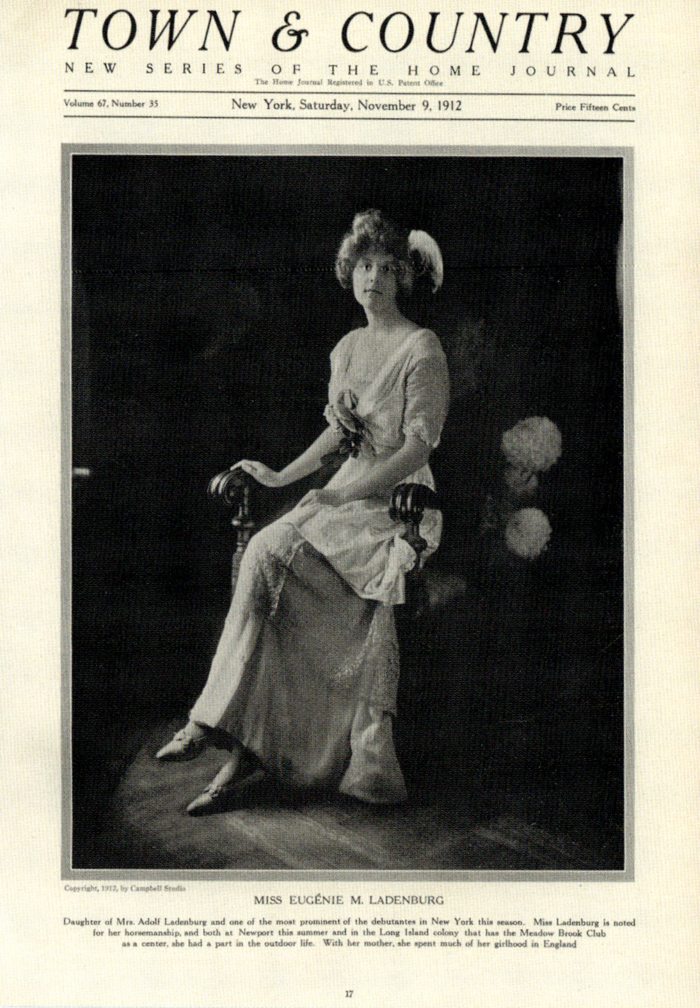

TOWN & COUNTRY

NEW SERIES OF THE HOME JOURNAL

The Home Journal Registered in U.S. Patent Office

Volume 67, Number 35 New York, Saturday, November 9, 1912 Price Fifteen Cents

Copyright, 1912, by Campbell Studio

MISS EUGÉNIE M. LADENBURG

Daughter of Mrs. Adolf Ladenburg and one of the most prominent of the debutantes in New York this season. Miss Ladenburg is noted for her horsemanship, and both at Newport this summer and in the Long Island colony that has the Meadow Brook Club as a center, she had a part in the outdoor life. With her mother, she spent much of her girlhood in England

17

ABOVE, LEFT

"Disarming debutantes." As seen in *Town & Country*, 1937.

ABOVE, RIGHT

Debutante Eugenie M. Ladenburg was considered one of the most prominent debs of her day. Daughter of Mr. and Mrs. Adolf Ladenburg of the banking house of Ladenburg, Thalmann and Company, the Ladenburgs were well known socially in both New York and Newport. As seen in *Town & Country*, 1912.

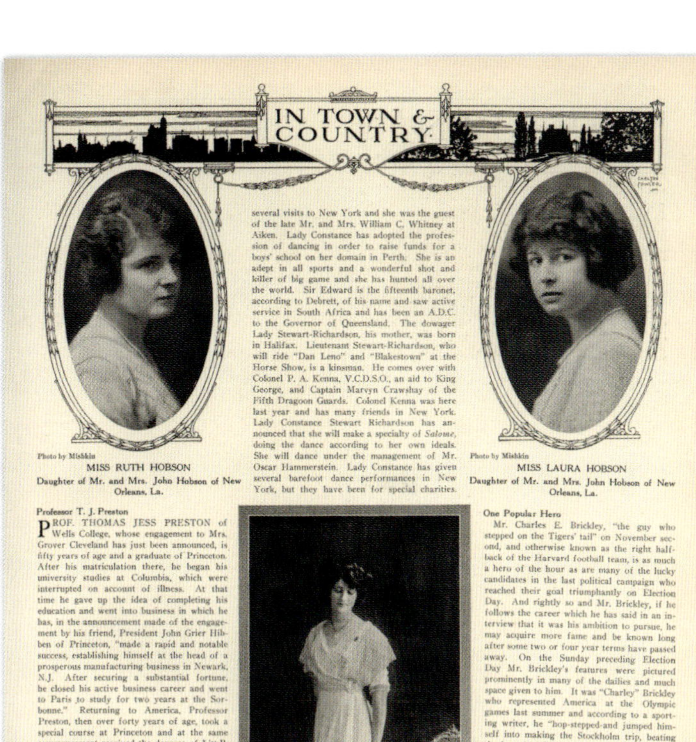

IN TOWN & COUNTRY

Photo by Mishkin

MISS RUTH HOBSON

Daughter of Mr. and Mrs. John Hobson of New Orleans, La.

Photo by Mishkin

MISS LAURA HOBSON

Daughter of Mr. and Mrs. John Hobson of New Orleans, La.

**Professor T. J. Preston**

PROF. THOMAS JESS PRESTON of Wells College, whose engagement to Mrs. Grover Cleveland has just been announced, is fifty years of age and a graduate of Princeton. After his matriculation there, he began his university studies at Columbia, which were interrupted on account of illness. At that time he gave up the idea of completing his education and went into business in which he has, in the announcement made of the engagement by his friend, President John Grier Hibben of Princeton, "made a rapid and notable success, establishing himself at the head of a prosperous manufacturing business in Newark, N.J. After securing a substantial fortune, he closed his active business career and went to Paris to study for two years at the Sorbonne." Returning to America, Professor Preston, then over forty years of age, took a special course at Princeton and at the same commencement received the degrees of Litt.B. and M.A., a very unique attainment. Then he went abroad again as Fellow of the American School of Classical Study at Rome and later won the Fellowship of the Archaeological Institute of America. After taking his degree of Doctor of Philosophy at Princeton, he was called to the chair of Archaeology and the History of Art at Wells College. Mrs. Cleveland was graduated from Wells and she has always been interested in the studies of which Professor Preston is the exponent. Mrs. Cleveland, who was a beautiful girl and young matron, is still an extremely handsome woman. Simple and gracious, she won the hearts of all Americans during the two terms of her husband at the White House.

**Sir Edward Austin Stewart-Richardson**

This is the third visit of Sir Edward Austin Stewart-Richardson to America and he is now at the St. Regis waiting the arrival of his wife, who will be remembered in New York as Lady Constance Mackenzie, daughter of the late Earl of Cromartie and a young woman who was the pioneer of barefoot dancing and who is now on the stage. Lady Constance Mackenzie, as she is known everywhere, made several visits to New York and she was the guest of the late Mr. and Mrs. William C. Whitney at Aiken. Lady Constance has adopted the profession of dancing in order to raise funds for a boys' school on her domain in Perth. She is an adept in all sports and a wonderful shot and killer of big game and she has hunted all over the world. Sir Edward is the fifteenth baronet, according to Debrett, of his name and saw active service in South Africa and has been an A.D.C. to the Governor of Queensland. The dowager Lady Stewart-Richardson, his mother, was born in Halifax. Lieutenant Stewart-Richardson, who will ride "Dan Leno" and "Blakestown" at the Horse Show, is a kinsman. He comes over with Colonel P. A. Kenna, V.C.D.S.O., an aid to King George, and Captain Marvyn Crawshay of the Fifth Dragoon Guards. Colonel Kenna was here last year and has many friends in New York. Lady Constance Stewart Richardson has announced that she will make a specialty of *Salome*, doing the dance according to her own ideals. She will dance under the management of Mr. Oscar Hammerstein. Lady Constance has given several barefoot dance performances in New York, but they have been for special charities.

Copyright, 1912, by Marceau

MISS GROVENE VAIL CONVERSE

The débutante daughter of Mrs. L. Grovene Converse of New York, a granddaughter of Theodore Vail and of Edmund Converse, of Boston and a relative of Mr. E. C. Converse of Greenwich, Conn.

**One Popular Hero**

Mr. Charles E. Brickley, "the guy who stepped on the Tigers' tail" on November second, and otherwise known as the right halfback of the Harvard football team, is as much a hero of the hour as are many of the lucky candidates in the last political campaign who reached their goal triumphantly on Election Day. And rightly so and Mr. Brickley, if he follows the career which he has said in an interview that it was his ambition to pursue, he may acquire more fame and be known long after some two or four year terms have passed away. On the Sunday preceding Election Day Mr. Brickley's features were pictured prominently in many of the dailies and much space given to him. It was "Charley" Brickley who represented America at the Olympic games last summer and according to a sporting writer, he "hop-stepped-and jumped himself into making the Stockholm trip, beating the best America could produce in that specialty at the Harvard stadium tryouts." At the Olympiad, Brickley finished second to Platt Adams in the hop-step-and jump event. The hero of the Harvard-Princeton game was born in Boston, Mass., and he played on the Everett High School eleven and then on the Exeter College team when he was preparing for Harvard. Brickley aspires to become an all-around athlete and he is also a star on the baseball diamond, having captained the Harvard freshmen nine last spring. One hundred and eighty-six pounds is the figure at which he tips the scales and he is five feet eight inches high.

**The New British Ambassador**

Sir Cecil Arthur Spring-Rice, the successor of the Honorable James Bryce, the British Ambassador at Washington, who has resigned his position, is well known in this country. During the term of the late Lord Pauncefote at Washington, he was Third Secretary and is an intimate friend of Colonel Roosevelt. Now he is British Minister to Sweden, to which post he was appointed in 1908, after he had served some years as British Minister to Persia. The new Ambassador is fifty years old.

17

IN TOWN & COUNTRY

Photo by Mishkin

MISS SUSANNE E. WARREN

The débutante-daughter of Mr. and Mrs. Charles Elliot Warren, of New York, and a granddaughter of Professor George William Warren of Columbia University

Photo by Boissonnas & Taponier

MISS EDITH LOGAN

The débutante-daughter of Mrs. John A. Logan, a granddaughter of General Logan, and a sister of Mrs. Henri St. Paul de Sincay of Brussels

**A Military Secretary**

Governor-elect William Sulzer has appointed Captain E. Gilbert Schermerhorn as his military secretary. Captain Schermerhorn is a member of the Seventh Regiment Veteran Association, the Thirteenth Regiment Veteran Association and the One Hundred and Twelfth Regiment Veteran Association. He also belongs to the Military Society and the Veteran Corps of Artillery, 1812; Sons of the Revolution, Society of Colonial Wars, St. Nicholas Society and the Holland Society. Captain Schermerhorn is the son of Mr. and Mrs. George Stevens Shermerhorn and his mother was a Miss Gilbert.

**A Possible Ambassador**

There have been suggestions that one of the new ambassadors to be appointed by President-elect Wilson will be Mr. Frederick Courtland Penfield and there could not be selected a gentleman more fitted to occupy such a position. Mr. Penfield is not only a diplomat of experience—having been United States Vice Consul-general at London in 1885 and Diplomatic Agent and Consul-general to Egypt with rank of Minister Resident in 1893 until 1897—but he is a writer of international reputation and a savant. Like President-elect Wilson, he is a Princeton man and after his graduation there had a thorough schooling in journalism on the editorial staff of the Hartford *Courant*. Mr. Penfield has received a number of decorations from different sovereigns, including the Sultan of Turkey and the Khedive of Egypt, the "Palmes Academique" and the Cross of the Legion of Honour from the French government and Servian and Russian orders. Among his books are "East of Suez" and "Present Day Egypt" and a later one on Eastern and Oriental travels. In 1908 Mr. Penfield married Mrs. Anne Weightman Walker of Philadelphia and they make their winter residence at 787 Fifth Avenue, where they entertain handsomely and they always make a long voyage in the East during the spring, taking with them a party of friends. Mr. and Mrs. Penfield have large wealth and social position.

**Count Guy de Lasteyrie**

THE fiancé of Miss Constance Warren, who arrived here this past week from Paris, is a son of the Marquis and Marquise de Lasteyrie and is thirty-three years old, good-looking and blond. In November, 1900, he was enlisted for a period of three years in the Twenty-ninth Regiment of Dragoons and is said to be a splendid horseman. It was his duty to break the hardest horses and he won a great reputation for his prowess all over the Continent. After a year of service, he was elevated to the rank of Brigadier, but he retired from the army after an accident caused by a fall from a horse. As already stated sometime ago, he is a descendant of the famous Lafayette. His mother was an English-woman.

**A New Master of the Household**

It is of interest to many Americans that the new Master of the Household to King George will be Sir Derek-Keppel, who has been equerry in ordinary to the King when he was Prince of Wales. Sir Derek is a brother of Mr. George Keppel, whose wife was one of the prominent figures in society during the last reign and who has last spring made a triumphant re-entry into London society. The new Master of the Household is a brother of the present Earl of Albemarle and he married a daughter of Lord Suffield. A sister is Lady Susan Townley whose husband was connected some years ago with the British embassy in Washington and who herself was one of the most popular hostesses there, during the term of her husband's service. The duties of the Master of the Household are varied and are principally concerned in the charge of the accounts and oversight of the servants.

Photo by Mishkin

MISS JESSON THAYER

The débutante-daughter of Mr. and Mrs. Benjamin B. Thayer of New York who will be presented at a reception on December sixth

**Diplomatic Changes**

On the eve of a new administration changes in the diplomatic corps by the party going out of power seem futile, but Civil Service these days manages to make a proper adjustment. President Taft has recently done some shifting and made some new appointments. In the first place he has changed the rank of Mr. Larz Anderson from Minister to Ambassador and appointed him to Tokio, which has recently been made vacant by Mr. Charles Page Bryan, who arrived in America recently and who has been a victim to ill health. Mr. Larz Anderson comes from historic stock in Ohio and he married the daughter of the late Commodore Perkins, U.S.N., of Boston. Until his appointment to Belgium, Mr. Anderson lived in Washington, D.C., where he and Mrs. Anderson were lavish in entertaining. During the time that they have been in Brussels they have interested themselves in many plans of a philanthropic nature such as a reading room and library for American students and they have kept open house. Mrs. Anderson was heiress to a large fortune.

17

ABOVE, LEFT

Miss Grovene Vail Converse (bottom) was a closely watched debutante in her day. Daughter of Mrs. L. Grovene Converse of New York, Miss Converse was presented with a group of the most noted debs of the season. Mrs L. Grovene Converses gave a tea for her daughter, to which *The New York Times* declared, " . . . [at that tea] many buds blossomed in to full blown social flowers." As seen in *Town & Country*, 1912.

ABOVE, RIGHT

Debutante Suzanne E. Warren (top, left) was presented to society in New York. Her grandfather, Professor George William Warren was one of the best-known Episcopal musicians of his time. As seen in *Town & Country*, 1925.

with at least some schooling—no matter their class—marriage remained the only viable option for a girl's secure future.

The formal practice of finding a suitable husband for a young and innocent—and naïve—lady took hold in both the industrial North as well as the antebellum South. This was called the "coming out."

Theirs was a world that moved very slowly compared to today. The telephone and the automobile had yet to be developed. Communication was face-to-face, or via letter written and delivered by messenger or post. Travel was by horse, by boat, or by foot. Socializing was limited to events, visits, and letters, and was usually local.

The coming out of a young lady to society began with a flurry of activity of meeting people. The debutante—*always* chaperoned (usually by her mother)—called on the matrons who presided over the social life. There were two social seasons—winter, stretching from mid-November through Lent, and summer.

In New York, a heavy schedule of formal calling, along with afternoon teas and opera going—also part of the process—required great attention to personal detail. First there was the appropriate wardrobe. There were exclusive formal dances, known as Patriarchs' balls, and subscription dances—attendance by invitation only, where the debutante would make an "appearance." A girl had to seriously prepare for these by taking dancing lessons to learn the complicated and numerous steps required in a cotillion. There, she would hopefully make a good impression.

The stiff and scrupulous traditions that young women of society faced during the Gilded Age, the late Victorian era, got its first inkling of "change" through a force of personality named Alva Erskine Smith. Alva, born in Mobile, Alabama, to a Southern businessman and his wife in the early 1850s, and her family summered in Newport. They moved to New York when she was a small child and on to Paris, where she grew up. When she was a teenager, she met and married young William Kissam Vanderbilt, the second son of William H., a grandson of Commodore Cornelius, and heir to the greatest fortune in the world.

Debutante Elsie Benkard wears a sleeveless dress with a bateau neckline and ruffled tulle skirt. Her mother, Mrs. Lewis Stuyvesant and her late father, J. Philip Benkard were prominent in New York society. New York, 1925.

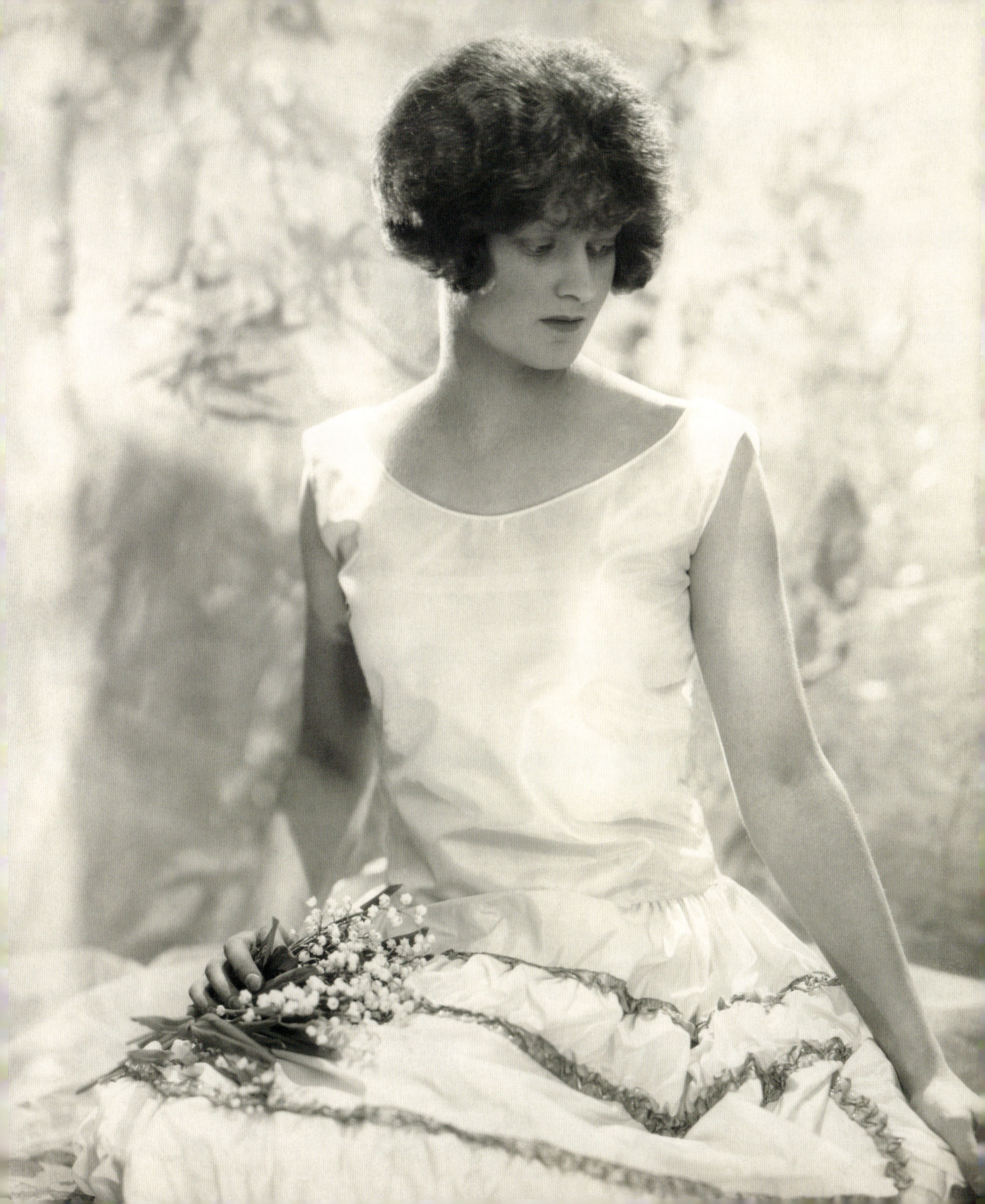

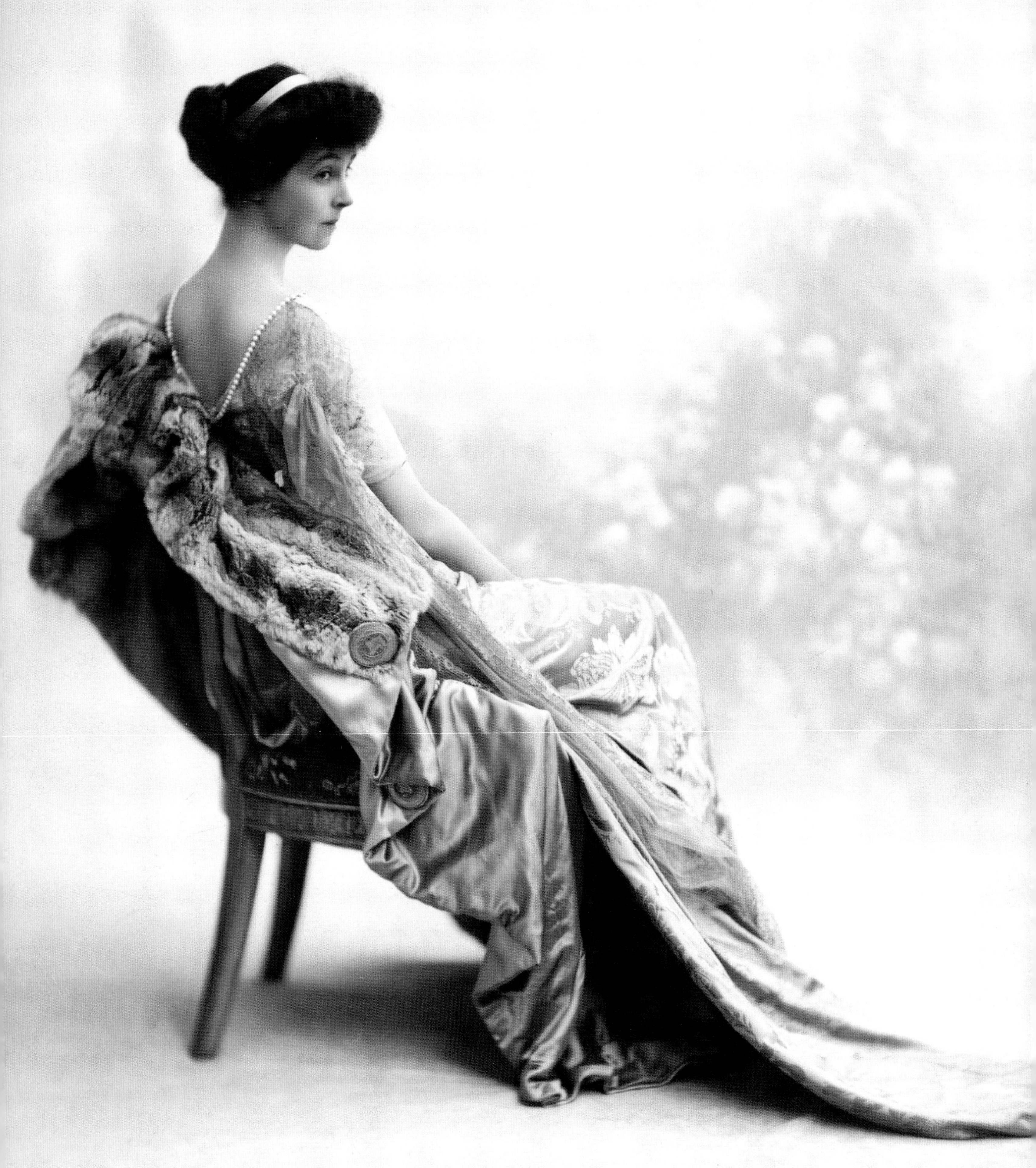

When Alva and Willie K.'s firstborn, a tall and slender daughter named Consuelo, was sixteen, Alva took her to Europe to find her a husband among the royalty and aristocracy. There, Mother beat the competition by having her daughter come out a year earlier than other young women of her age. Rich American girls were considered a good bet for a landed and/or titled European aristocrats saddled with debts and empty coffers.

In her memoir, *The Glitter and the Gold* (Harper & Brothers, 1952), Consuelo Vanderbilt Balsan referred to her "coming out" as exhausting—lasting weeks, with trans-Atlantic voyages and trips from London to Paris for fittings, followed by all the social events including the actual debut (which took place in London).

Mother's plan to nab a king, a prince, or a high-ranking duke succeeded. When the girl was introduced to dance with the 9th Duke of Marlborough, Charles Spencer-Churchill, she had no idea (although he did) that the plan had already been set in motion. With the family not exactly penniless but with a big overhead, the duke's marriage contract would bring much-needed millions into the Churchill family coffers. And so, at age eighteen, the year her friends were coming out, Consuelo Vanderbilt was forced against her wishes to marry, and she became the Duchess of Marlborough.

Although the alliance was a great social coup for her mother—an American girl marrying into British aristocracy—the marriage was a loveless one. The bride produced an heir (and a spare), but after several years, the couple separated.

*The Glitter and the Gold* is the classic drama in the history of debutantes—a domineering, social-climbing mother uses her daughter to secure social prestige. Alva Vanderbilt never questioned her own ambitions. She felt the girl's future was none of the girl's business, and she wasn't the only one who felt the same way. But years later, after Consuelo had divorced the duke and married Jacques Balsan—with whom she lived happily for the rest of his life—Alva confided that her early demands had been unfair. Alva by then had moved on to become a leading suffragette. Ironically, Consuelo, remarried happily and living as a woman of great independent wealth, admitted that her mother's ambition had provided her a very interesting life.

OPPOSITE

The Duchess of Marlborough, born Consuelo Vanderbilt to William K. Vanderbilt and his wife, Alva. 1911.

FOLLOWING PAGES

The Waldorf-Astoria Hotel opened in 1931 and played host to exceptionally lavish parties, even boasting its own in-house professional hostess, Elsa Maxwell. Dinner dance for debutante Jane Aldred at the Waldorf-Astoria Hotel seen here. New York, 1934.

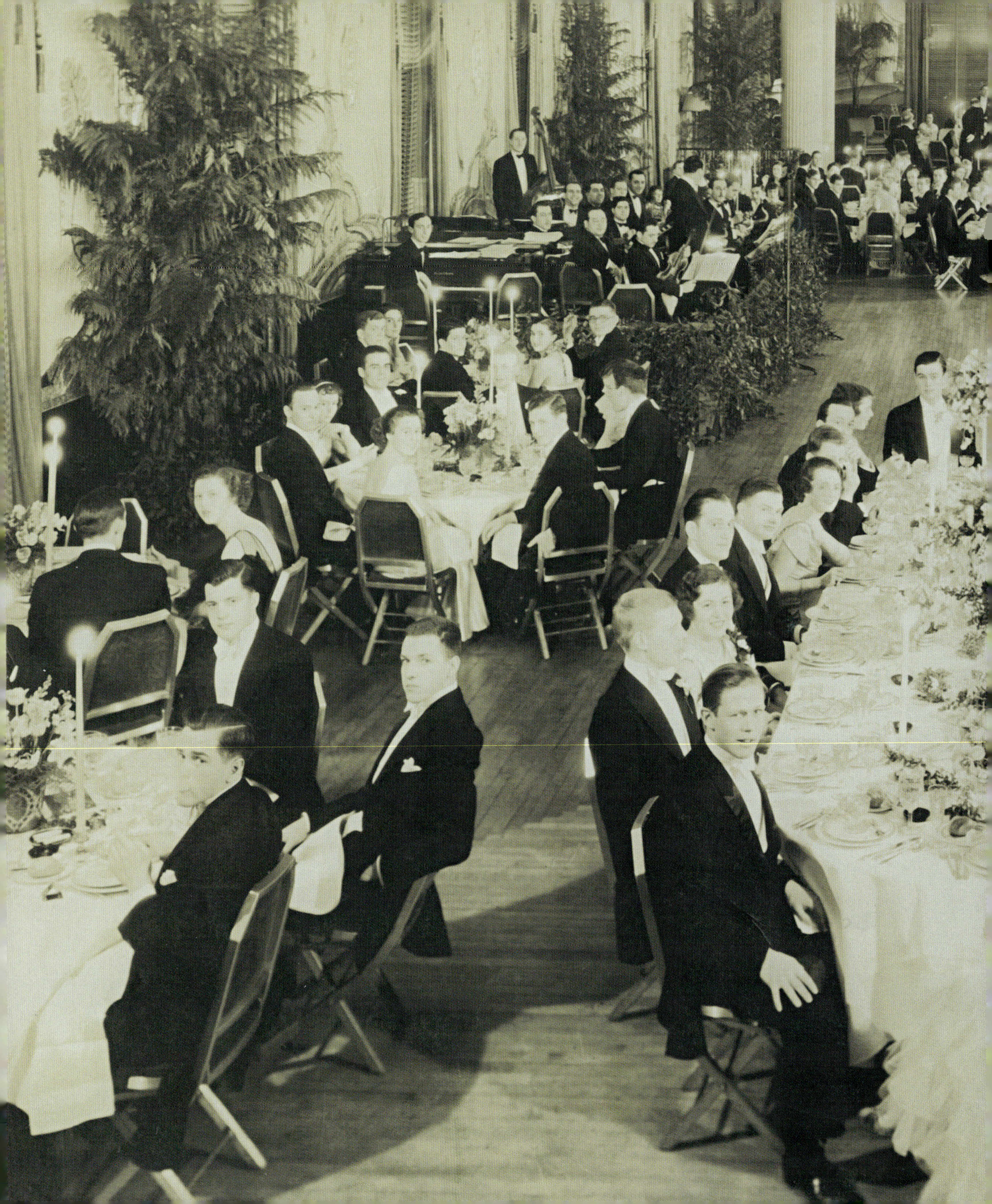

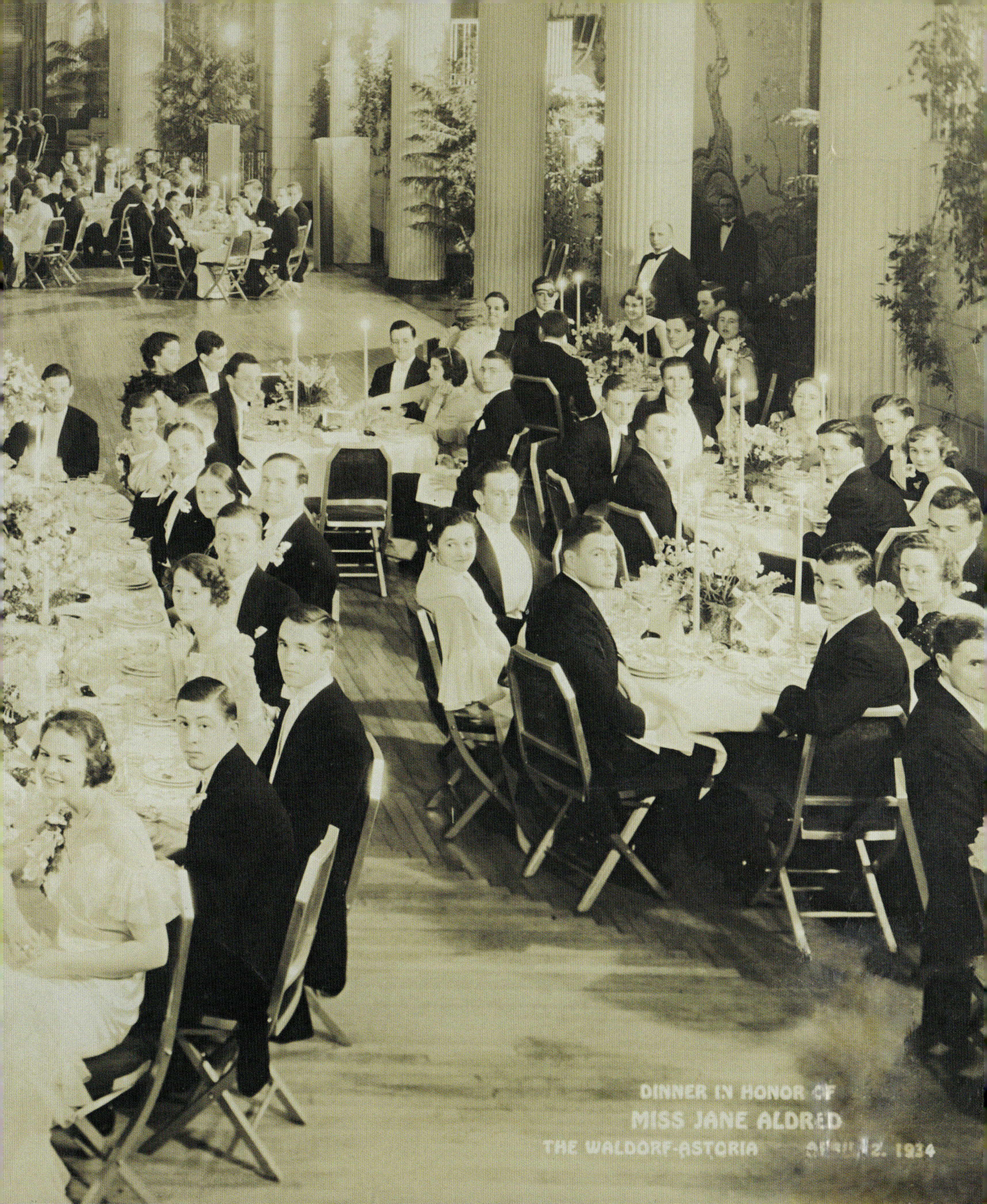
DINNER IN HONOR OF
MISS JANE ALDRED
THE WALDORF-ASTORIA
12. 1934

The generation following Consuelo Vanderbilt ushered in the Roaring Twenties, the Jazz Age, Prohibition, the stock market crash. When Alva Vanderbilt Belmont died in 1933 at age eighty, her funeral service was planned by her suffragette sisters, who referred to God as "She." By then the modern world had begun and the past was the past.

In 1930, the debutante image was forever stripped of almost all the old rules in the persona of Miss Barbara Woolworth Hutton, the only child of Edna Woolworth—one of the three daughters of F. W. Woolworth, founder of the five-and-dime chain. Barbara's mother had committed suicide when the girl was no yet five years old (she discovered her mother's body), and her father, Franklyn Hutton (brother of E. F. Hutton), had already divorced the mother. The child was brought up by relatives. Not surprisingly, little Barbara was withdrawn and introverted.

However, like her friend and contemporary Doris Duke, Barbara was also one of the richest girls in the world. On her eighteenth birthday, November 14, 1930, Barbara was given a coming-out party at the Ritz-Carlton Hotel (demolished in 1951) in New York. It was the party of the year for New York. Long gone were Mrs. Astor, the Patriarchs' balls, the cotillions, the high teas, and the complicated dancing lessons. It was a new world, moving much faster—even flying. Maurice Chevalier and Rudy Vallee, two of the biggest singing stars of the day, entertained. The guest list included all the big society names like the Vanderbilts, Whitneys, Astors, and Rockefellers. The flowers alone cost $50,000 (or $1 million dollars in today's currency).

The stock market crash in late October 1929 had caused a major dislocation for business and for working people, but the full effects of the Great Depression were not yet apparent. However, the New York press had a field day covering Barbara Hutton's lavish debut, and the upshot was very negative. They called Barbara the "Poor Little Rich Girl." Fifty thousand bucks on flowers while ordinary Americans didn't have fifty cents a day to feed themselves? The press gave her a new name: Rich Bitch. She was only eighteen, and a complete innocent, but the publicity was so bad that she was sent to Europe to get away from the clawing press.

When Barbara turned twenty-one, in 1933, as the world was really entering the depths of the Great Depression, she came into her inheritance: about $45 million (approximately $1 billion today).

That same year, still in Europe, she married her first husband, Alexis Mdivani (a self-style prince, one of three brothers from the country of Georgia, famously known as the "marrying Mdivanis"). She eventually had six more husbands after the prince, whom she divorced less than two years later: first a German count who gave her a son, Lance Reventlow; then movie idol Cary Grant; then a Russian prince, Igor Troubetzkoy; then Dominican playboy Porfirio Rubirosa (the shortest marriage—a couple of months); then a German baron, Gottfried von Cramm; and then finally to Vietnamese prince Pierre Raymond Doan Vinh na Champassak (for two years). Barbara died at age sixty-six in 1979 in her suite in the Beverly Wilshire Hotel. She had three thousand dollars left in her bank account and a great fortune in jewels.

In 1938, eight years after Barbara Hutton made her debut at the Ritz-Carlton, as the nation had begun to raise itself out of the depths of the financial debacle of the 1930s, another young heiress, Brenda Frazier, was introduced to the world of society (and the press) in the same ballroom of the Ritz.

Frazier was a stunner and she would soon become the debutante of the century—the *New York Times* declared her "the most glamorous, black-haired, gardenia-skinned, ruby-lipped debutante who ever wore a strapless dress."

Brenda's mother, born Brenda Williams-Taylor, was the child of a woman with great pretensions toward society. Brenda's grandmother kept a portrait of Hitler given to her by the Nazi dictator and no amount of history prevented her from prominently displaying it in her house. The grandparents—grandfather was a knighted Canadian diplomat—lived between New York and Ottawa.

Brenda's mother, after whom she was named, had been presented to society at Buckingham Palace during the brief reign of Edward VII. Encouraged by *her* mother, the young woman developed a taste for society in New York.

Little Brenda's mother and father divorced when she was four years old. When father died a few years later, his young daughter inherited a little over $4 million (or more than $50 million in today's currency).

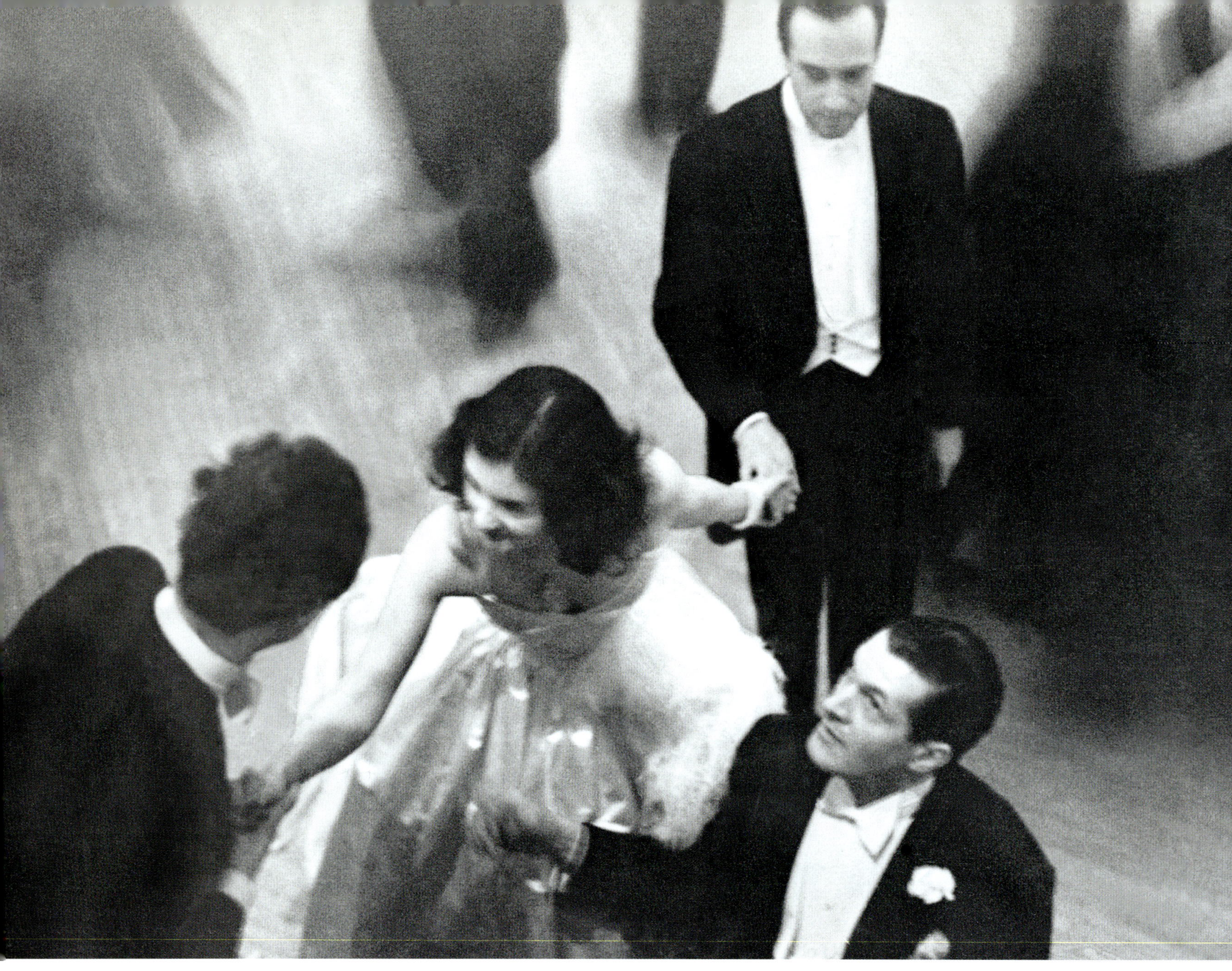

Peter Arno (bottom right) and other admirers vie for a dance with Brenda Frazier at her debut at the Infirmary Ball. The Waldorf-Astoria Hotel, New York, 1938.

The emergence of Brenda Diana Duff Frazier, debutante and glamour-girl millionaire, was what today would be called a major marketing event. She was as famous as Paris Hilton or the Kardashians today. Like them, she developed a yen for the nightlife in her early teenage years. By the time she was fifteen, Maury Paul, writing the Cholly Knickerbocker society column for the *Journal-American,* predicted that she would become famous when she made her debut. And he was right.

She created the white powdered look, her face contrasting with the red of her lipstick and making her dark brown hair look black. The strapless gown, again a new look, became her signature. Her coming-out party—she made bows at several—turned into one big, long night at El Morocco. Soon she was not only on the cover of *Life,* but in Walter Winchell's column in the Hearst papers (thirty million daily readers), as well as in magazine ads for soaps, cars (although she couldn't drive), and cigarettes. Her fame surprised her more than anybody: "I don't deserve this. I haven't done anything at all; I'm just a debutante."

On the night of her official bow, she'd come down with the flu and her legs were swollen painfully from edema. Begging her mother to cancel the party was ineffective. The show went on, and it was later reported that Brenda went with it: she danced all night, with the party winding down at six the following morning.

Fame brought her dates with famous men like Howard Hughes, among others, but the results of her spectacular "debut" were slow in materializing. "Unless I married well, the whole year [of coming out] would have passed in vain," she later said, adding, "I was bred and trained to be married, run a household, give parties, and rear daughters to have their own debuts and sons to dance with a new generation of debutantes."

Finally, three years after her coming out, in 1941, Brenda married John "Shipwreck" Kelly. Eleven years older than his bride, the tall, handsome all-American track and football star from Kentucky played halfback in the NFL and five seasons in the 1930s for the New York Giants and the Brooklyn Dodgers football club. With a charming, charismatic personality and as a frequent habitué of "21" and El Morocco, Kelly was the darling of the social set and was said to be unfazed by it, although his social pals became his security blanket.

The star-studded lives of the newlyweds had its limits, and their wedding also marked the peak of their personal success and popularity. This did not bode well for either. "Shipwreck" Kelly's athletic career had brought him all kinds of accolades from supporters and fans, including mentoring by rich bankers and business tycoons. But his off-field business ventures never had the success or the sensational turns he experienced as an athlete. His business prowess was unsteady. His greatest achievements had come in youth, and disintegrated thereafter into memories hailed most enthusiastically at cocktail parties or long martini lunches at "21."

By 1950, the marriage was over, although they didn't divorce until 1956. The world's most celebrated debutante was no longer in the circle of interest. The crowd had moved on and she was alone, isolated by her defunct fame. She got involved in volatile relationships, particularly one with Count Pietro Mele, a wealthy Italian, a man given to unpredictable mood swings. After one especially volatile public scene, the couple broke up. A week later Brenda was admitted to a hospital for treatment of a severe nervous breakdown. After recovery she attempted suicide and failed—the first of many unsuccessful attempts to end her own life.

A marriage to Robert Chatfield-Taylor ended in divorce in 1962. In December 1963, *Life* magazine, which had made her famous with a cover twenty-five years before, revisited the famous debutante. The attention buoyed her briefly, and she appeared several times on television talk shows decrying the emptiness of her former celebrated life. Those televised moments, however, were only the appearance of stability in the woman's life. For the next two decades, Brenda Diana Duff Frazier Kelly Chatfield-Taylor would be in and out of hospitals treated for chronic pain, alcoholism, and habitual drug use. In February 1982, she was finally diagnosed with inoperable bone cancer. Three months later, on May 3, 1982, she died.

Nine years after Brenda Frazier made her spectacular debut, a very pretty girl named Jackie Bouvier, who grew up in New York, East Hampton, and Newport and loved horses, came out during the 1947–48 debutante season. She was not a stand-out debutante like Brenda Frazier or Barbara Hutton before her, nor was that probably even on her mind. Her name found its way into the *New York Times* as a volunteer or committee member for various charities, but there were no interviews asking her what she thought of her future.

Jacqueline Lee Bouvier was like her contemporaries—going through the motions of preparing herself for a future in "society." In late January 1952, in

OPPOSITE

Jacqueline Lee Bouvier with her friend Jack Sterling, who dons what looks like a dinner napkin around his head. Newport, Rhode Island, 1947.

FOLLOWING PAGES

Sisters Lee and Jacqueline Lee Bouvier in their coming out dresses. *Hearst* writer Igor Cassini dubbed Jackie "Debutante of the Year" in 1947.

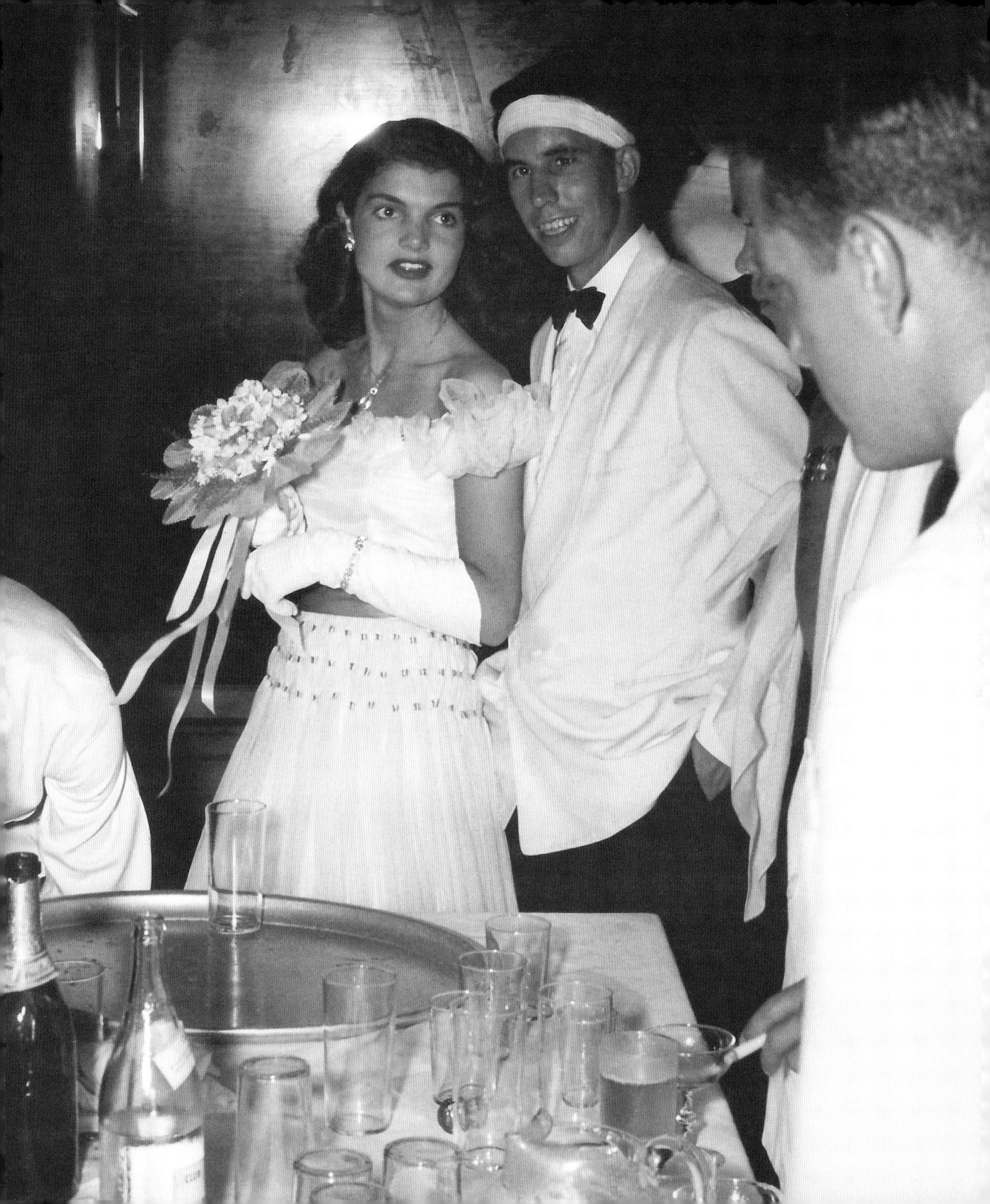

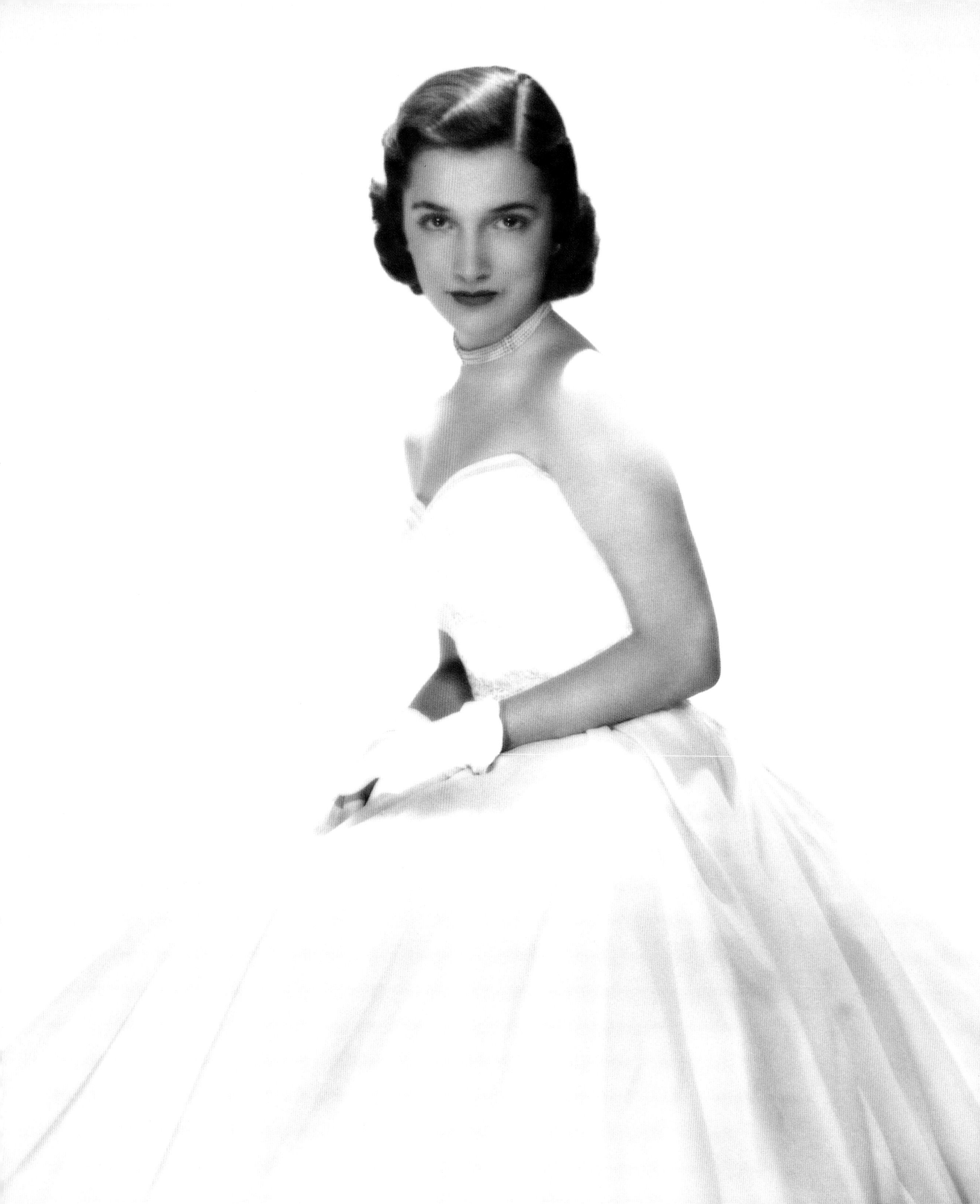

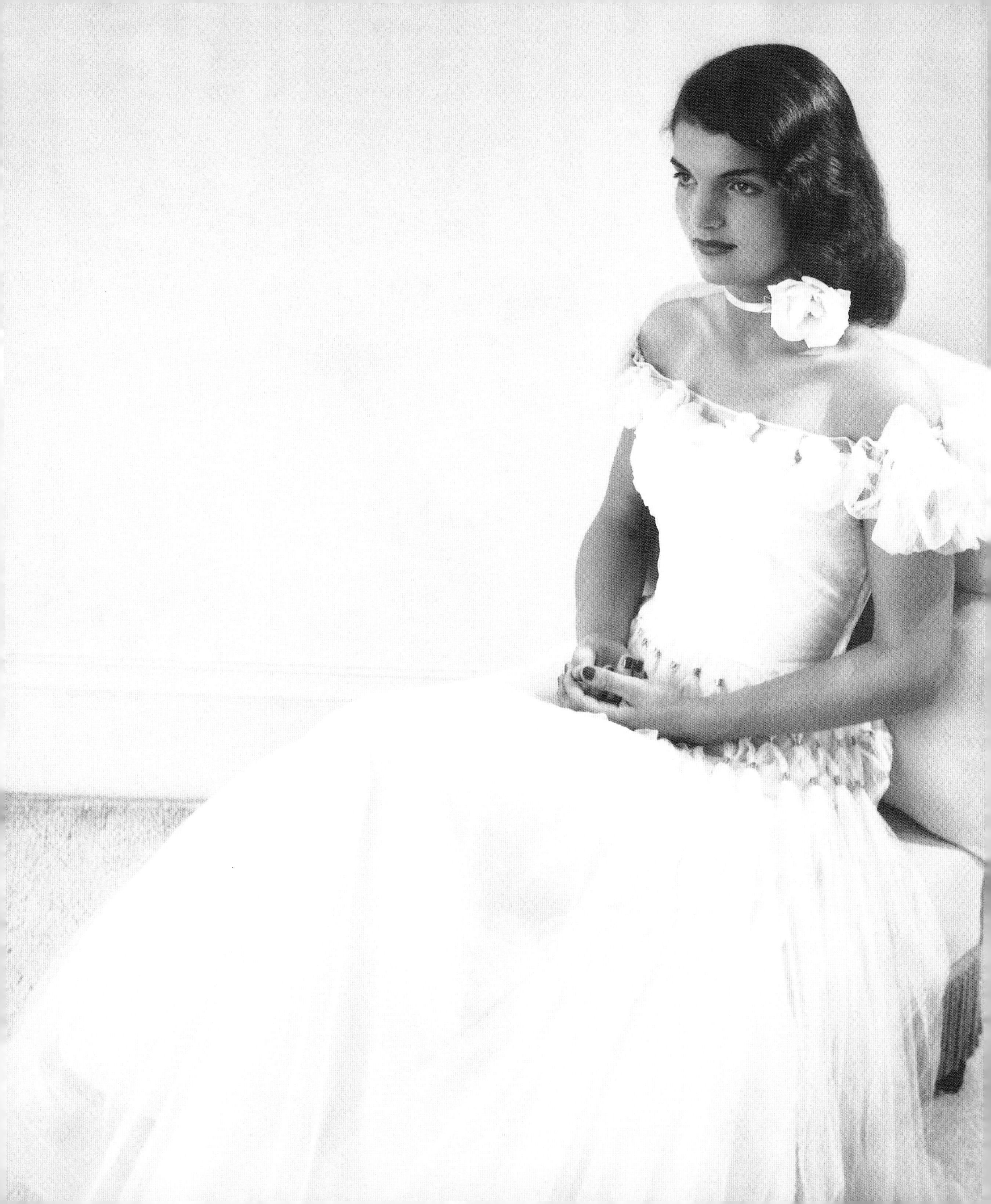

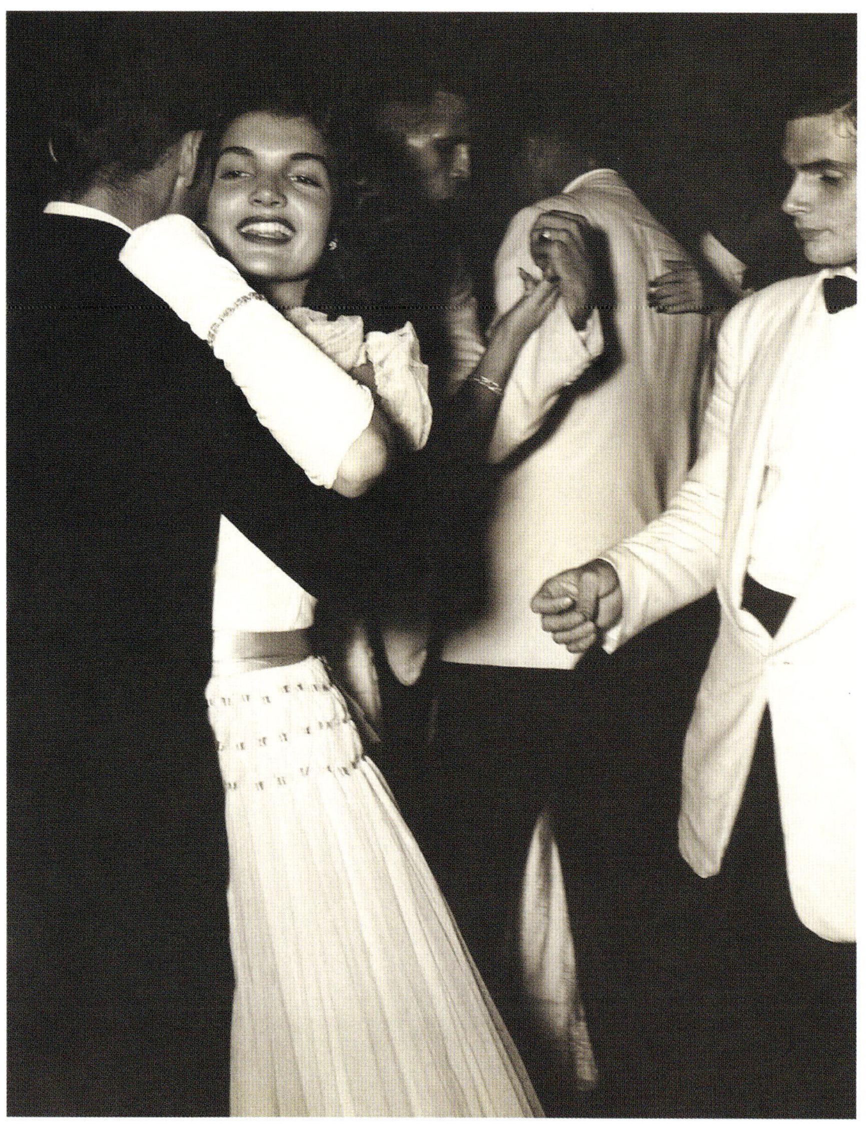

the wedding section of the *New York Times,* it was announced that Jacqueline Lee Bouvier had become engaged to John G. W. Husted, Jr. Besides listing the schools the girl attended (Chapin, Miss Porter's, Vassar, Sorbonne), the article stated that she was "a debutante of the 1947 season." (Mr. Husted was a graduate of St. Paul's and Yale.) However, fate in the form of a young senator from Massachusetts named Jack Kennedy stepped in, and the girl's life took a different course.

The world of Jacqueline Bouvier, like the world of debutantes, had begun changing when the boys came home from the war in Europe. Those soldiers' children, the first postwar/post-Depression babies, the so-called

Jacqueline Bouvier enjoys a dance with her stepfather Hugh Auchincloss as a somewhat eager gentleman looks ready to cut in. Newport, Rhode Island, 1947.

Boomers, would be brought up with other ideas, including civil rights and women's lib. The children of Jacqueline Bouvier's generation would complete that change.

The great era of the debutante had a dazzling finale in America in 1959 when Charlotte Ford came out at a party given by her parents in Grosse Pointe. It was covered in the national press, in *Time* and *Newsweek*. The whole world read about it—mainly because the party was reported to have cost $500,000, which would be like $15 million today. Charlotte's sister, Anne, came out at another dazzler the following year, but the press reaction was a little lower key: a kind of "been there, done that."

Charlotte's famous party catapulted her into celebritydom so that she was almost as famous as her automotive-heir father, Henry Ford II. Although later in life she and her sister had multiple marriages, like so many of their contemporaries, neither had a taste for the fast life (Charlotte never in her life took a drink) nor the wild side. As they matured, besides parenting their children, they devoted themselves to their friends and their philanthropies. Neither had been led to expect (or desire) anything more from a coming-out party than the party itself. So there were no personally ambitious mothers and there were no disappointments.

Debutante balls in the days of yore went out about the same time John and Jacqueline Kennedy moved into the White House in 1961. After the assassination of President Kennedy, Mrs. Kennedy's life changed dramatically and decisively, as did fashion and culture. The Vietnam war's effect on the national dialogue killed the concept of elite girls coming out (along with a lot of other concepts). From 1964 onwards through the '70s, through the liberation movements and the hippie movement, debutantes and their parties were either nonexistent or dullsville even for the girls making their bows. In the mid-'70s there was the noticeable exception of Cornelia Guest, the daughter of C.Z. and Winston Guest. But the traditions that her mother and father were brought up under and adhered to were no longer applicable. Cornelia had a young woman's taste for the nightlife of New York in the 1970s but also, like her mother and her father, for the equestrian life.

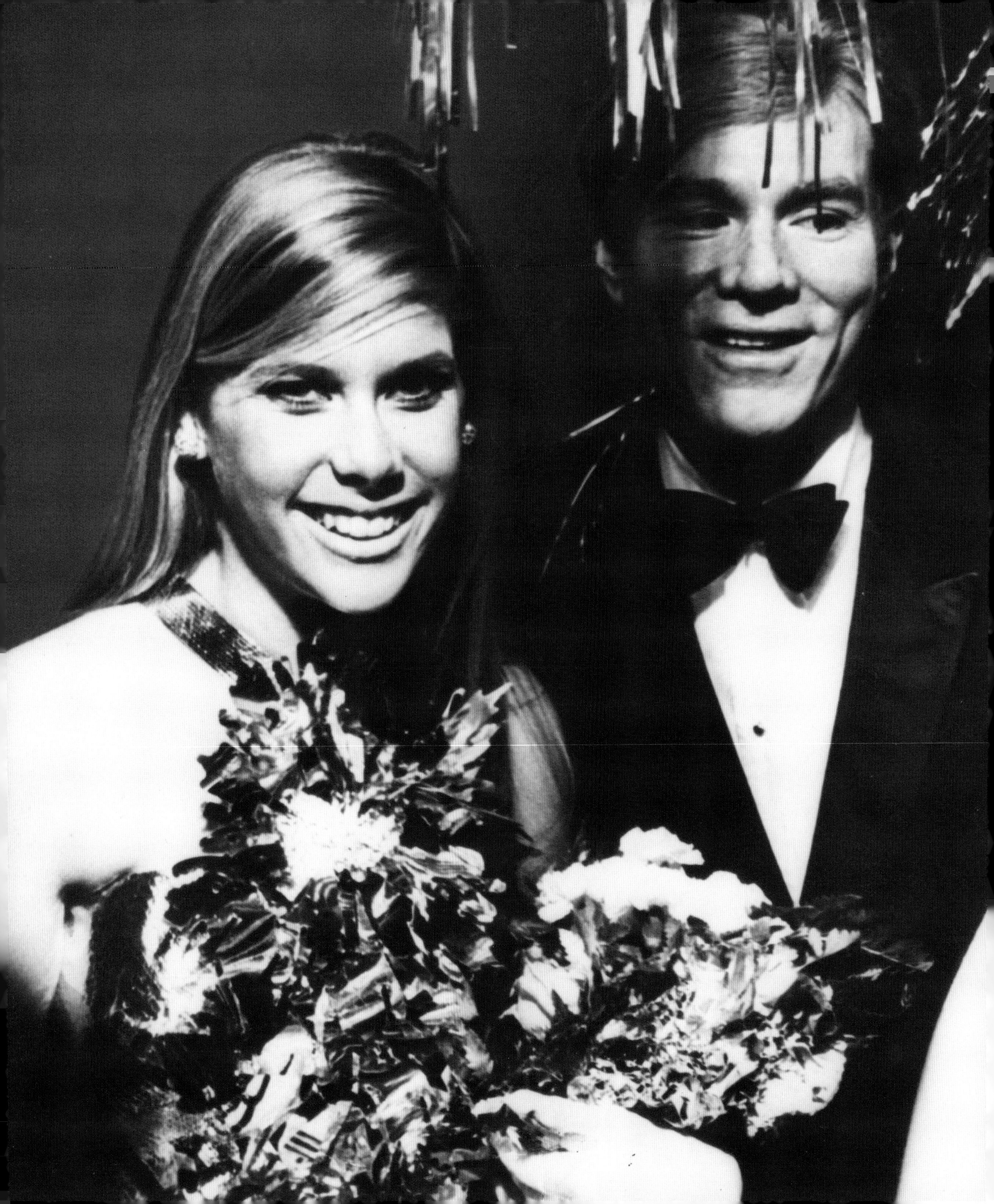

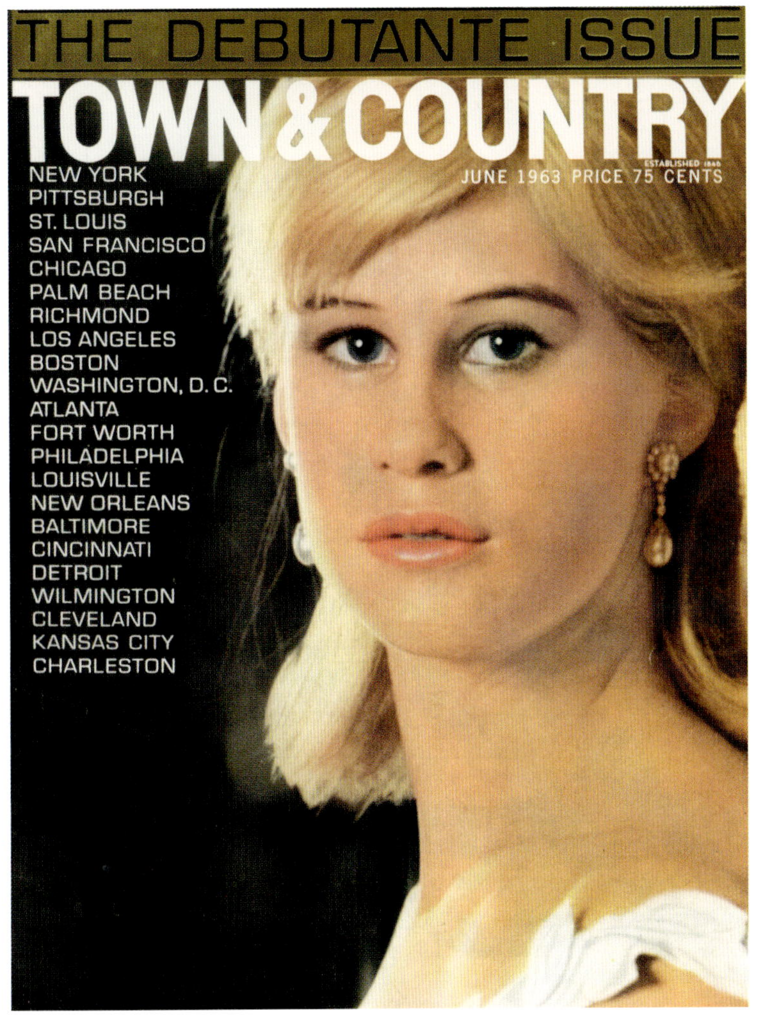


ABOVE

Mazie Cox featured on the cover of *Town & Country*'s "Debutante Issue." June, 1963.

OPPOSITE

The much publicized debutante Francine LeFrak—daughter of New York real estate developer Samuel LeFrak—is escorted by her great friend Andy Warhol at her coming out party. Francine wears a foil paper dress (a popular trend in the late '60s and early '70s). Arthur's Discotheque, New York, circa 1967.

FOLLOWING PAGES, LEFT

Justine Vilgrain, Hôtel Crillon, Paris, 2012.

FOLLOWING PAGES, RIGHT

Filippa Brandolini d'Adda, Zoe-Bleu Sidel, and Justine Vilgrain make their debut at the famous Crillon Ball. Hôtel Crillon, Paris, 2012.

In the first decade of the twenty-first century, the public image of the debutante has risen somewhat from its oblivion in what has now become a media circus of both young women and men pursuing publicity and branding rather than marital alliances that support community and family traditions. Young women today, however, have different role models than their antecedents. They expect to advance themselves through education and careers, rather than marriage. They often want full-time careers besides, or as well as, motherhood.

They also live in a world where the word "marketing," as much as education, is a key to accomplishment and achievement. The word "debutante," aside from its social intimations, is, as it always was, an opportunity, but now it is for the experience of meeting people, of going out into the world, of gathering. And so it remains the ritualistic tradition that it always was but with some major alterations. What has changed is the world—changed to suit the debutante, the young woman of tomorrow.

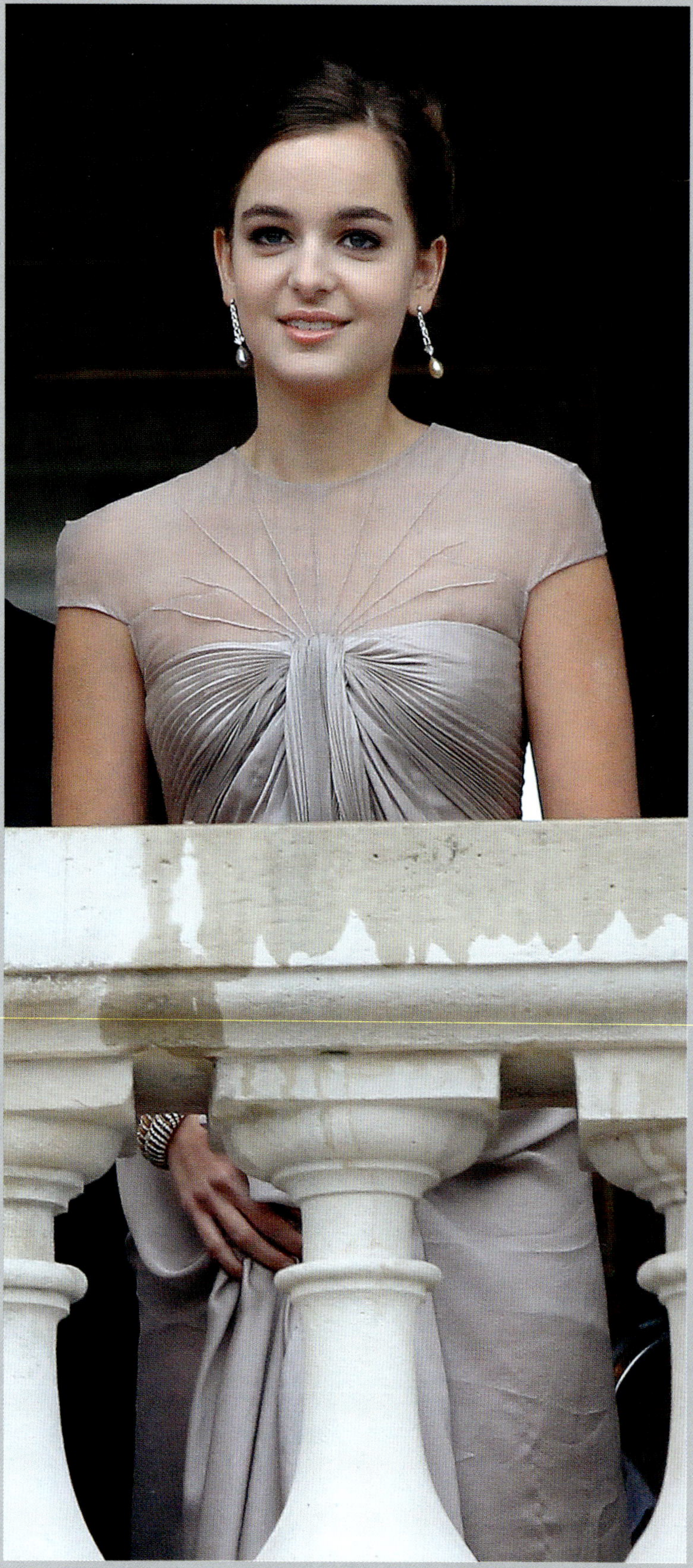

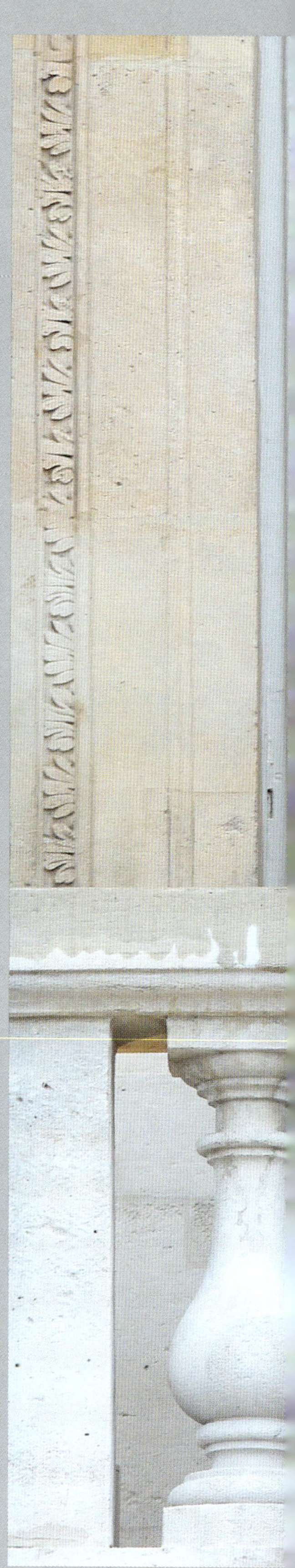

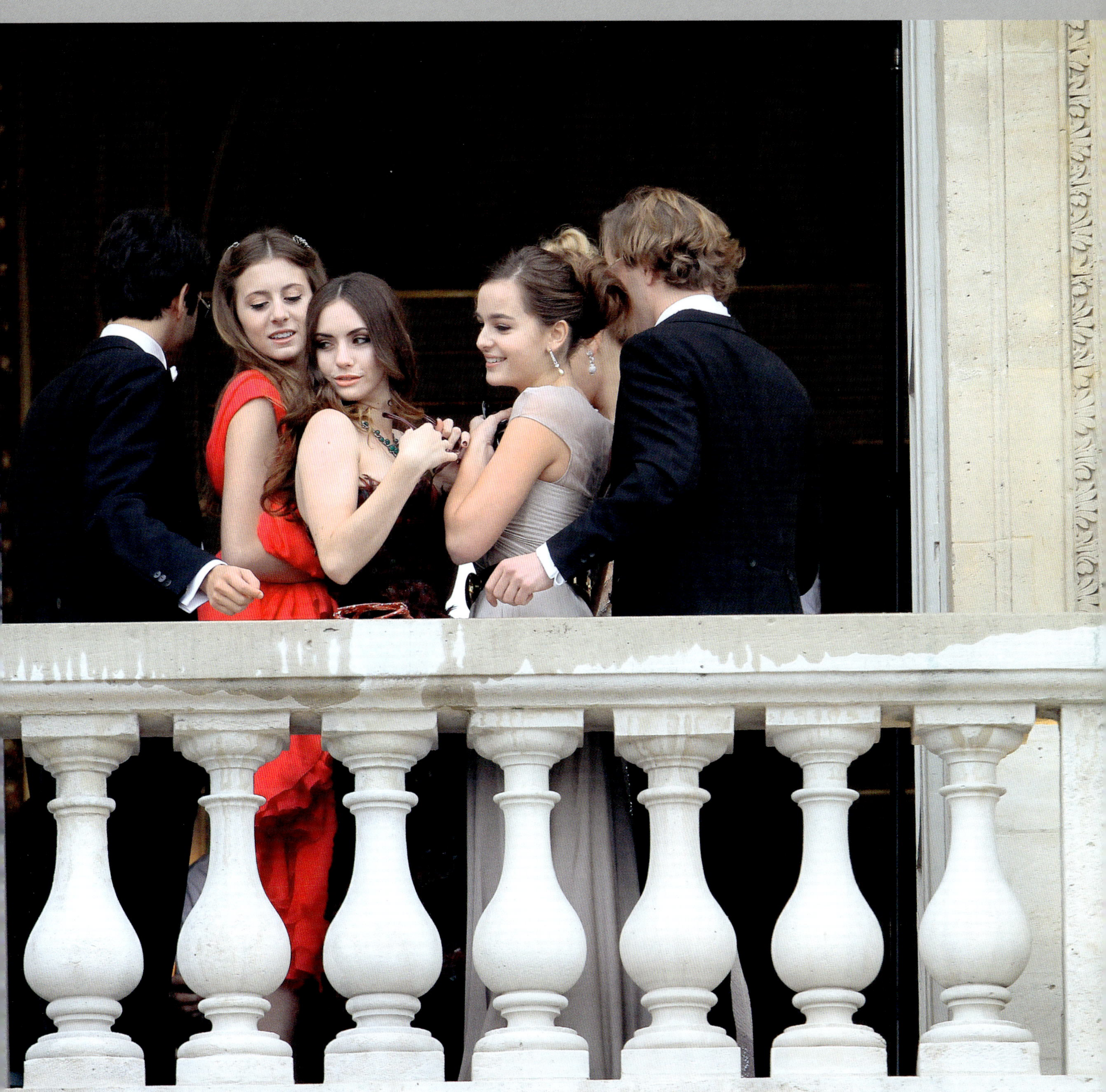

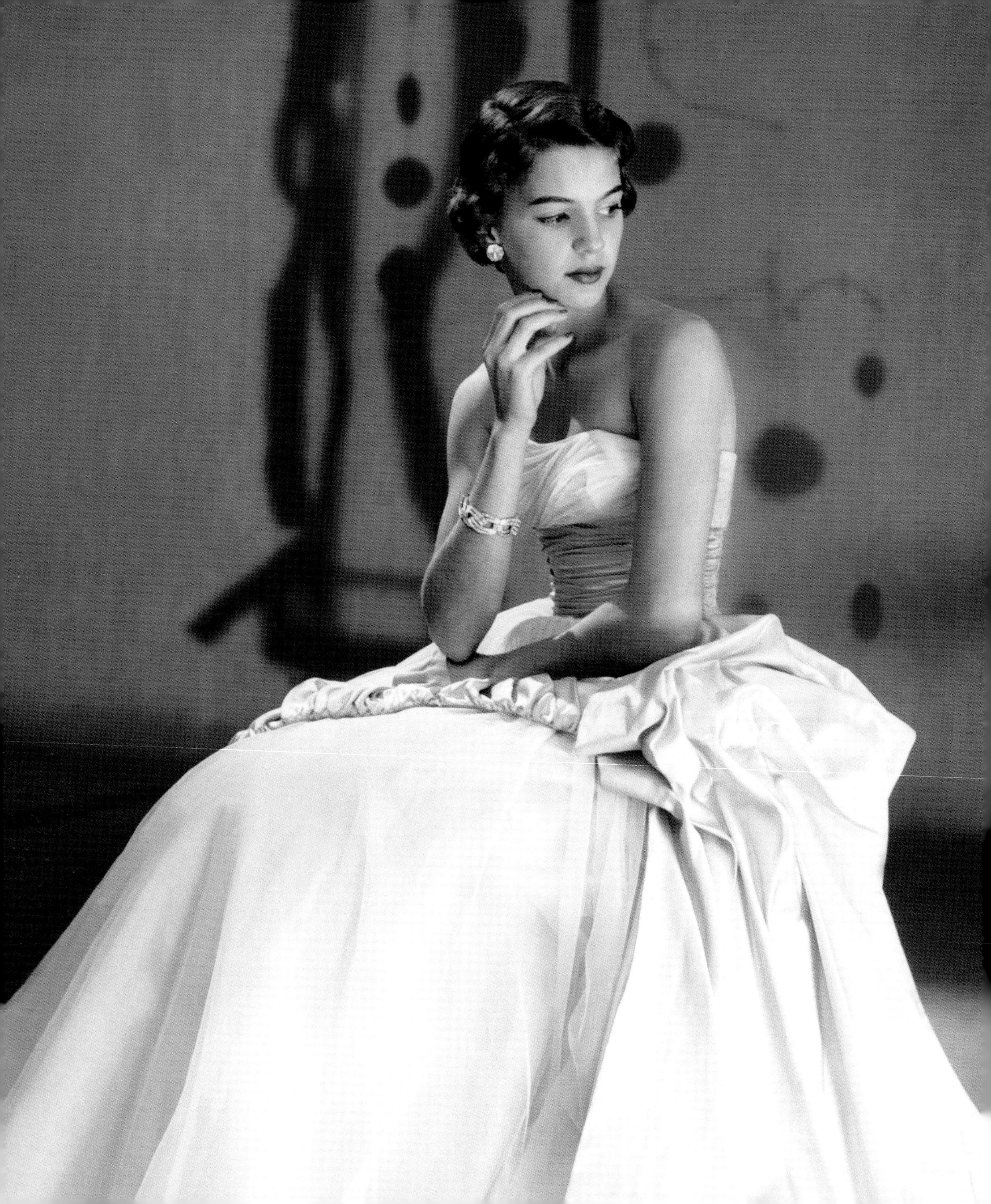

# A FINE ELEGANCE

*Elegance is good taste plus a dash of daring.*

—CARMEL SNOW

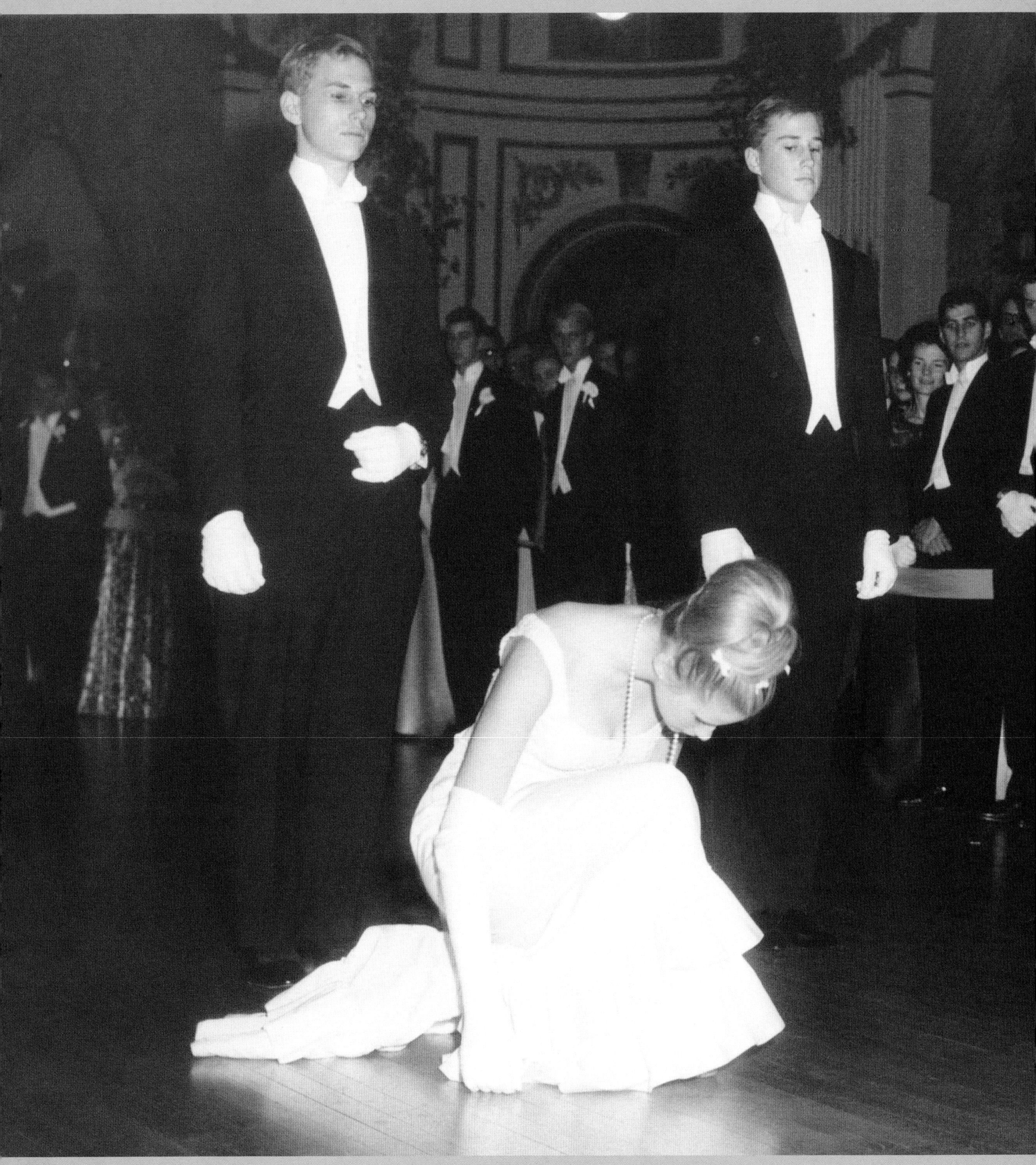

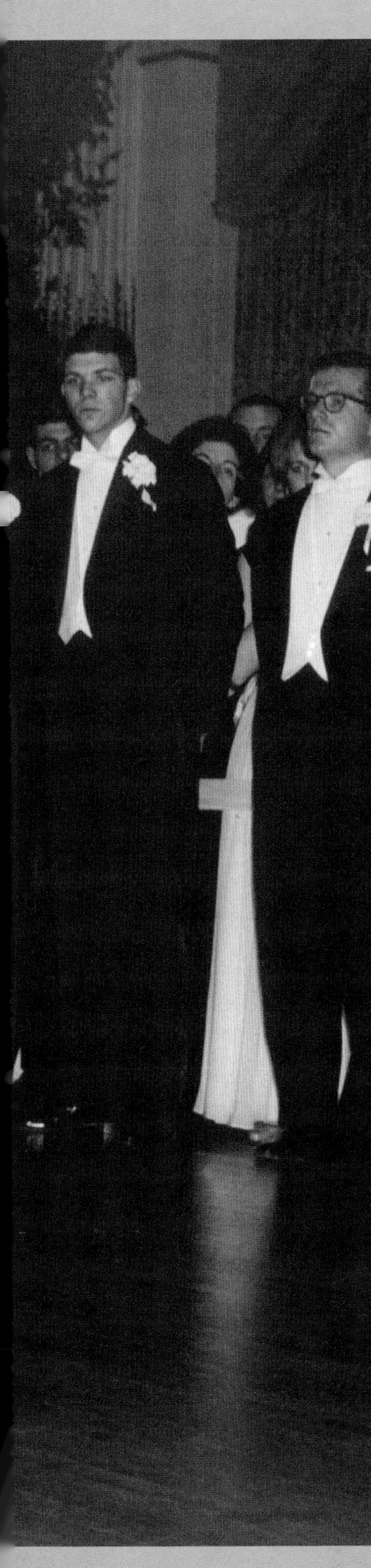

PREVIOUS PAGES

One of the most beautiful debs of her year, Beatrice Wagstaff wears a glamorous Ceil Chapman dress, 1953. Ceil Chapman was noted for her focus on the female form. Her artistry in draping and layering fabric to accentuate the figure made her one of the most popular dress designers from the 1940s to the 60s.

OPPOSITE

Mazie Cox strikes the perfect curtsey at the Waldorf-Astoria Hotel, 1963.

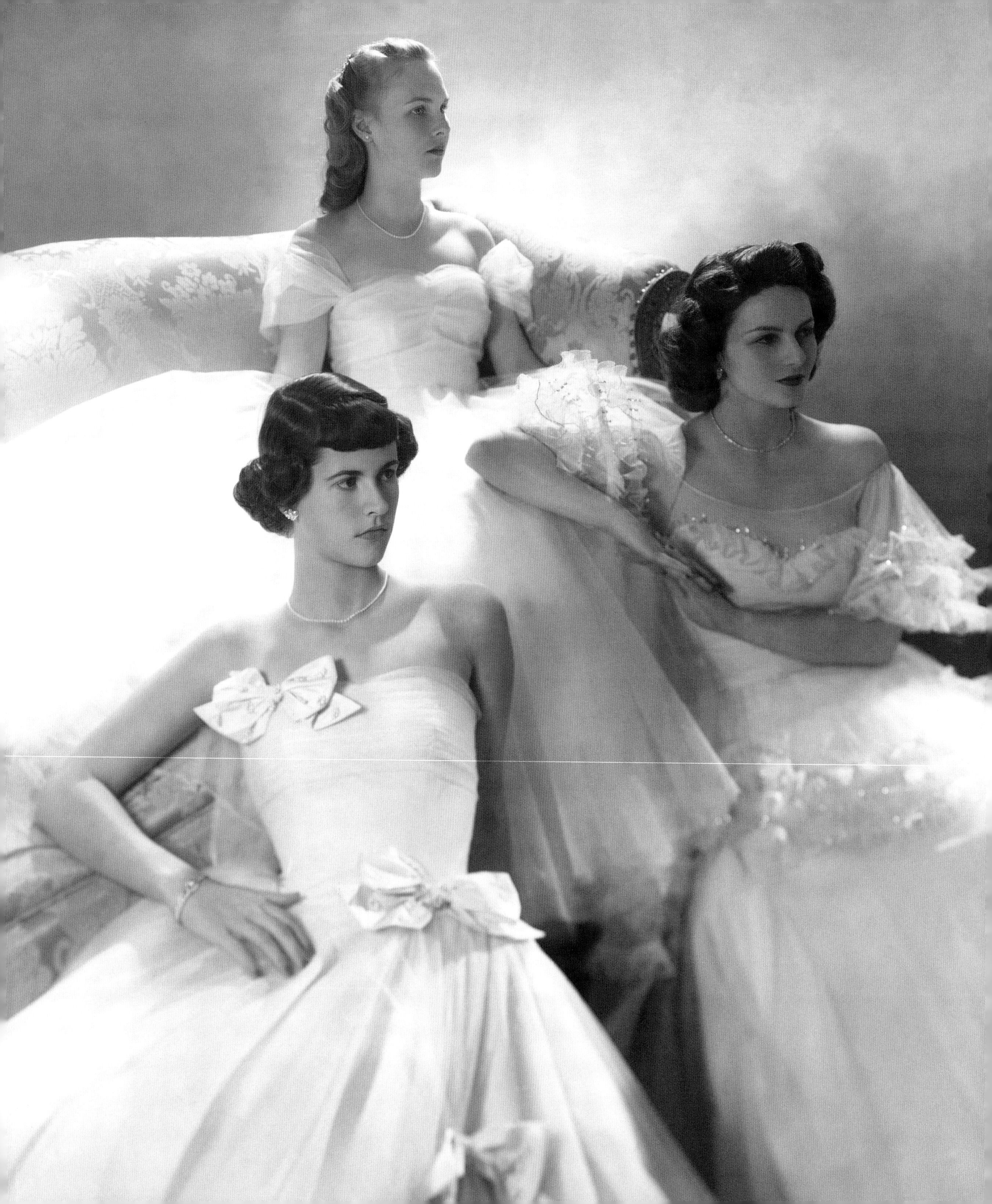

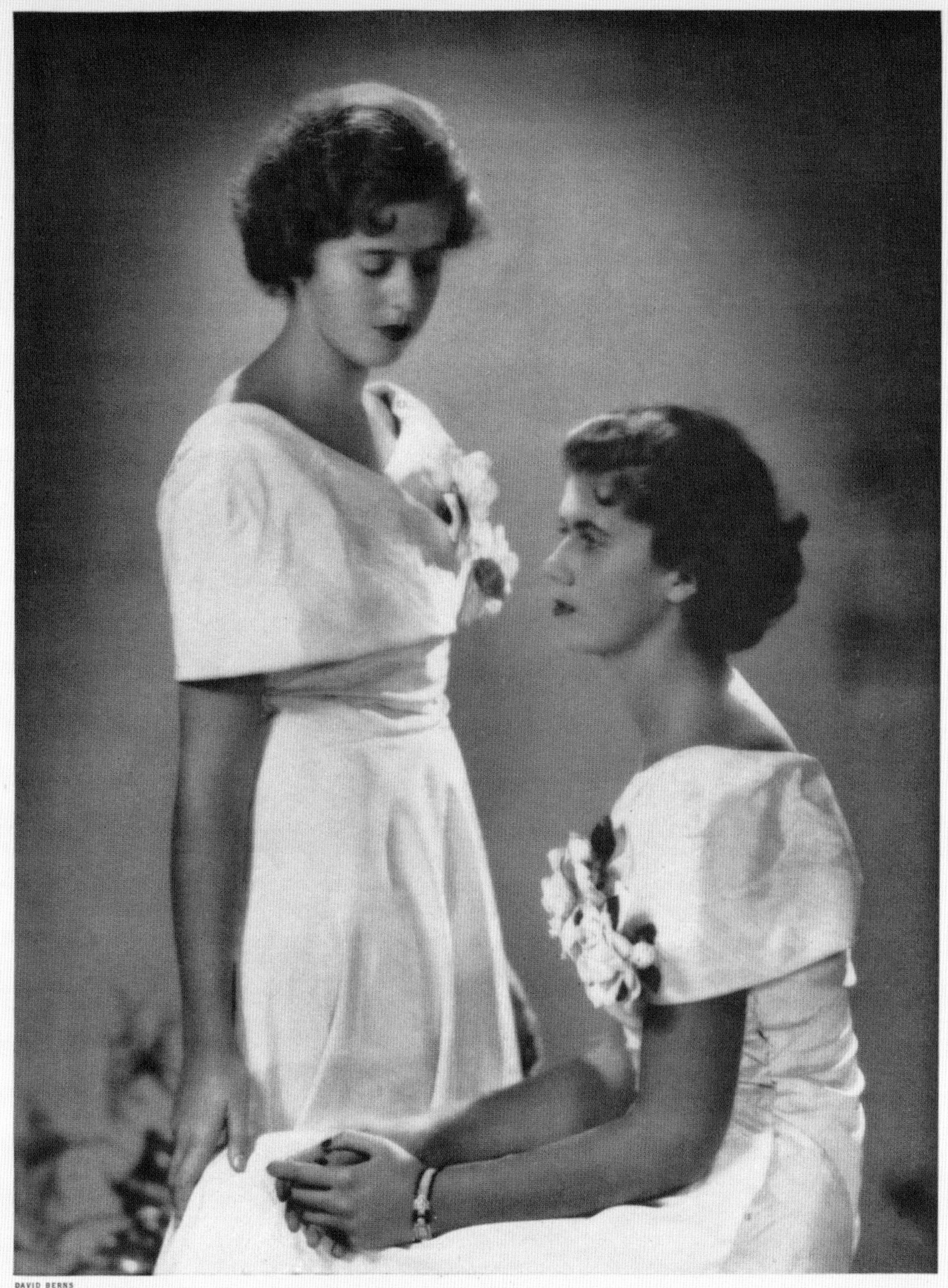

DAVID BERNS

# JOAN AND KATHERINE BLAKE

The débutante daughters of Dr. Joseph Blake and the late Mrs. Katherine Duer Blake will be presented on the twenty-second of this month at a supper dance, in the Crystal Room of the Ritz, by their half-sisters and brother, Mrs. Kenneth O'Brien, Mrs. Irving Berlin and John Mackay

PREVIOUS PAGES, LEFT

Debutantes Ann Burton, Nancy Young, and Marilyn Mueller are presented at the Las Madrinas debutante ball in Los Angeles, 1947. Founded in 1933, the Las Madrinas Ball devotes much of its financial support to the Los Angeles Children's Hospital.

PREVIOUS PAGES, RIGHT

Joan and Katherine Blake, the debutante daughters of Dr. Joseph Blake and the late Mrs. Katherine Duer Blake, presented by their half sisters Mrs. Irving Berlin and brother Mr. Kenneth O'Brien at a supper dance at the Crystal Room of the Ritz Carlton. Torrington, Connecticut. As seen in *Town & Country*, 1933.

OPPOSITE

Debutante Tess D'Erlanger wears a white organdy gown by Irene, 1952. Irene began her career as a costume designer and catered to both high society and Hollywood royalty.

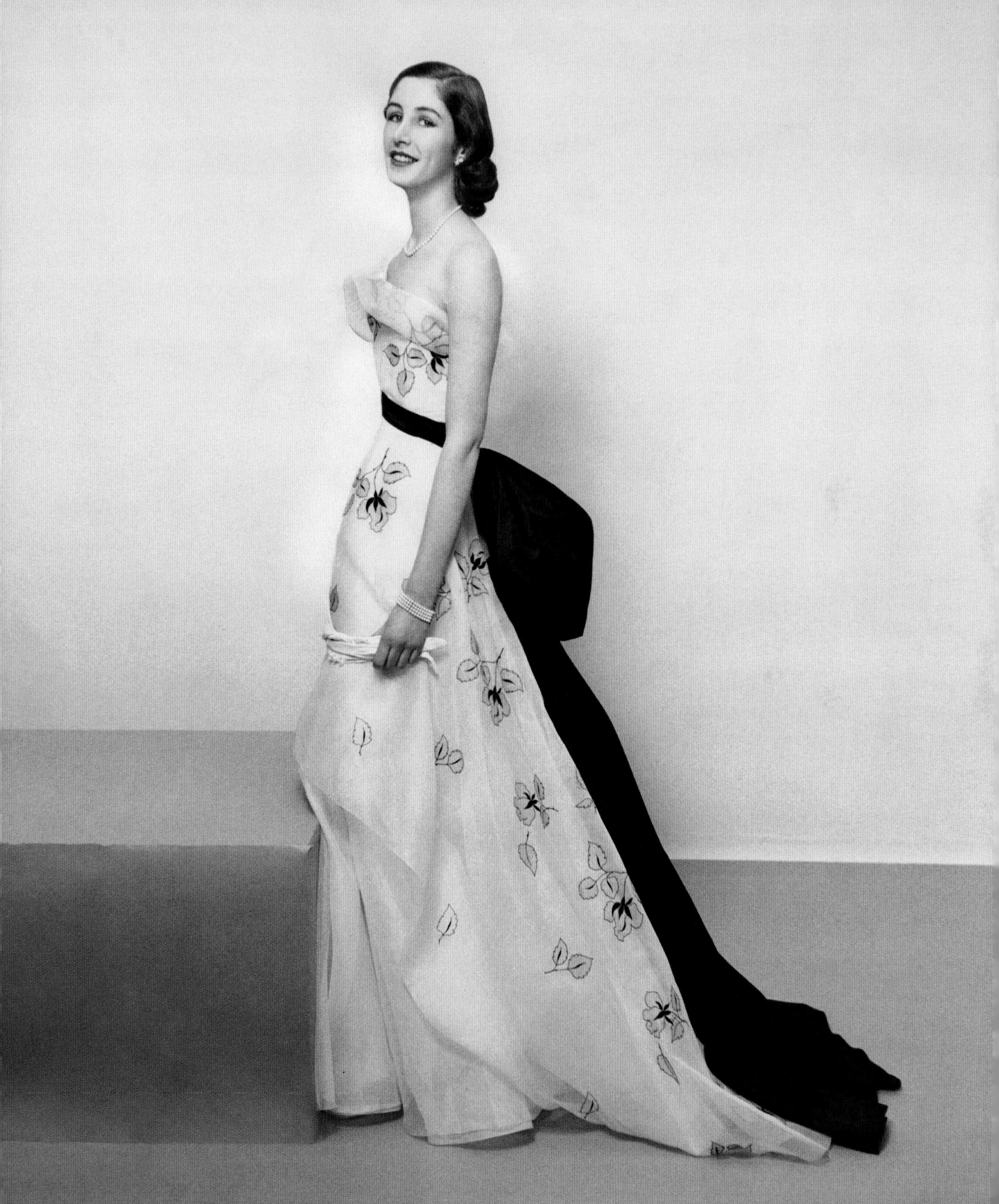

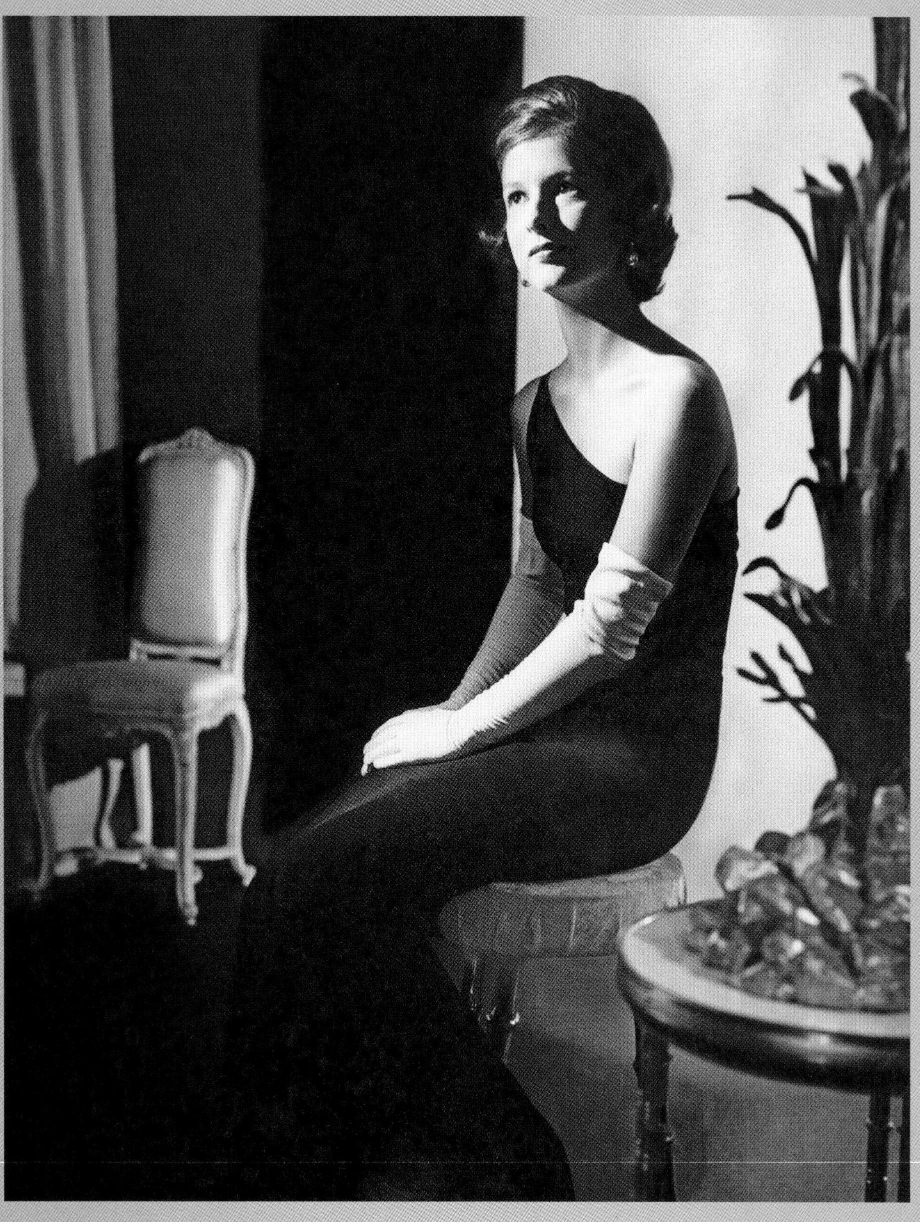

ABOVE
One of the most stunning debutantes of the early '60s, Daphne du Pont wears a dress by Norman Norell, 1961. Norell's creations were brilliant in both simplicity and form.

OPPOSITE
Born Catherine Conn in New Orleans, Kitty Carlisle Hart was brought up by a mother who placed great importance on Kitty's entrance and elevation in to society. A debutante herself, Kitty's hairstyle, shown here, was referred to as the "debutante roll." 1934.

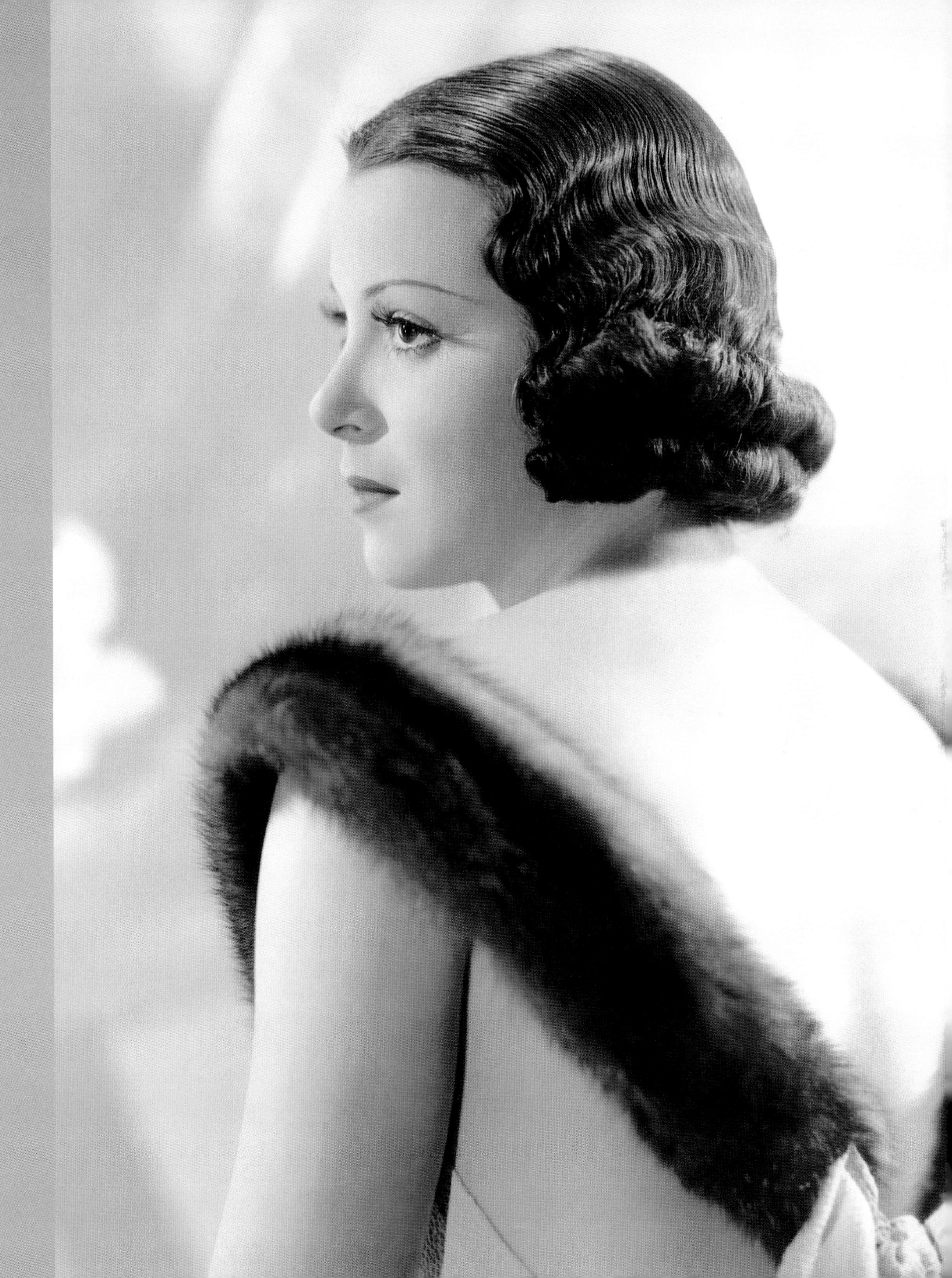

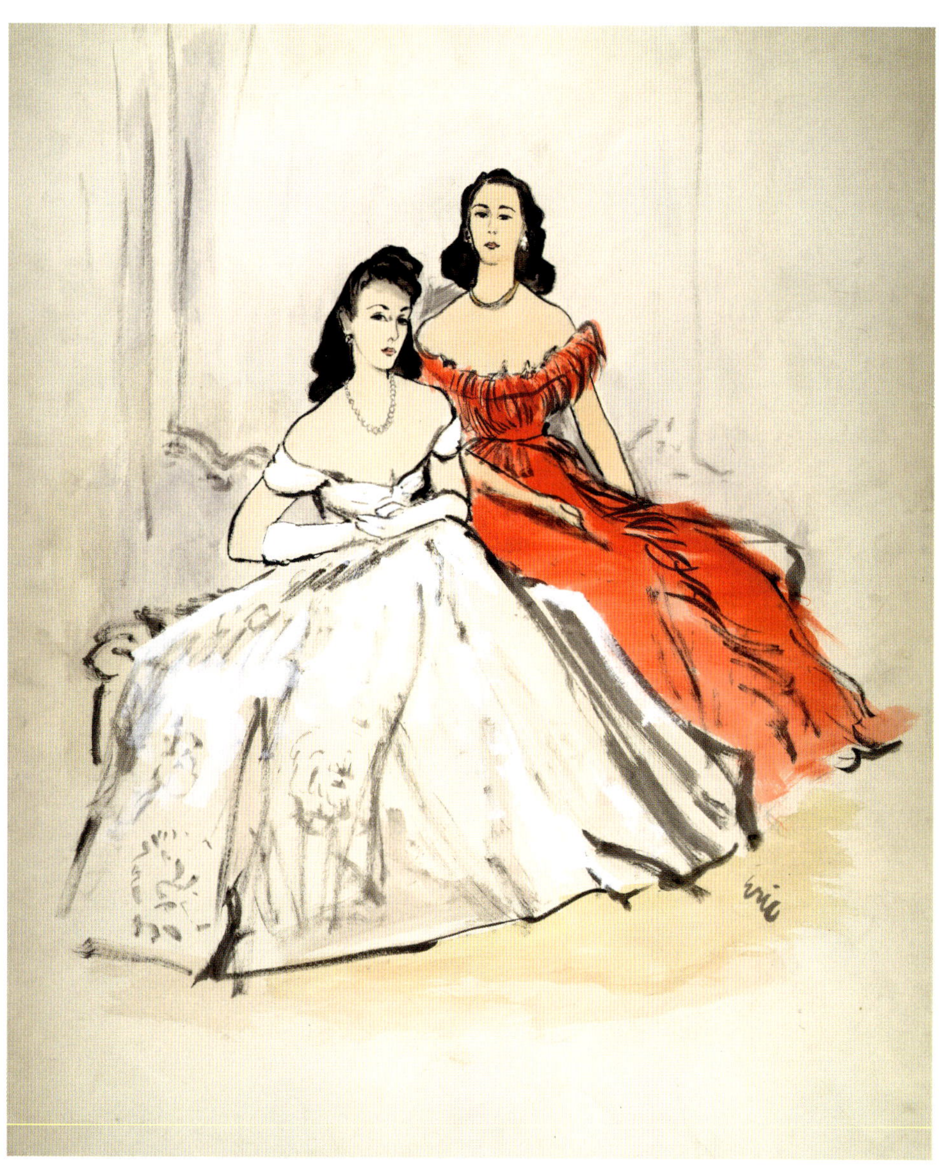

ABOVE

Joan Metzger and Sylvia Whitehouse, presented at the Waldorf-Astoria Hotel's Victory Debutante Cotillion Ball. Miss Metzger wears an off the shoulder satin gown with iridescent sequins. New York, 1945.

OPPOSITE

Debutante Pamela Lehman is escorted to the International Debutante Ball by her close friend Tony Cointreau of the Cointreau liqueur family. Pamela's father, Robert Lehman (Bobbie), who headed up Lehman Brothers, was arguably the most influential and powerful moguls of his time. It took Mr. Lehman's gift of persuasion to finally encourage a reluctant and shy Pamela to come out. New York, 1959.

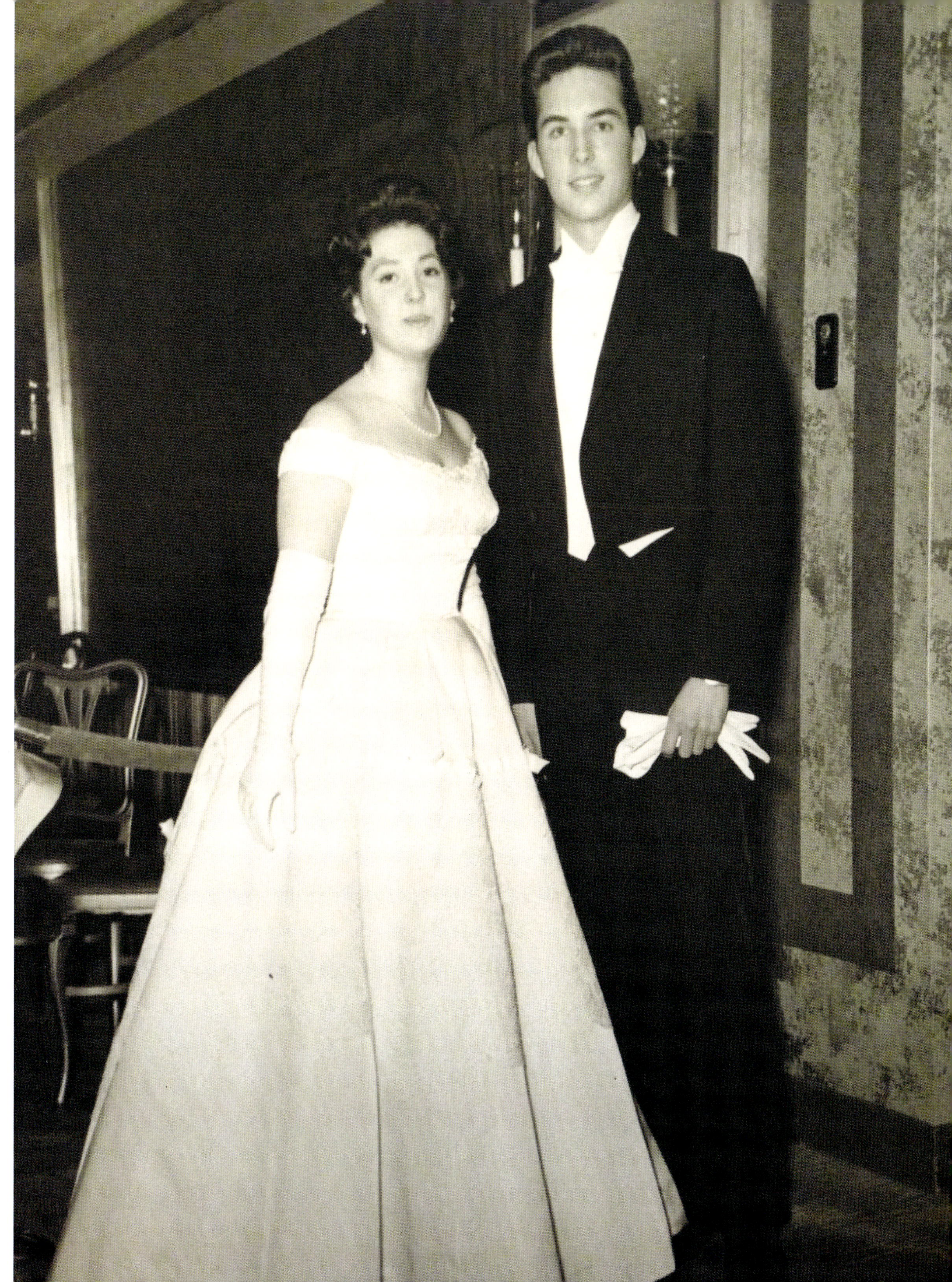

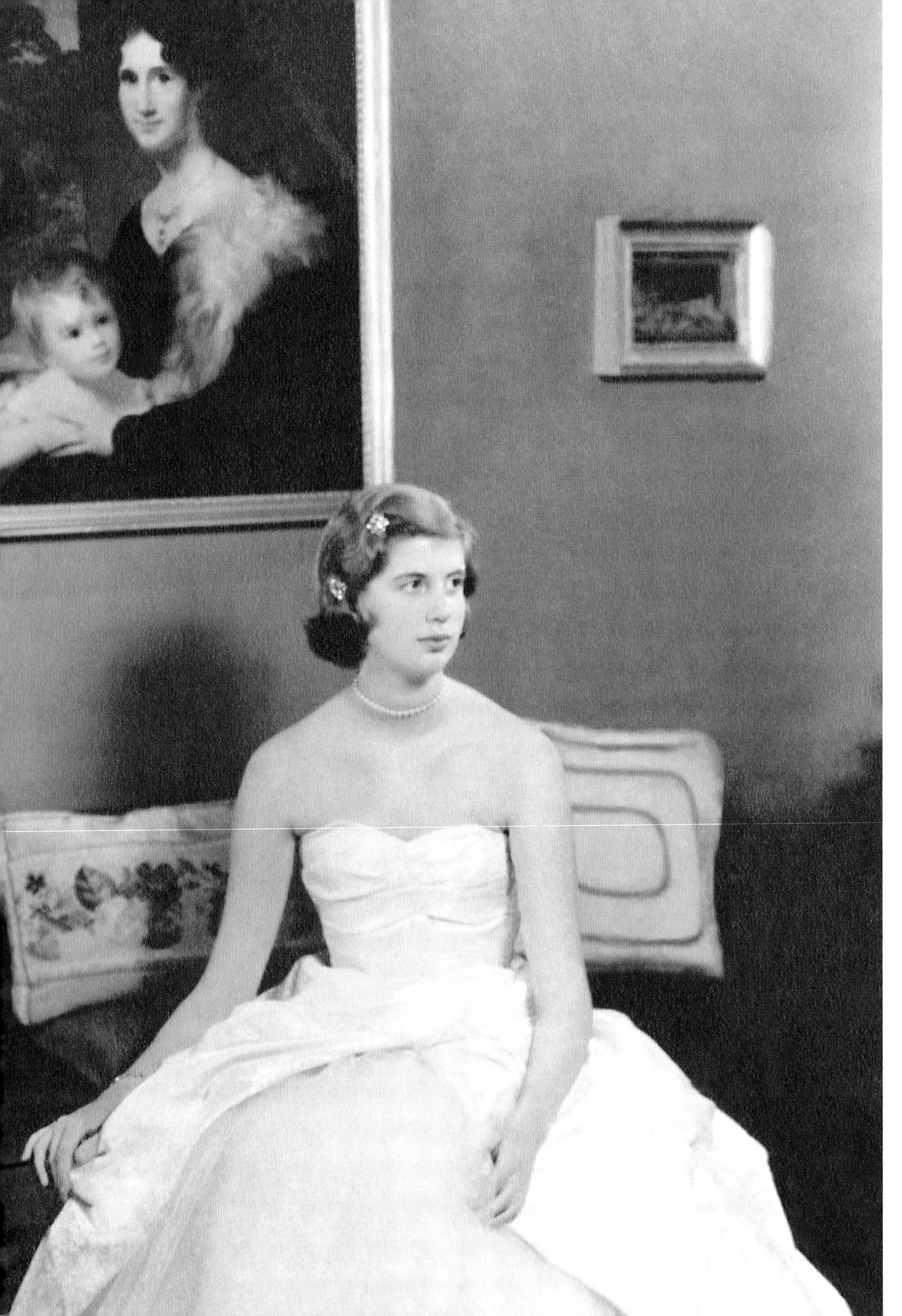

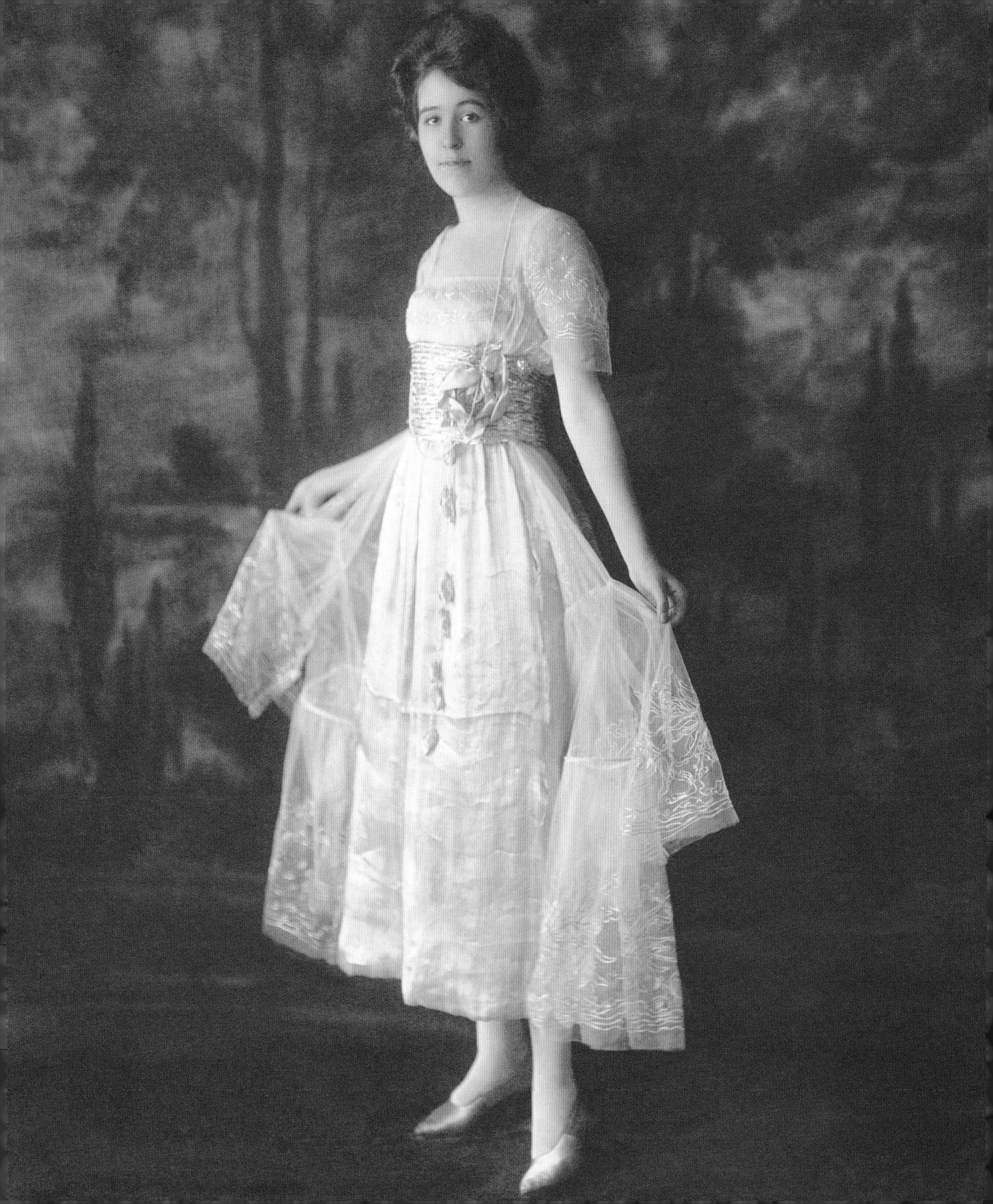

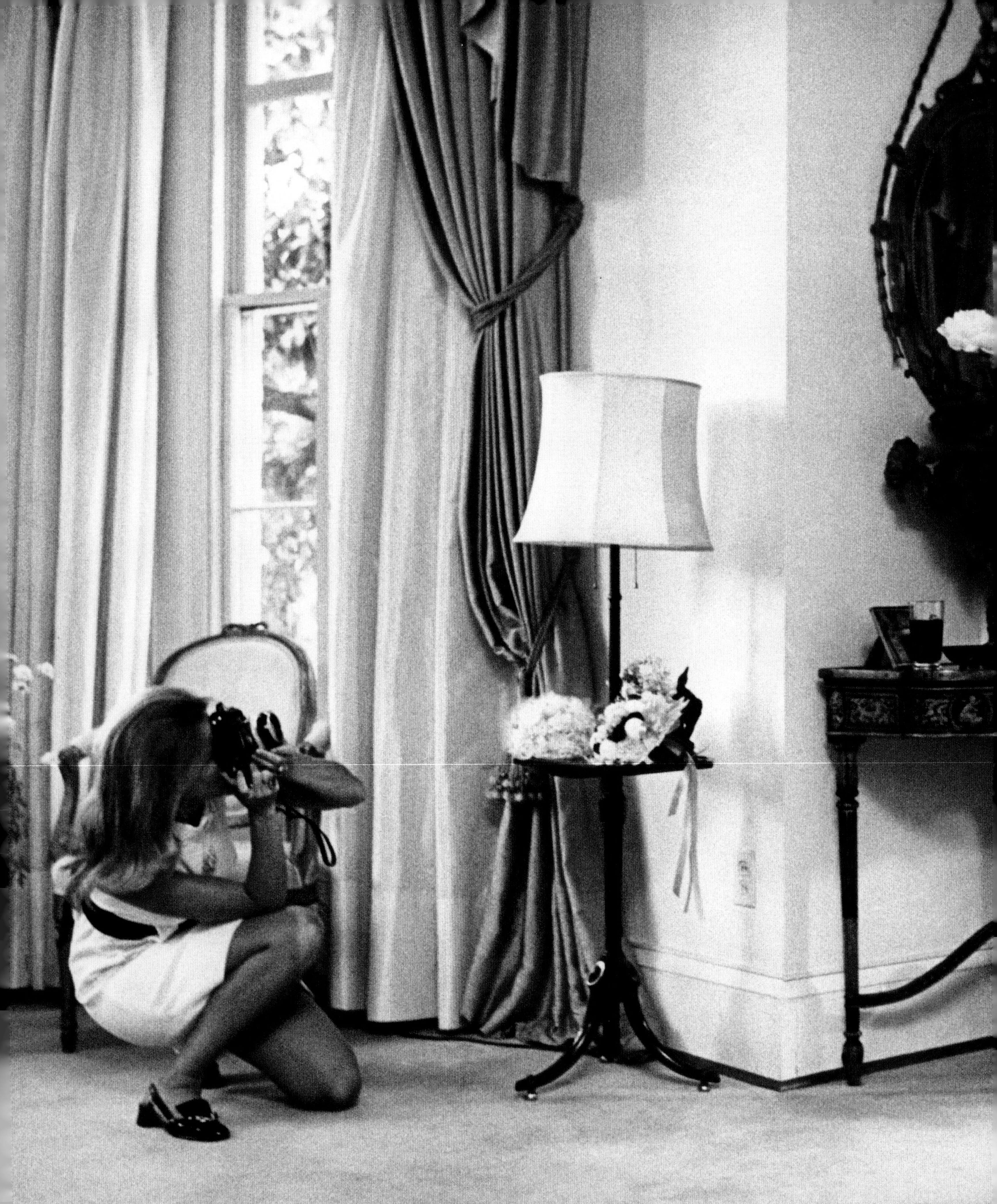

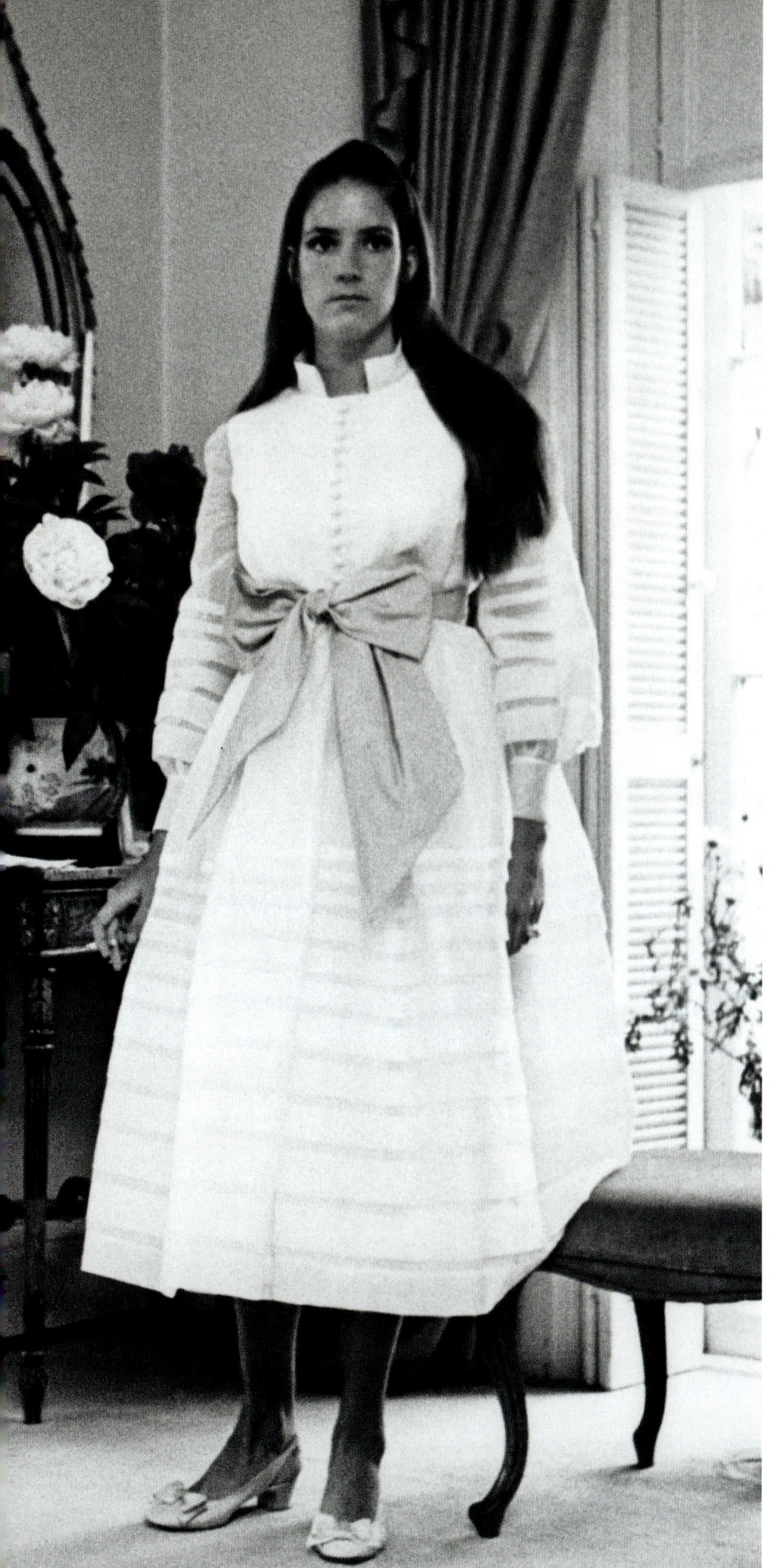

PREVIOUS PAGES, LEFT

Audrey Clinton sits underneath a portrait of her great-great grandmother, Mrs. George Hoffman before making her debut at the Junior Assemblies. New York, 1951.

PREVIOUS PAGES, RIGHT

Dresses of the early 1900s were often loosely tailored and simple with a slightly raised waistline. During the years between 1915 and the early 1920s, it wasn't uncommon for a debutantes dress to be short. Audrey Hoffman, mother of Audrey Clinton, in her coming out dress made of silk, satin, and lace. New York, 1915.

LEFT

As the photographer snaps the perfect shot, debutante Victoria Leiter gets ready for her tea dance. Washington, D.C., 1968.

FOLLOWING PAGES, LEFT

Seen here in a stunning Hattie Carnegie dress, debutante June Buffinton, daughter of Mrs. Elise Buffinton, was considered one of the most beautiful post-war debs. As seen in *Town & Country*, 1948.

FOLLOWING PAGES, RIGHT

Debutante Frances Kearsley Mitchell as painted by Hungarian painter Philip De Laslo, known especially for his portraits of the aristocratic set. Miss Frances Kearsley, daughter of Mrs. J Kearsley Mitchell of Villanova PA, was given a debutante dance at her grandparents Mr. and Mrs. Edward T. Scotesbury's residence, "Whitemarsh Hall." Chestnut Hill, Pennsylvania. As seen in *Town & Country*, 1926.

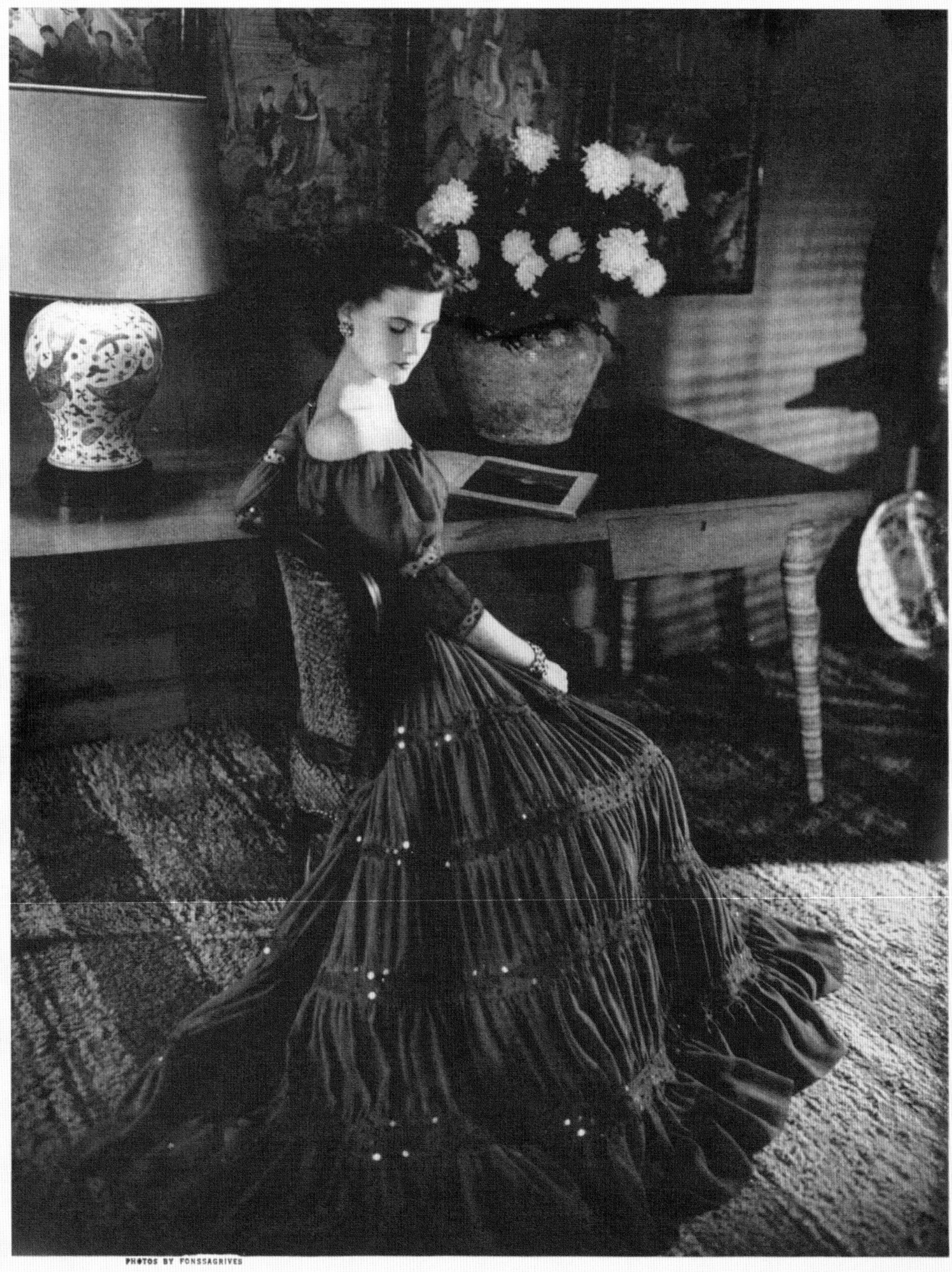

PHOTOS BY FONSSAGRIVES

ONE of the most charming postwar debutantes is June Buffinton, daughter of Mrs. Eliot Buffinton, who wears a debutante's dream of a dress. The tiered sleeves start from bare shoulders, the waist is snug and small, and the skirt is made of foaming royal chiffon gathered onto sequin-studded strips of net. Custom made at Hattie Carnegie

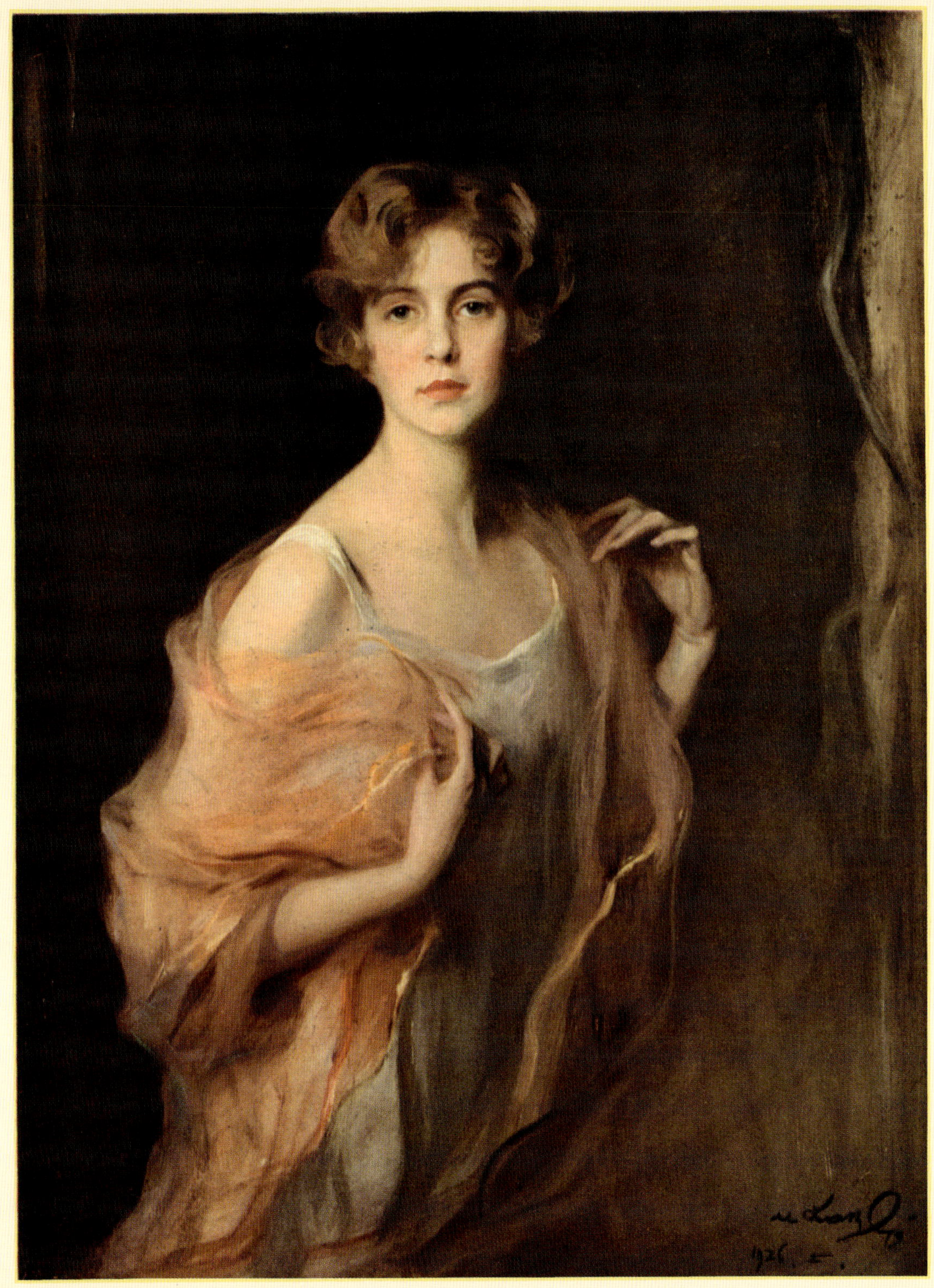

MISS FRANCES KEARSLEY MITCHELL

From the portrait by Philip A. De Laszlo

*Miss Frances Kearsley Mitchell, the very charming daughter of Mr. and Mrs. J. Kearsley Mitchell, of Villa Nova, Pennsylvania, will make her début this autumn at a dance given for her at "Whitemarsh Hall," the estate of her grandparents, Mr. and Mrs. Edward T. Stotesbury, at Chestnut Hill*

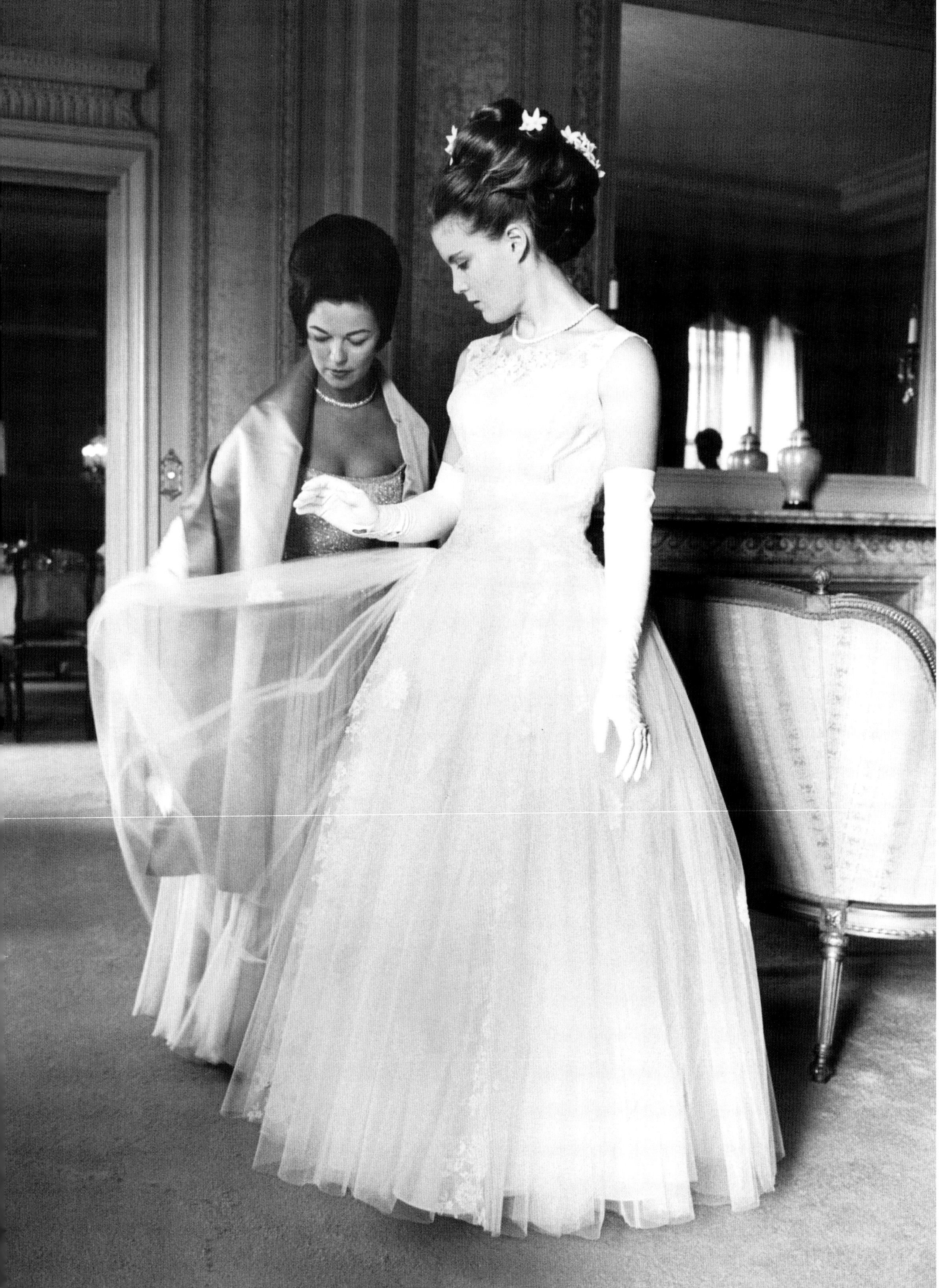

# CELEBUTANTES

*I was plunged in to what was known as the debutante social whirl. This was one of the ways fathers justified their own hard work and sacrifices.*

—GENE TIERNEY

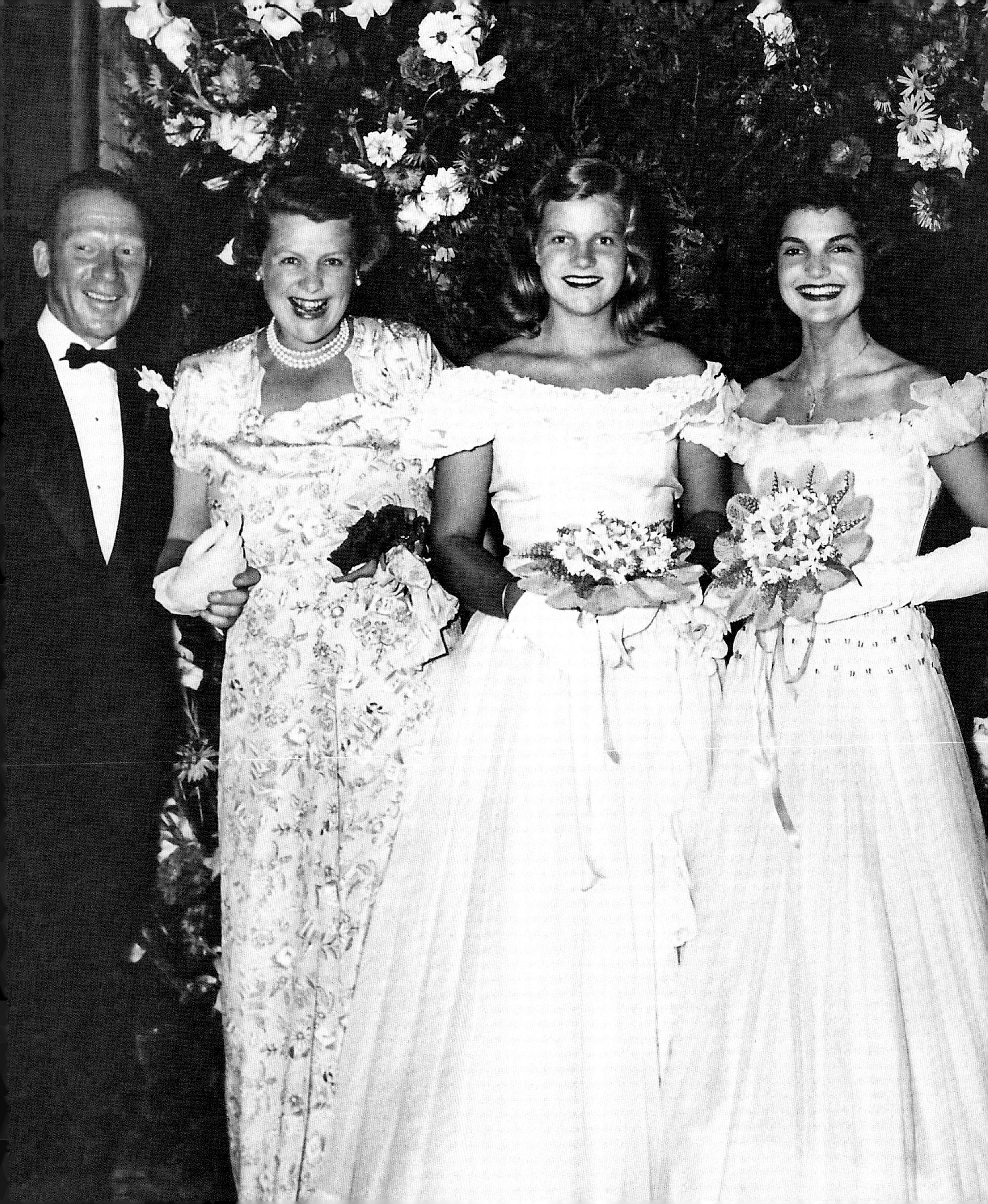

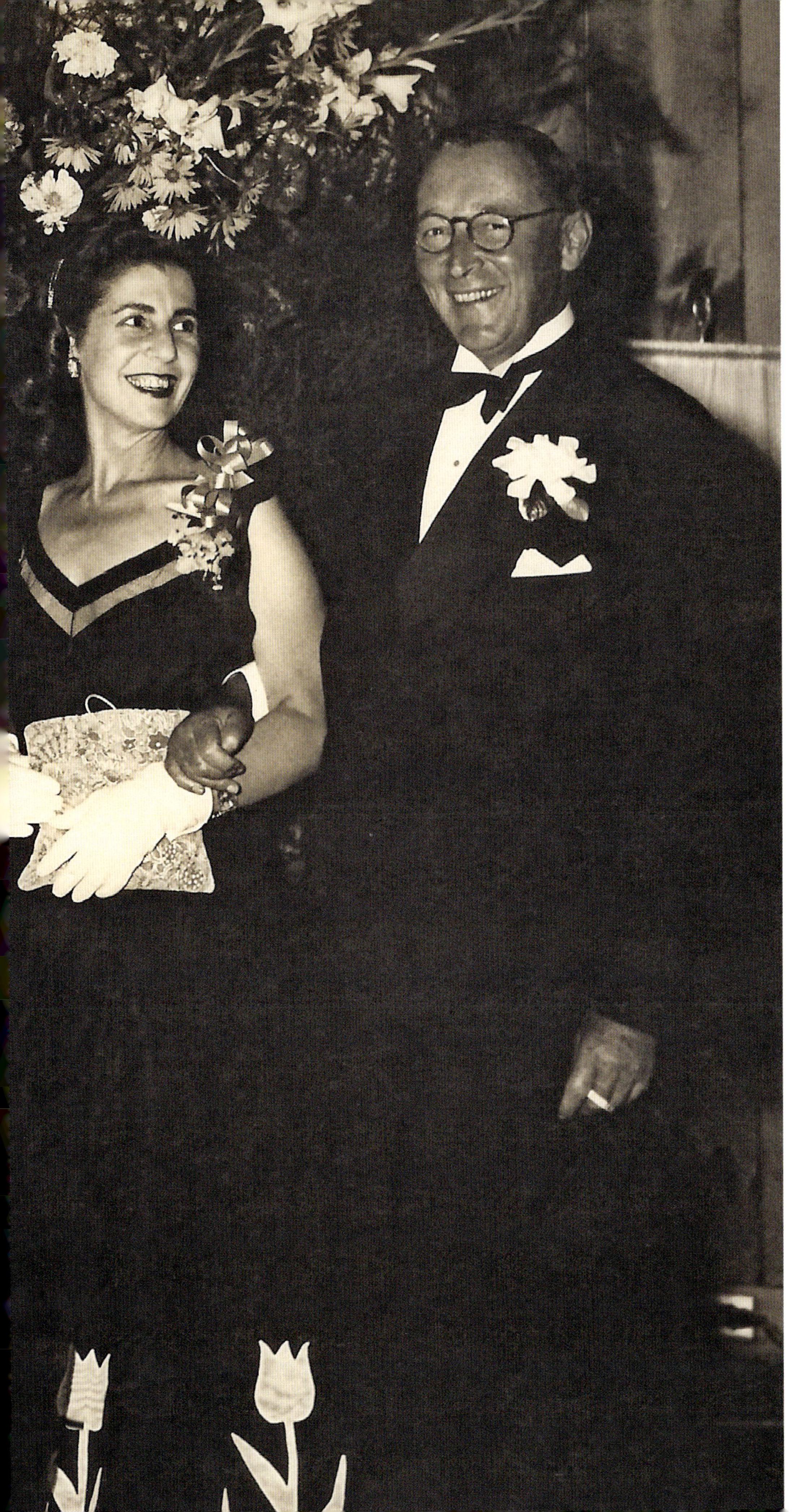

PREVIOUS PAGES
Shirley Temple inspects her daughter Sue Black's gown before her debutante party at the Sheraton Palace Hotel. San Francisco, 1965.

LEFT
Jackie Lee Bouvier and Rosie Grovesnor with their their parents, Mr. and Mrs. Theodore Grovesnor and Mr. and Mrs. Hugh Auchincloss. Newport, Rhode Island, 1948.

FOLLOWING PAGES, LEFT
Debutante Honora Winthrop Mason, was considered one of the most attractive debutantes in Boston. She was presented to society by her aunt Mrs. Joeseph Grafton Minot. Miss Mason's parents, Philip Dana Mason and Mary Emma (Winthrop) Mason, had both died when she was an infant. As seen in *Town & Country*, 1925.

FOLLOWING PAGES, RIGHT
Debutante Miss Martha Louise Aldrich (bottom), "one of the most popular debutantes of the season." As seen in *Town & Country*, 1925.

# EVENTS IN SOCIETY

THE winter season for New York, as for other cities, is rich with promise in social plans. It is a vital, rushing prospect, which is going to be gayly electric, throbbing with more interest than the individual can absorb, and productive of a general breathlessness, as one regards it from a distance up the brightly carpeted aisle of autumn's approach. In this blessed autumn interval, before getting into the winter whirl, there is something very lazy in the atmosphere, something very pressing about the temptation to go leisurely, enjoying the peace before the pace begins; talking disconnectedly of this thing or that, as it comes to mind. Whatever appears on this page in this October issue will appear just as it comes to mind, a few notes of the things that have occupied our thoughts in the news recently, and out of it—just leaves—some gay, some somber—as they've droppped on the leaf-carpeted aisle of the autumnal approach to winter.

### Miss Mason Introduced

OF the outstanding introductions to society this season the début of Miss Honora Winthrop Mason is important and interesting. The niece and ward of Mrs. Joseph Grafton Minot, of 175 Beacon Street, Boston, will be presented by Mrs. Minot, in Boston, at a ball at the Hotel Somerset, December seventh. On December twenty-ninth Mr. Grafton Minot will give a small dance for her at Pierre's, in New York. Due the privileges of a highly delightful social connection, the winter's outlook for Miss Mason is a happy one. A comparative stranger to New York as well as to Boston—she has been at Miss Windsor's School for the last two or three years, and has spent the intervals mostly abroad and in California—she will make her bow under the most favorable conditions, with the Newport-Boston-New York friends of her family standing ready to open their doors and give her cordial greeting.

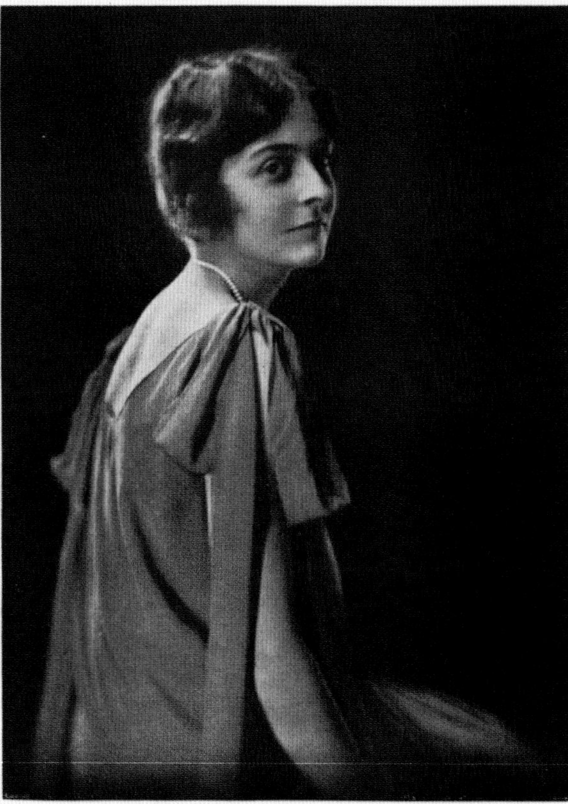

**MISS HONORA WINTHROP MASON**

**An exclusive photographic study, made abroad, of one of the most attractive of next winter's débutantes, the niece and ward of Mrs. Joseph Grafton Minot, of Boston, by whom she will be presented to society. An accompanying note appears on this page**

### The Dearborns' Return

IT is always a heart-warming thing to contemplate when a man and woman with widely declared charm, having lived sufficiently to prove their capacities for good and loyal friendships, decide at length to join forces on the great highway of matrimony. Neither Beth Evans nor David Dearborn—both charming, both having hosts of good friends—had been married before, up to the time they took their vows in Paris, last August, in the apartment of Mrs. William Astor Chanler, the scene of many a happy gathering in years past for the former Miss Evans. Mr. and Mrs. Dearborn have recently returned from their honeymoon and are at the Hotel Chatham for awhile. Their first week-end at home was spent at the country place of Mr. Dearborn's sister, Mrs. Lewis Lapham, at New Canaan, Connecticut, after which they made a visit to Maine, where they were guests of his cousins, the Sewalls. An account of the wedding comes with the arrival of the couple from Europe, as recorded in the Paris *Herald*. After the simple ceremony in the Chanler apartment, a reception followed at the Ritz. The guests gathering there were Mrs. Newbold Edgar, Mrs. Henry Alexander, Mrs. Philip Rhinelander, Mr. and Mrs. Allan McLane, Mr. and Mrs. Eugene Lentilhon, Mr. and Mrs. Robert Langdon, Mrs. Joseph B. Thomas, Miss Dorothy Fellowes Gordon, Miss Muriel Dundas—who was maid of honor—Mr. and Mrs. Edward Choate, Dr. and Mrs. Francis Murray, Nathan Gibson Clarke, Miss Belle Greene, Major and Mrs. Helmsley, Miss Mary Louise Emmet and Mr. Jan Boissevain.

### Folding Their Tents

BORN in the winter home of his parents, on Fifth Avenue, December 19, 1880, it was a touching circumstance that of all his family Reginald Vanderbilt's mother should have been alone with him—with the exception of doctors, nurses and attendants—when he made his final departure at his summer home, Sandy Point Farm, at Newport. So many of those who'd been at Newport for the Vanderbilt-Church wedding, the tennis matches, and all the accompanying parties—not to speak of numberless other parties which gave the place a great season this year—little expected to be brought back so quickly and, in the dignity which the Church offers, pay him the tribute and the fealty of their presence at the last great event in his honor. His daughter, Cathleen, rushed back from the Canadian Rockies with her husband, Harry Cushing; the W. K. Vanderbilts—Mrs. Vanderbilt, Mrs. Church and Consuelo Vanderbilt—gathered with the rest of the large Vanderbilt family in St. Mary's Church at Portsmouth. The widow, the former Gloria Morgan, and her mother, Mrs. Harry Hayes Morgan, and the Vanderbilt baby, Gloria Laura, were brought back from New York, where they were about to sail for South America, to join Mr. Morgan. Brigadier-General Vanderbilt and Mrs. Vanderbilt, Miss Grace Vanderbilt and Mr. and Mrs. Harry Payne Whitney were among the close relatives who helped support the senior Mrs. Vanderbilt in her ordeal. Following the services—as has already been written in detail in the newspaper accounts—the funeral party boarded the train for New York and at New Dorp, on Staten Island, the last of what remained of a genial, convivial friend was laid to rest with his fathers in the Vanderbilt tomb.

### Walking in Grief

EXCEEDINGLY tragic has been the summer for Mrs. Woodbury Langdon. We have read notes of the death of her sister, Janet Tillotson Floyd, widow of John Gelston Floyd, but little has been said in the press regarding the significance in a cable dispatch from London, in June, which simply stated that news had been received in the English capital of the finding of the body of John Langdon, an American, in a river in Kashmir, in Northern India. John was one of the family of children born to Mrs. Langdon and the late Woodbury G. Langdon. He was in his early twenties, was handsome and, like his brothers and sisters, had inherited great wealth. The Langdon Hotel, if we are not mistaken, is one of the Langdon properties. Young Mr. Langdon left last spring, or early in the summer, to go on a world tour. He was missing nineteen days from his headquarters in India before a body, later identified as his, was discovered in the river. Distance was an element of hardship to the family at home, but it was at length found out that he had been walking an embankment and there had been a cave-in. His body will probably be returned to America, but, owing to official stipulations, not for some time. A brother, Dudley, was drowned several years ago. Mrs. Floyd, Mrs. Langdon's sister, died at Rhinebeck. There is another sister, Miss Adelaide H. Montgomery. The well-known New York clergyman, the late Reverend Henry E. Montgomery, was the father of Mrs. Langdon, the late Mrs. Floyd and Miss Montgomery.

### Having Joined the Vast Majority

EDWARD R. STETTINIUS has left a very vivid vacancy to mark his place in the world. A man with the force and personality to have accomplished what he has, does not step out of the company of his associates, or the close circle of his relatives and friends, and leave behind no form, no reminder he is no longer there. This second member of the Morgan firm, to join the vast majority in the last few years, undermined his health during the strenuous war period and reduced his resistance to such a point that when he was operated upon for appendicitis, in 1920, he never regained hs full quota of strength. He was born in St. Louis in 1865.

# EVENTS IN SOCIETY

IT is not everyone who dances in a Paul Jones who has the chance of gaining a Princess as a partner. But such was the case at the Thé Dansant given at the Hyde Park Hotel in aid of the Middlesex Hospital. The Princess in question was Princess Arthur of Connaught, who entered into the fun and danced indefatigably with all the stage celebrities, including Sir Gerald du Maurier, George Grossmith, Joseph Coyne, Henry Ainley and Richard Bird. Lady Alexander and Lady Wyndham organized the affair and conceived the brilliant idea of having stage stars present so one could dance with a celebrity by paying five shillings, and Misses Gladys Cooper, Peggy O'Neil, Tullalah Bankhead, Heather Thatcher and Viola Tree did so well they were almost exhausted. Mrs. Kendal beamed serenely at the proceedings. Poor Joseph Coyne was auctioned so often for a pound that it looked as if it would be impossible for him to tear himself away to go to "No, No, Nanette." Mrs. Philipson, M.P., the one-time Mabel Russell, as a Cockney flower-girl, complete in straw hat and shawl, recited the poem that is such an appeal to Londoners at present, "Middlesex 'Ospital's Fallin' Down." Later, Mrs. Philipson changed into an afternoon dress and joined the dancers. Many well-known people had tables and the hospital profited greatly.

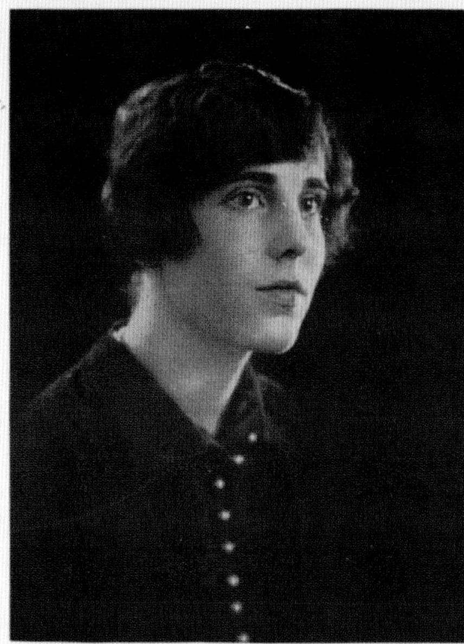

Pach Brothers

MISS BESSIE BELMONT

Daughter of Mrs. John D. Wing, 2d, and the late August Belmont, Jr., a débutante on the New York scroll of '25-'26

### Mrs. Houghton "At Home" Again

MRS. HOUGHTON has resumed her Thursday afternoon receptions at Crewe House, which are so much appreciated by the members of the American colony in London. The American Ambassador and Mrs. Houghton spent a recent week-end as the guests of the Marquis and Marchioness of Salisbury at that marvelous Elizabethan mansion with its Tudor relics and memories, Hatfield House.

### An Interesting Exhibition

A MOST interesting autumn exhibition being held at the Royal Academy is that of the International Society of Sculptors, Painters and Gravers. The Private View day was almost as crowded with important people as the real exhibition of the year in May. Lord Birkenhead made the opening address. To the humble lover of pictures, and all that is beautiful, some of the canvasses gave one the feeling of needing a sedative and a desire to haunt the galleries where, between the examples of ultra-modern art, there was a peaceful, beautifully-executed bit of work that did not make the bewildered art lover feel that many of the artists represented were in for a really bad time if they went out unattended. One of the most pleasing portraits was that of Miss Elsie de Wolfe by Oswald Birley. It really looked like the person it was intended to represent. Two portraits that were equally delightful were Sir William Orpen's, R.A., "The Irish Volunteer" and "Miss Jill Martin," by Ambrose McEvoy, R.A. Of the more modern school the many pictures by Jacovleff were among the most interesting, while, of course, Sir John Lavery, R.A.'s work was excellent. Mme. Merry del Val, the Duchess of Atholl, Sir Hamar and Lady Greenwood, Mrs. Avery Robinson, who had a case of her exquisite sculptured flowers on exhibition, the Rt. Hon. David and Dame Lloyd George, Lady Birkenhead, Lady Lever and Mrs. Wesley Watson were some of the private viewers.

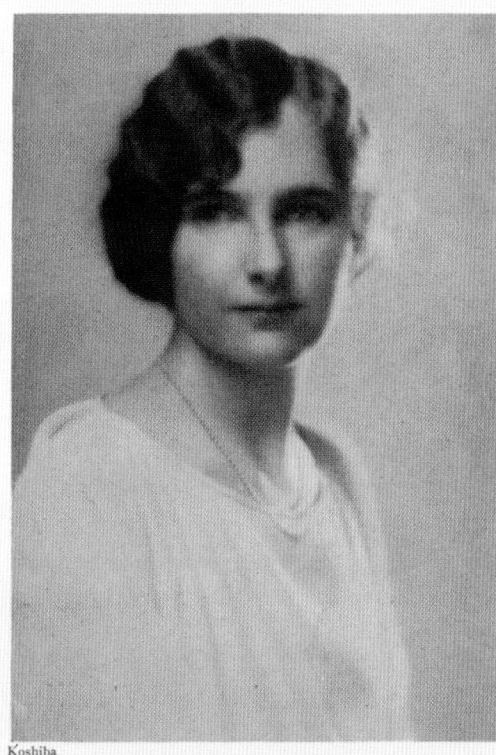

Koshiba

MISS MARTHA LOUISE ALDRICH

A Providence, Rhode Island, débutante of the season, daughter of Mrs. Stuart Aldrich of that city and niece of Mrs. John D. Rockefeller, of New York

### Party for Chaliapine

THE Hon. Mrs. Henry McLaren gave one of the most interesting parties of the week for Chaliapine, after his concert at the Albert Hall. It was a sort of farewell affair and after singing through a long program at the concert he accommodatingly sang half the night to Mrs. McLaren's guests at her home in South Street, Park Lane, which boasts of one of the few marvelous drawing-rooms in London. There were many interesting guests, among them Lady Colfax, who sailed the following day for America; Mr. H. G. Wells, Mr. and Mrs. John Galsworthy, Sir Phillip Sassoon, Sir John and Lady Lavery, Baroness Ravensdale, Mr. A. E. Mason, the novelist, Mr. and Mrs. Benjamin Guiness, Lady Evelyn and Colonel Walter Guiness, Mme. Lopokova and Mr. Gilbert Russell.

### The Queen of Spain a Great Hostess

THE Queen of Spain is being entertained and entertaining every minute of the day and night and still finds time to go from shop to shop in the most democratic way. Claridge's seems her favorite place to give dinners and luncheons, and the Queen has given quite a number, usually followed by an informal theater party. The Spanish Ambassador and Mme. Merry del Val gave a huge dinner party in honor of Her Majesty, followed by a dance. Princess Mary Viscountess Lascelles, the Duke and Duchess of Sutherland, Countess of Pembroke, Lord and Lady Wimborne, Viscountess Curzon, Lord and Lady Louis Mountbatten, Lord and Lady Alastair Innes-Kerr and Major and Lady Zia Werner were among the dinner guests. The Prince of Wales came in later for the dance. Mrs. Spears (Mary Borden) returned from America and by way of greeting had most of her jewelry and other valuables stolen from her lovely home in Westminster. Colonel and Mrs. Spears are giving a large party on November twelfth.

### Plays and Russians, Etc.

MISS FRANCES CARSON, Lawrence Grossmith and J. H. Roberts labor in vain with "The Silver Fox" at St. Martin's, and they are all too finished artists not to have a play worthier of their efforts. Miss Carson gives an excellent performance of a very unsympathetic character. "La Chauve Souris," those delightful Russians, are packing the Strand Theater and are giving a new program. They remain in London until after Christmas.

### California Note

DEL MONTE society folk well-comed the Prince and Princess Asaka recently, on their visit to Pebble Beach. Of course there was no entertaining in connection with the visit of the Japanese Royalty, but the entire Peninsula took a keen interest in their golf. Incidentally Prince Asaka won over the "home town people" by stating that in their travels all over the world they had yet to see a golf links that compared with Pebble Beach. Mrs. C. Templeton Crocker, of Burlingame, has made reservations for a large party of guests at Del Monte over the holidays.

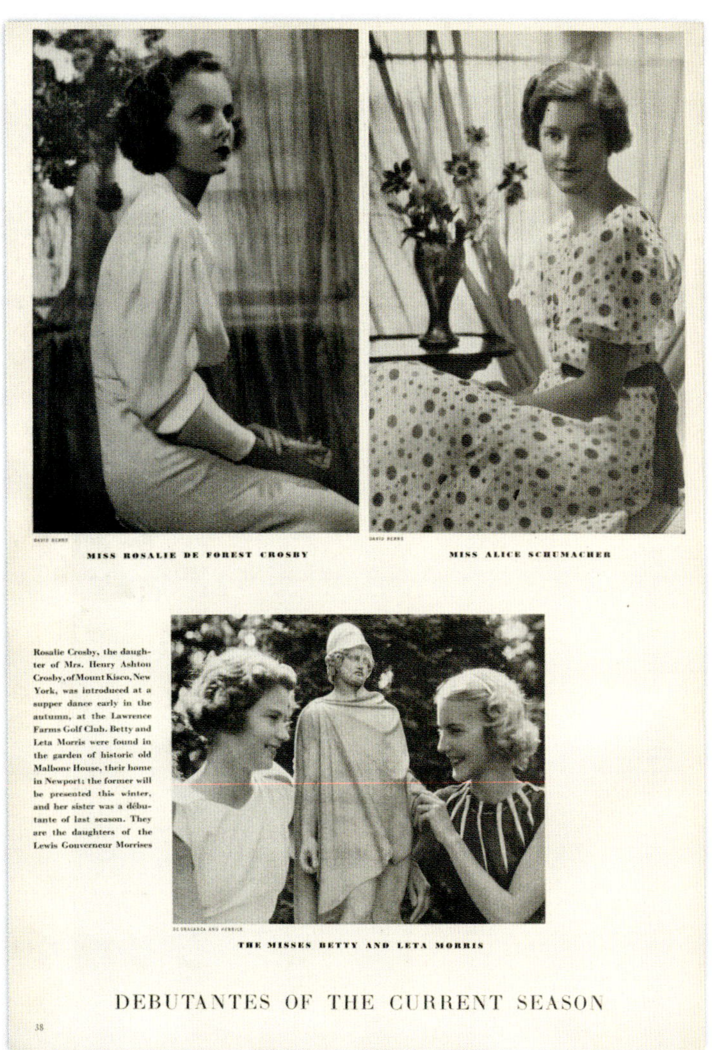

MISS ROSALIE DE FOREST CROSBY

MISS ALICE SCHUMACHER

Rosalie Crosby, the daughter of Mrs. Henry Ashton Crosby, of Mount Kisco, New York, was introduced at a supper dance early in the autumn, at the Lawrence Farms Golf Club. Betty and Leta Morris were found in the garden of historic old Malbone House, their home in Newport; the former will be presented this winter, and her sister was a débutante of last season. They are the daughters of the Lewis Gouverneur Morrises

THE MISSES BETTY AND LETA MORRIS

DEBUTANTES OF THE CURRENT SEASON

38

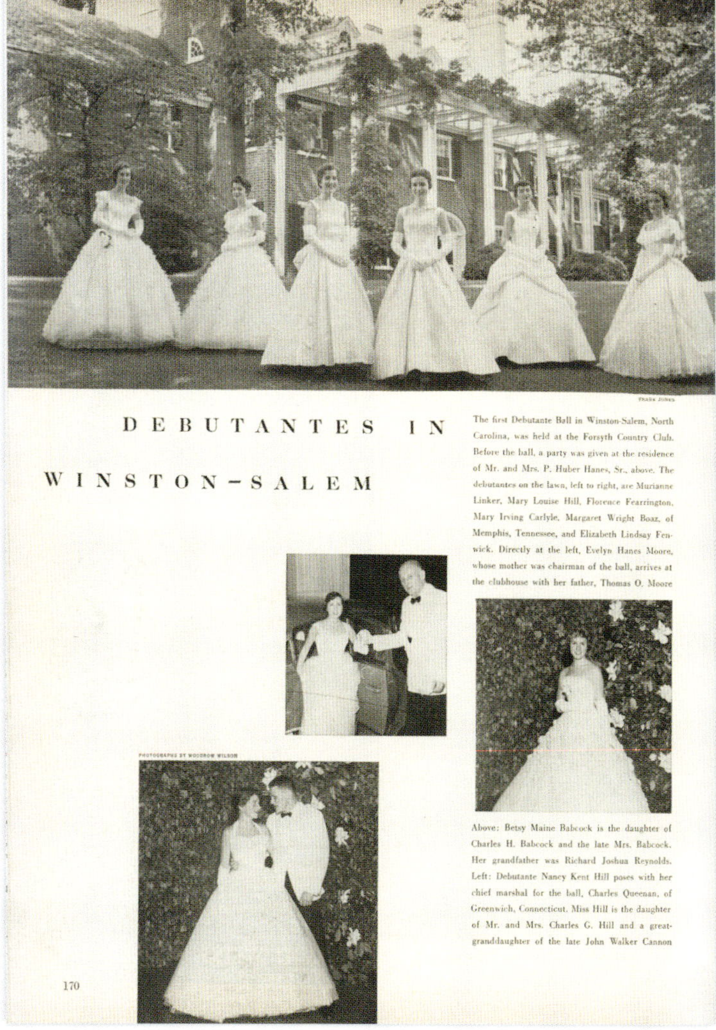

DEBUTANTES IN WINSTON-SALEM

The first Debutante Ball in Winston-Salem, North Carolina, was held at the Forsyth Country Club. Before the ball, a party was given at the residence of Mr. and Mrs. P. Huber Hanes, Sr., above. The debutantes on the lawn, left to right, are Murianne Linker, Mary Louise Hill, Florence Fearrington, Mary Irving Carlyle, Margaret Wright Boaz, of Memphis, Tennessee, and Elizabeth Lindsay Fenwick. Directly at the left, Evelyn Hanes Moore, whose mother was chairman of the ball, arrives at the clubhouse with her father, Thomas O. Moore

Above: Betsy Maine Babcock is the daughter of Charles H. Babcock and the late Mrs. Babcock. Her grandfather was Richard Joshua Reynolds. Left: Debutante Nancy Kent Hill poses with her chief marshal for the ball, Charles Queenan, of Greenwich, Connecticut. Miss Hill is the daughter of Mr. and Mrs. Charles G. Hill and a great-granddaughter of the late John Walker Cannon

170

LEFT

The debutantes of the current season were often pictured in a more casual setting for the press. Debutante Rosalie de Forest Crosby made her debut in Mt. Kisco, New York at a large supper dance given by her mother. Sisters Betty Morris and Leta Morris from Newport, Rhode Island were presented in New York City. It was pointed out in the press that Betty Morris was among the only debutantes of her group to wear an American designer when she was presented. As was observed, all the other debutantes wore the latest fashions from Paris. As seen in *Town & Country*, 1933.

RIGHT

Featured debutantes of the 1956 season in Winston Salem, North Carolina: Murrianne Linker, Mary Louise Hill, Florence Fearrington, Mary Irving Carlyle, Margaret Boaz, and Elizabeth Fenwick. As seen in *Town & Country*, 1956.

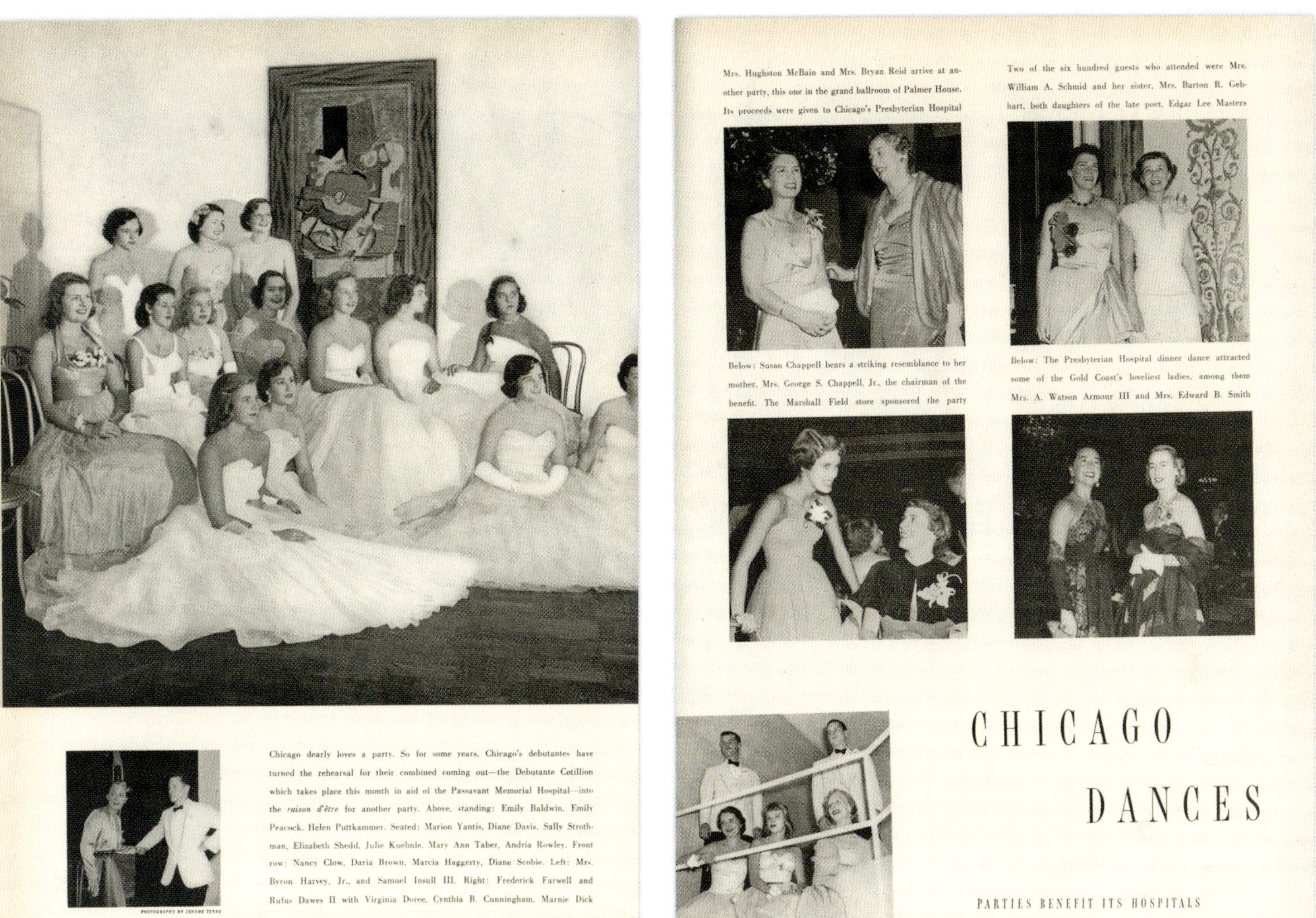

Chicago dearly loves a party. So for some years, Chicago's debutantes have turned the rehearsal for their combined coming out—the Debutante Cotillion which takes place this month in aid of the Passavant Memorial Hospital—into the *raison d'être* for another party. Above, standing: Emily Baldwin, Emily Peacock, Helen Puttkammer. Seated: Marion Yantis, Diane Davis, Sally Strothman, Elizabeth Shedd, Julie Kuehnle, Mary Ann Taber, Andria Rowley. Front row: Nancy Clow, Daria Brown, Marcia Haggerty, Diane Scobie. Left: Mrs. Byron Harvey, Jr., and Samuel Insull III. Right: Frederick Farwell and Rufus Dawes II with Virginia Doree, Cynthia B. Cunningham, Marnie Dick

54

Mrs. Hughston McBain and Mrs. Bryan Reid arrive at another party, this one in the grand ballroom of Palmer House. Its proceeds were given to Chicago's Presbyterian Hospital

Two of the six hundred guests who attended were Mrs. William A. Schmid and her sister, Mrs. Barton R. Gebhart, both daughters of the late poet, Edgar Lee Masters

Below: Susan Chappell bears a striking resemblance to her mother, Mrs. George S. Chappell, Jr., the chairman of the benefit. The Marshall Field store sponsored the party

Below: The Presbyterian Hospital dinner dance attracted some of the Gold Coast's loveliest ladies, among them Mrs. A. Watson Armour III and Mrs. Edward B. Smith

CHICAGO DANCES

PARTIES BENEFIT ITS HOSPITALS

55

LEFT AND RIGHT

Debutantes enjoying the highlight of the Chicago social season: the Debutante Cotillion. As Seen in *Town & Country*, 1959.

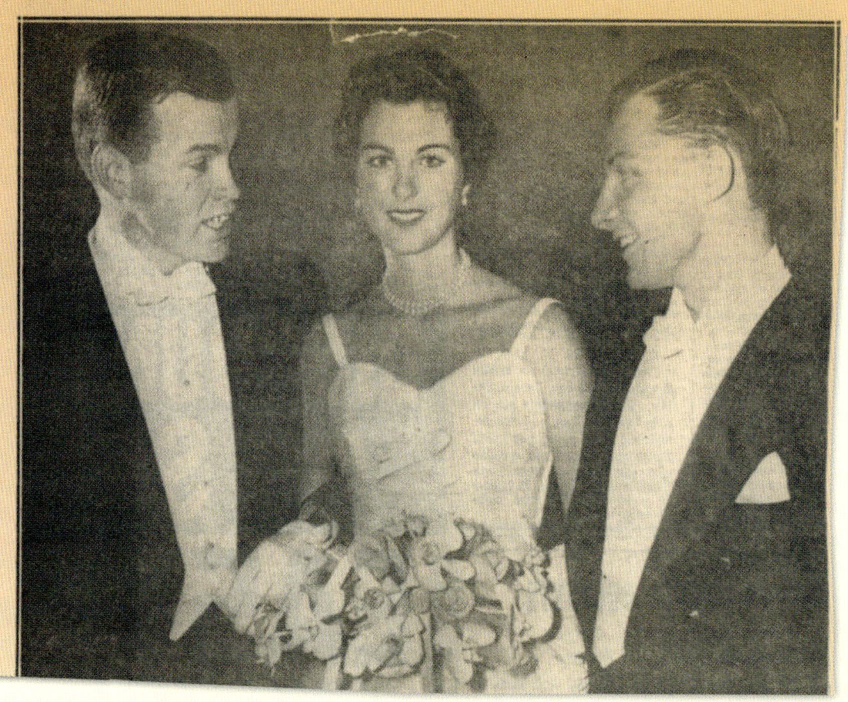

## Pretty Debs Bow At Cotillion

Sean McDonnell (left) and John F. Curry, 3d, pay court to lovely Maria Cooper, daughter of actor Gary Cooper, at the Debutante Cotillion and Christmas Ball, in the Grand Ballroom of the Waldorf-Astoria. One hundred and twelve debs were presented at annual fete which benefits the New York Infirmary. Miss Cooper is the granddaughter of Mrs. Paul

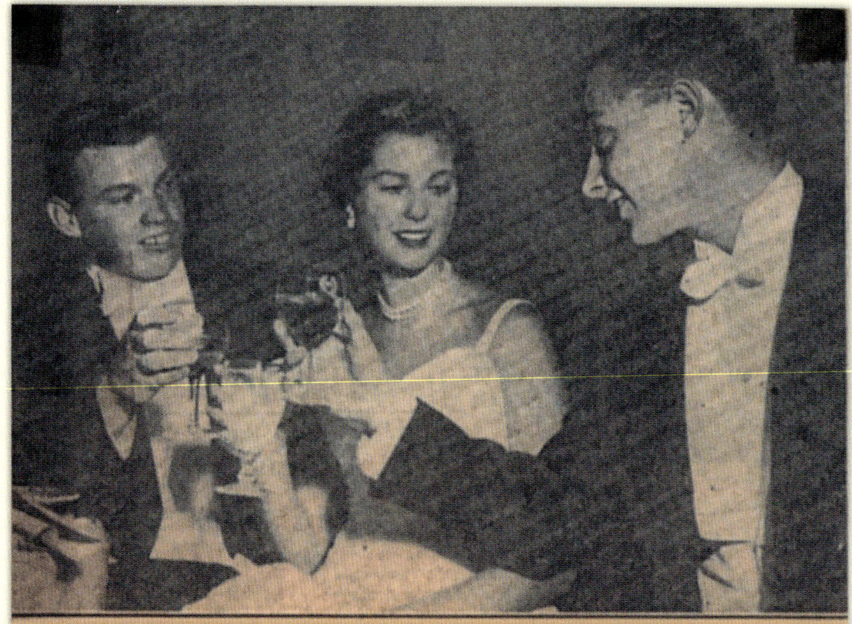

(NEWS foto by John Duprey)

## Yup, It's Gary's Daughter!

Maria Cooper, debutante daughter of Gary Cooper, is toasted by a couple of swains, Sean McDonnell (left) and John F. Curry, at last night's swank Debutante Cotillion and Christmas Ball at the Waldorf-Astoria. In all, 112 debs made a mass debut at the gala, a benefit for the New York Infirmary. —*Story on page 5*

Debutante Maria Cooper came out with considerable publicity given her Hollywood lineage. While her father Gary Cooper was raised in the quiet and reserved state of Montana, Maria's mother, Veronica Balfe or "Rocky" lived for a time in Paris and was quite entrenched in the social world. Maria made her debut at the Christmas Ball at the Waldorf-Astoria Hotel. New York, 1945.

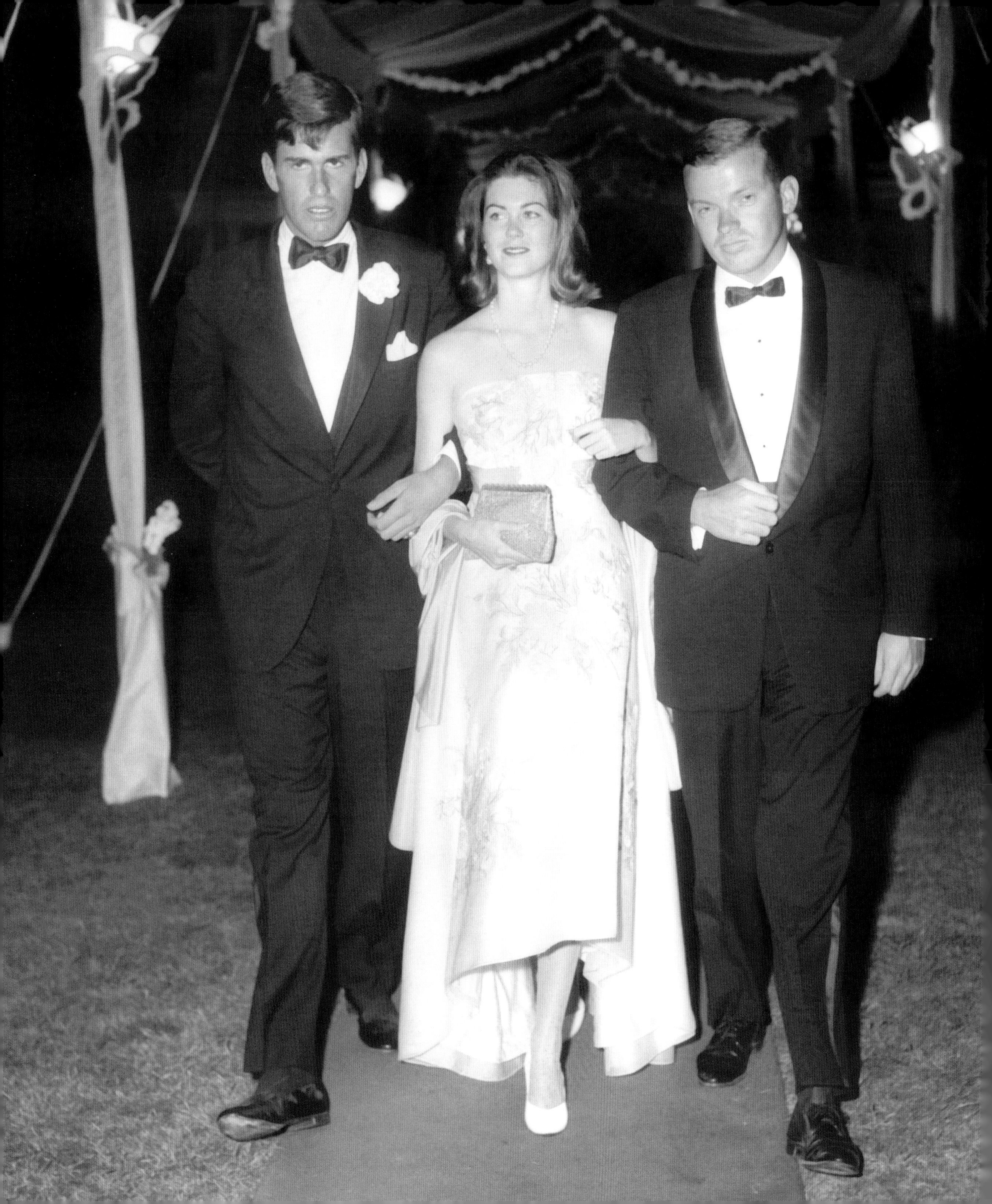

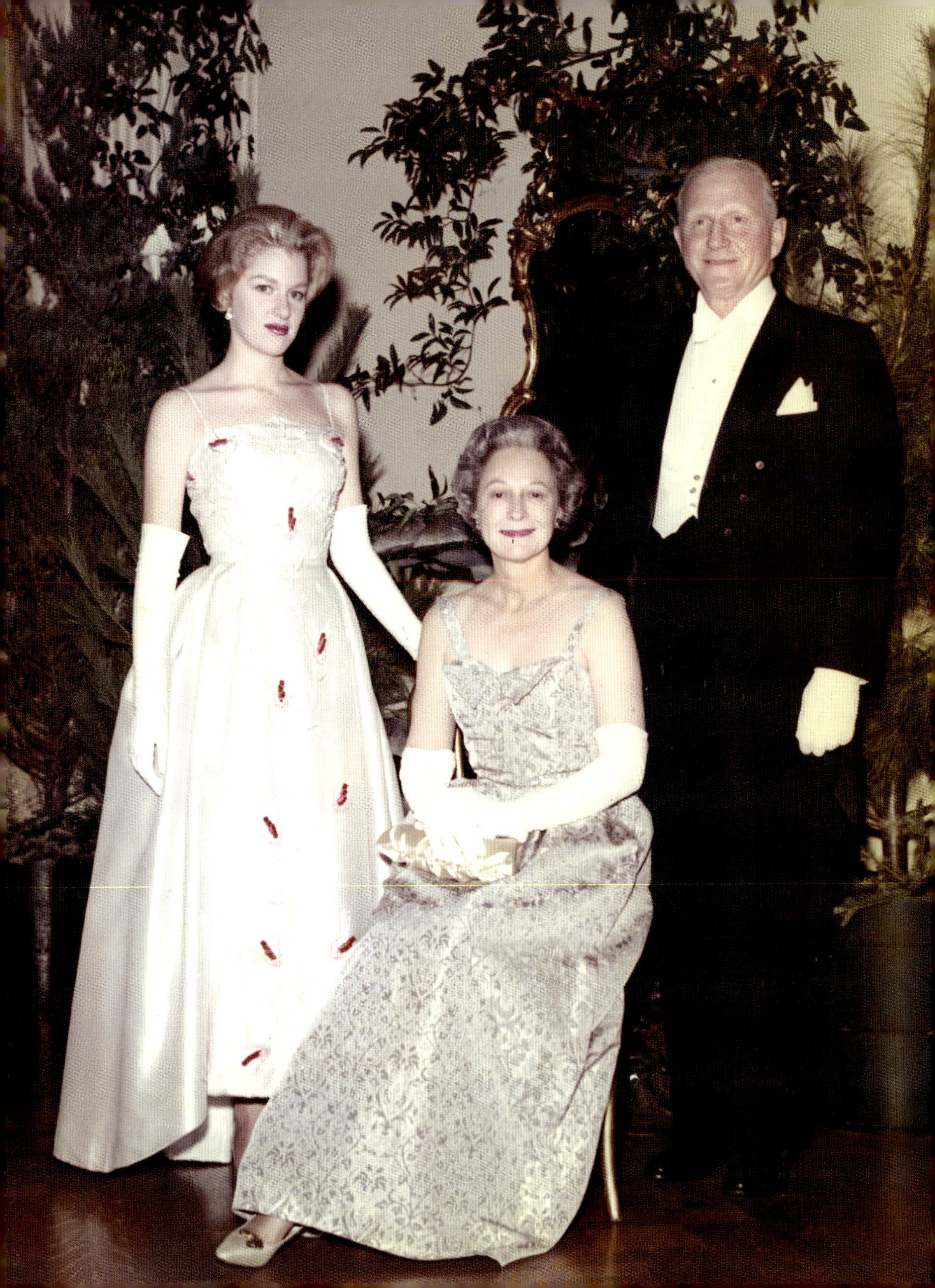

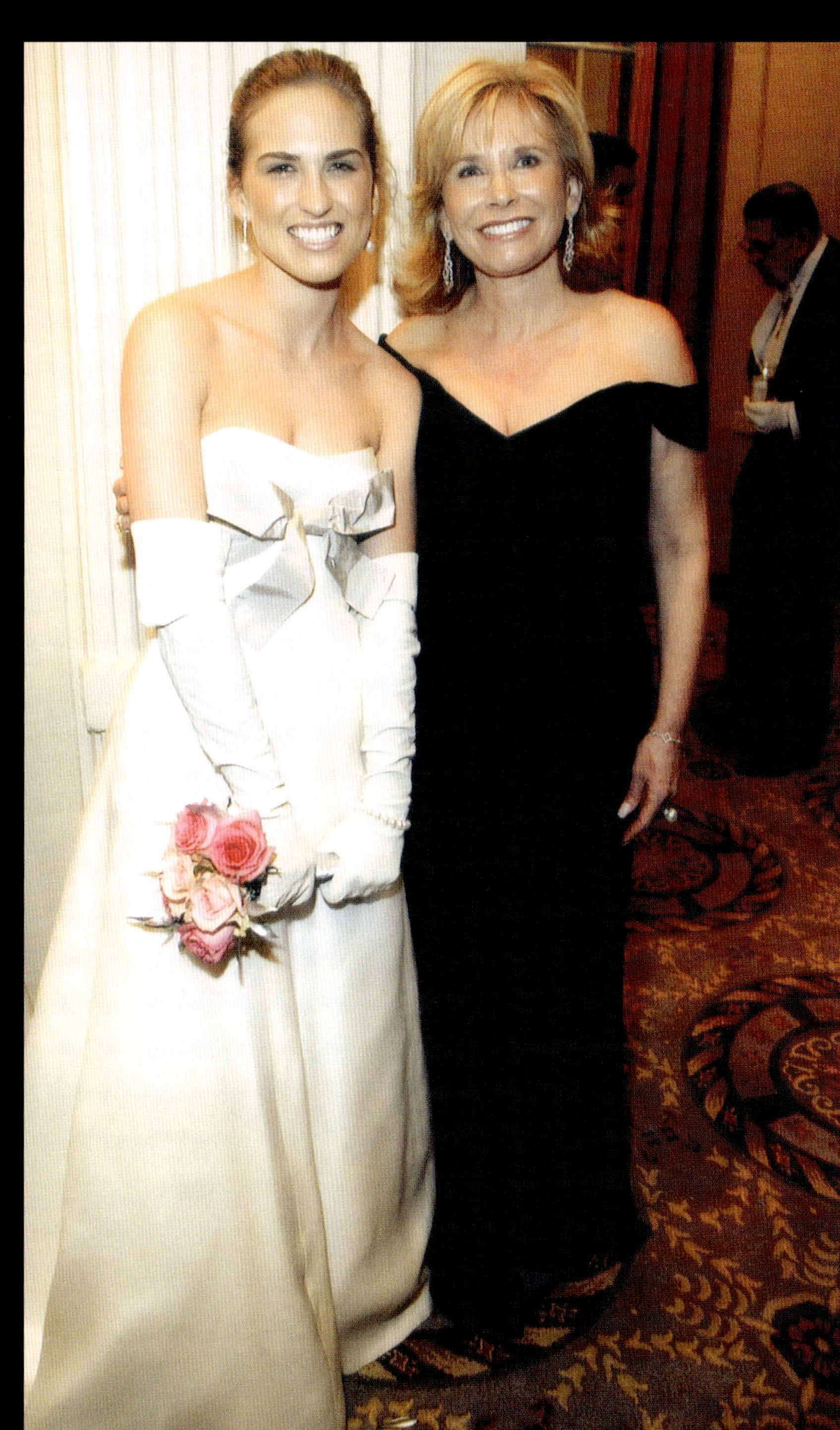

**OPPOSITE**
Mr. and Mrs. William Cutchins with their debutante daughter Alexandra Booth Cutchin. Pendennis Club Ball, Louisville, Kentucky, 1961.

**RIGHT**
Sharon Bush with her daughter Ashley Walker Bush. Ashley's father Neil, is the younger brother of George W. Bush. The International Debutante Ball, New York, 2006.

Eisenhowers attend the International Debutante Ball at the Waldorf-Astoria Hotel. (Left to right) Dwight David Eisenhower II; Barbara Anne Eisenhower; Don Stolper; and Julie Nixon, Eisenhower's fiancée. New York, 1967.

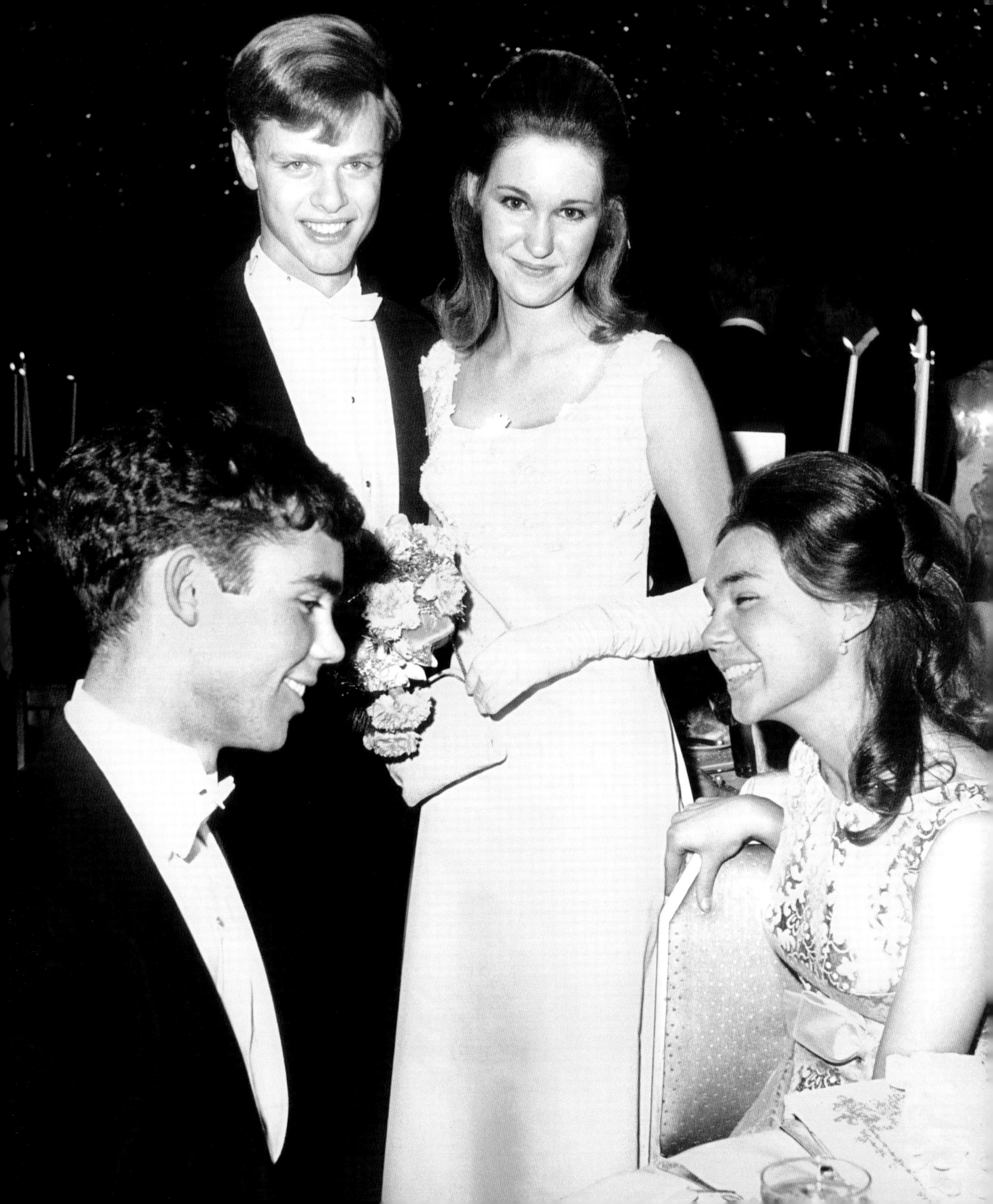

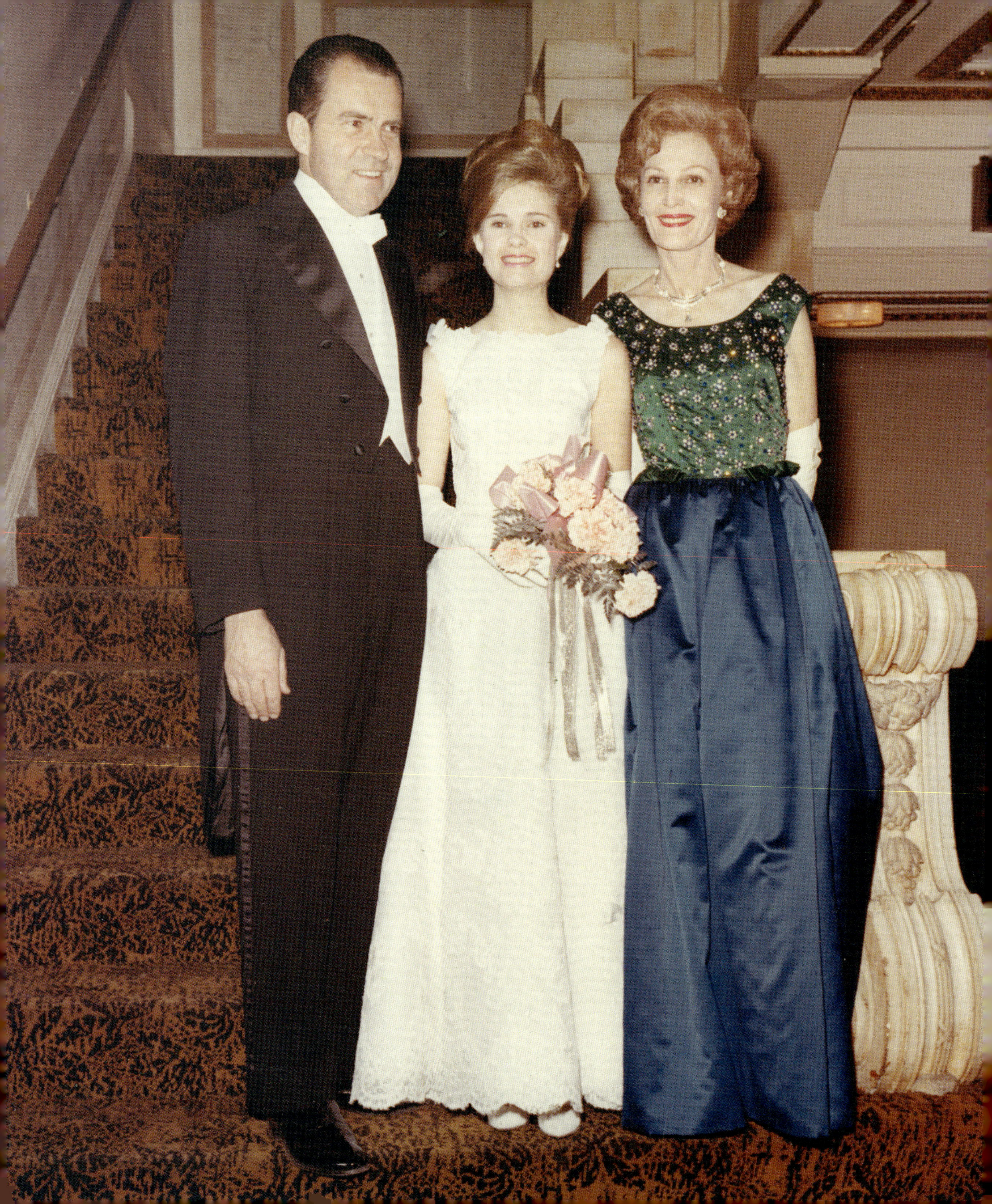

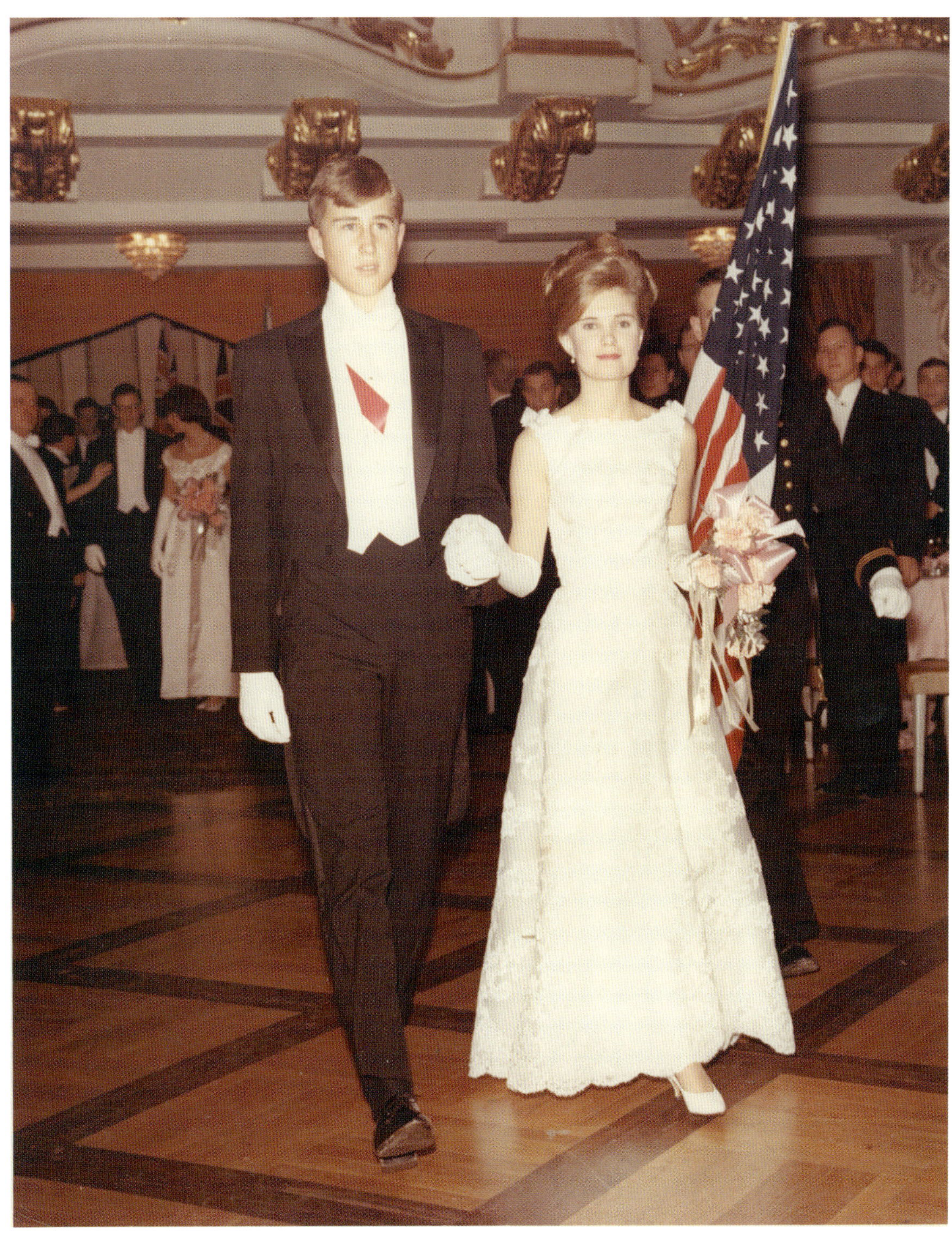

OPPOSITE
Then future President Nixon and Mrs. Nixon with their debutante daughter, Tricia Nixon. New York, 1964.

ABOVE
Tricia Nixon with her escort, Edward Cox, at The International Debutante Ball. New York, 1964.

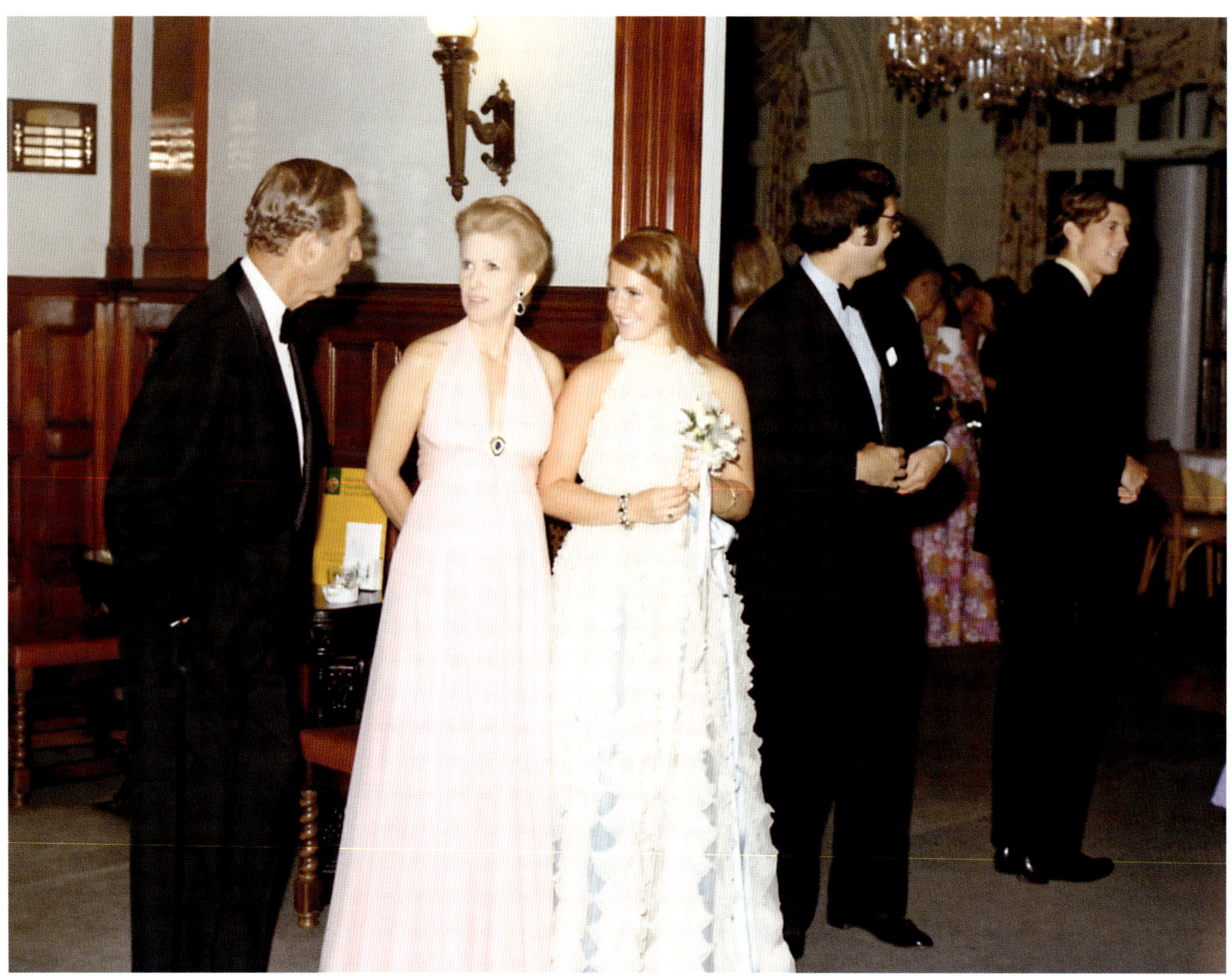

ABOVE

Cornelius Vanderbilt "Sonny" Whitney and Mary Lou Whitney with their daughter Heather, at her coming out party. Saratoga, New York, 1972.

OPPOSITE

Gloria Vanderbilt was perhaps among one of the more famous young debutantes of her day. Her family background combined with her scandalous custody trial, defined the younger days of Gloria Laura Vanderbilt's childhood. Gloria's aunt, Gertrude Vanderbilt Whitney finally received custody of "little Gloria." Gloria made her debut in New York, 1940.

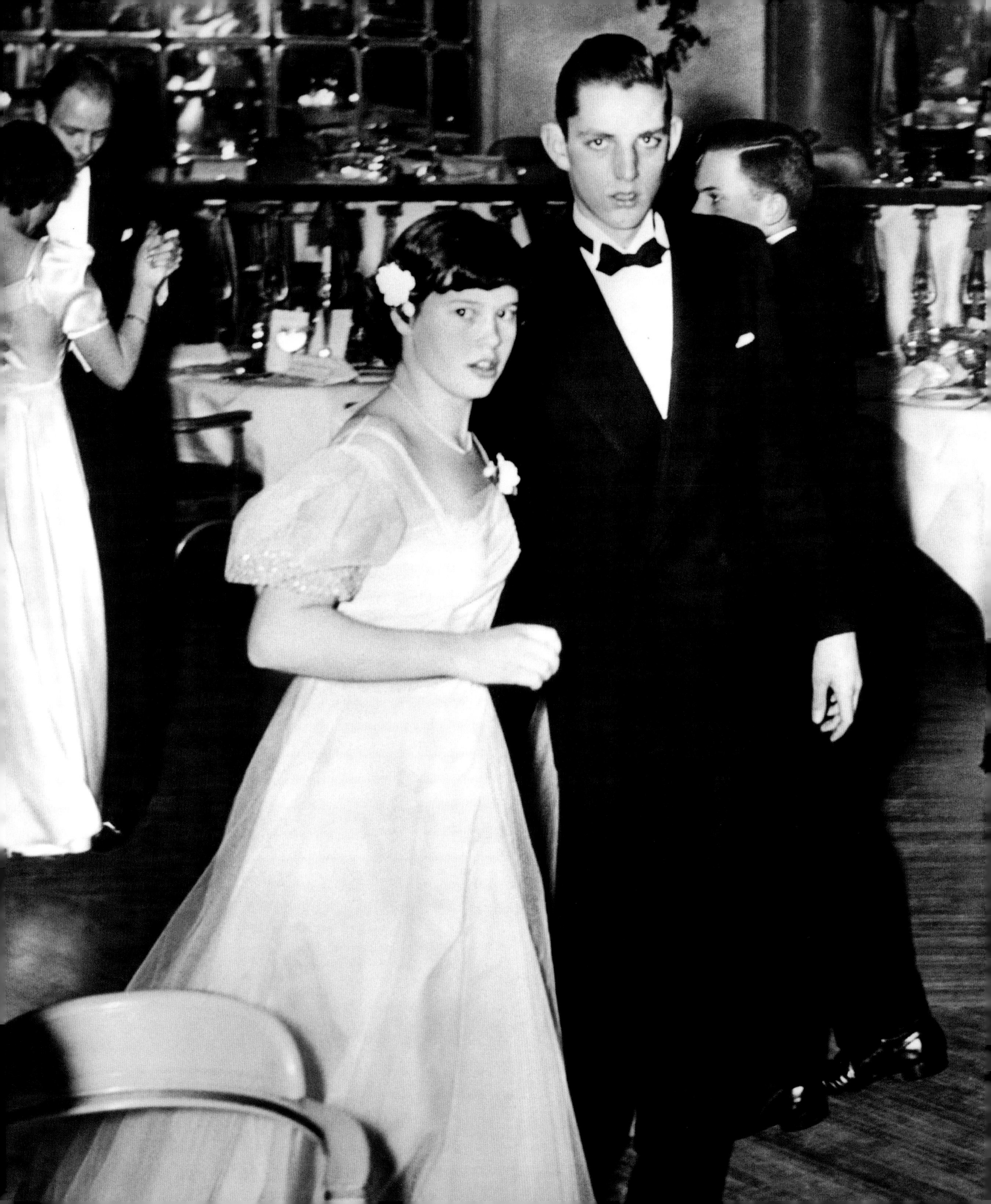

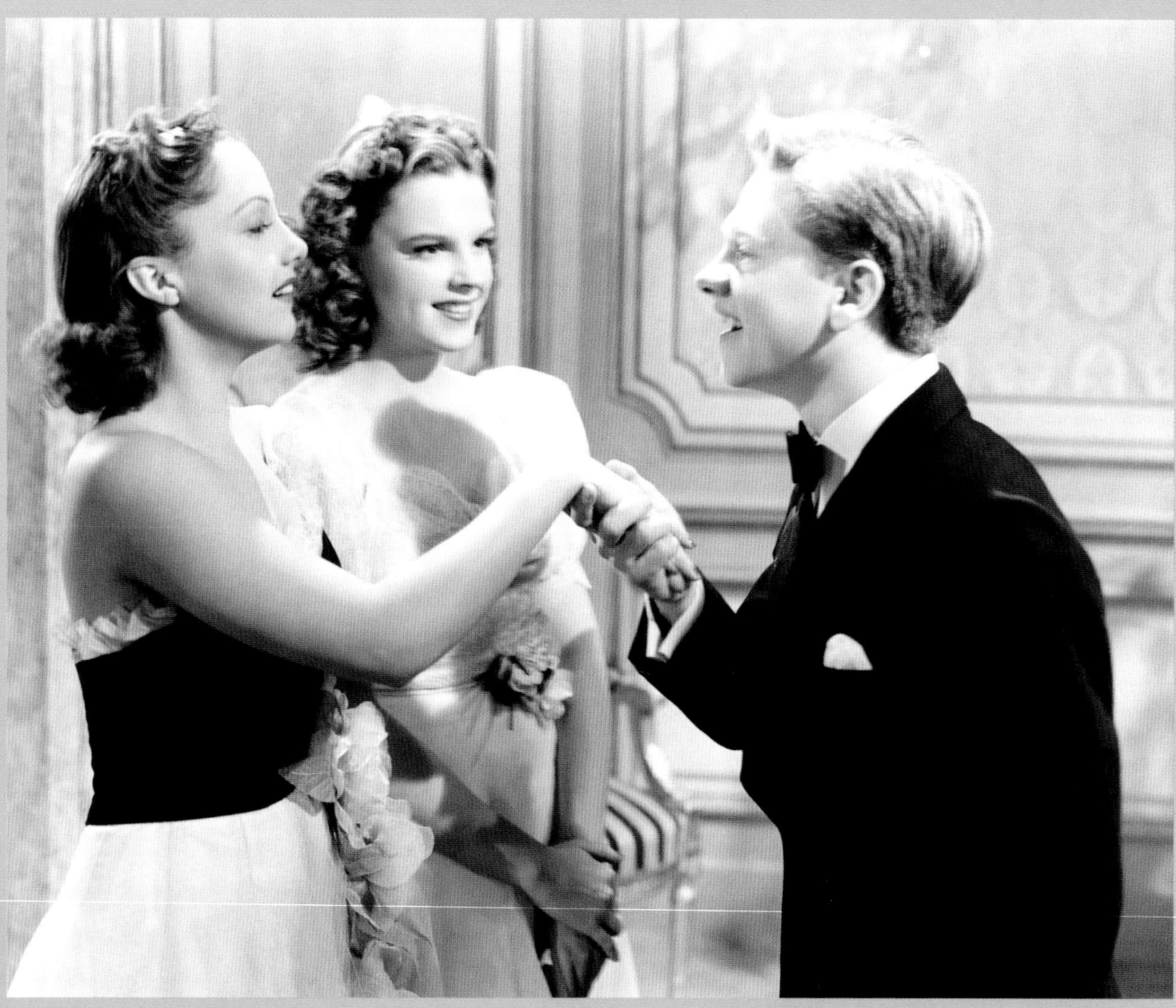

ABOVE
Judy Garland (Frances Ethel Gumm) had a rather modest upbringing in Grand Rapids, Michigan, far from the epicenter of high society and debutantes; however, she went on to star as "Betsy Booth" opposite Andy Rooney in the 1940 film *Andy Hardy Meets Debutante*. Garland's character facilitates Andy Rooney's introduction to the fictitious deb of the day, "Daphne Fowler." Hollywood was rabid with intrigue and interest in the antics of high society, and *Andy Hardy Meets Debutante* was among the films that depicted the fiascos a debutante might encounter.

OPPOSITE
Brooke Hayward making her debut at the Debutante Cotillion and Christmas Ball at the Waldorf-Astoria Hotel. New York, 1955.

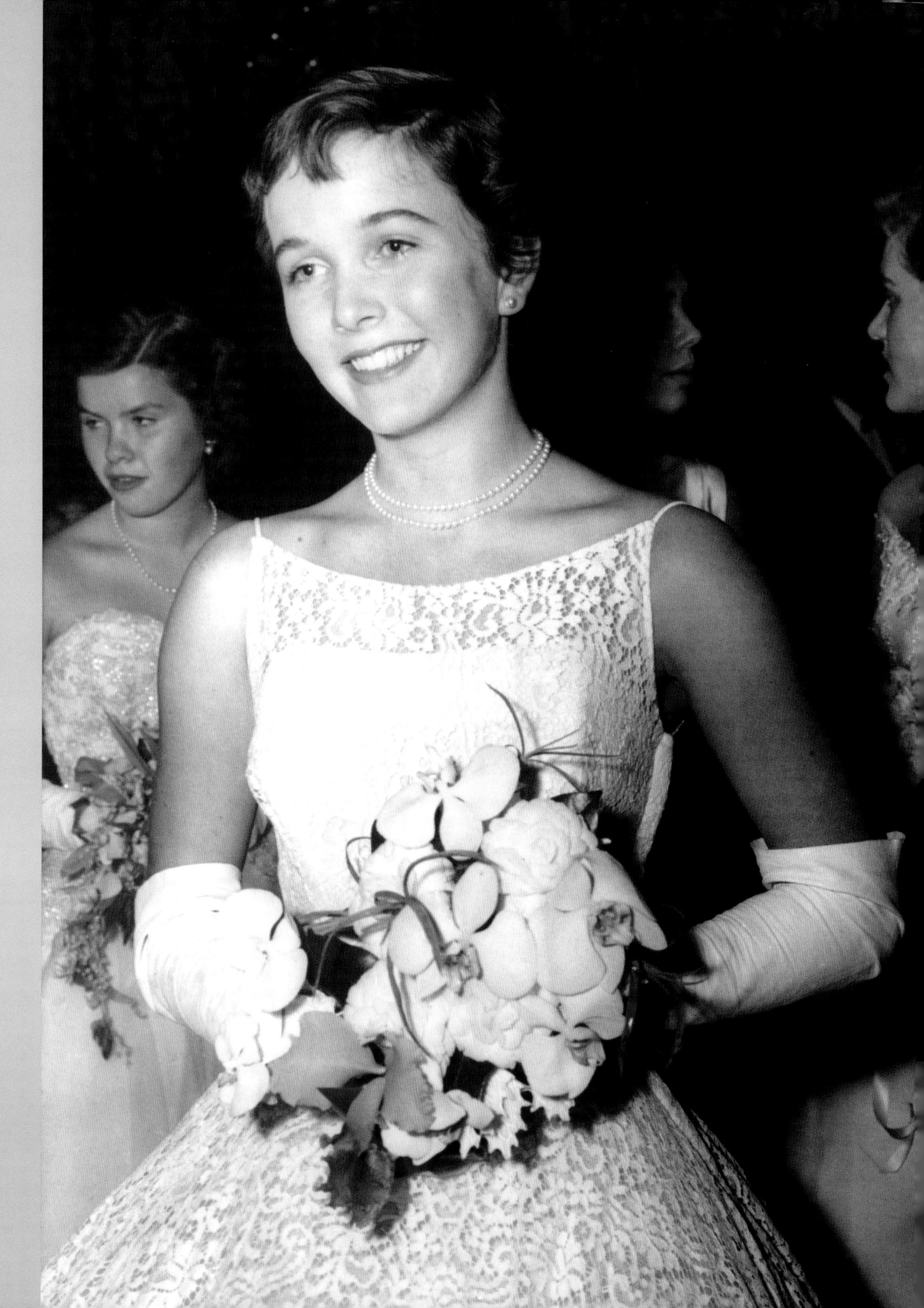

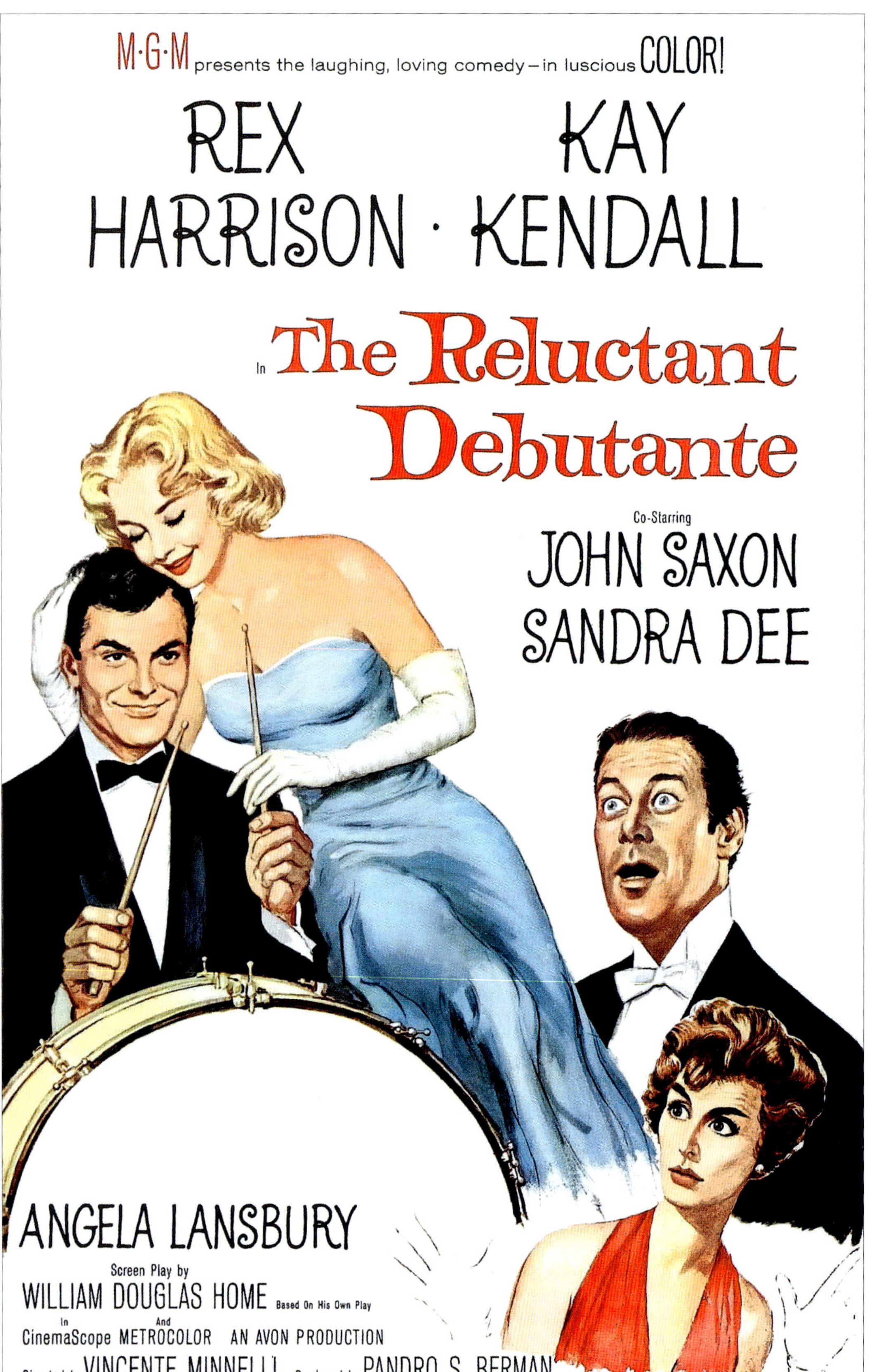


ABOVE AND OPPOSITE
A more sophisticated take on debutantes was the Rex Harrison and Kay Kendall comedy, *The Reluctant Debutante* (1958), directed by Judy Garland's second husband, Vincente Minelli. Based on a play of the same name, seventeen-year-old Jane Broadbent feels immense pressure from her social climbing step-mother to join the ranks of the beautiful debutantes. Bored of the entire process, Jane rebels and mayhem ensues. *The Reluctant Debutante* plot rings true to many of the real life pressures put on some young debutantes who found the process far too exhausting and all too consuming.

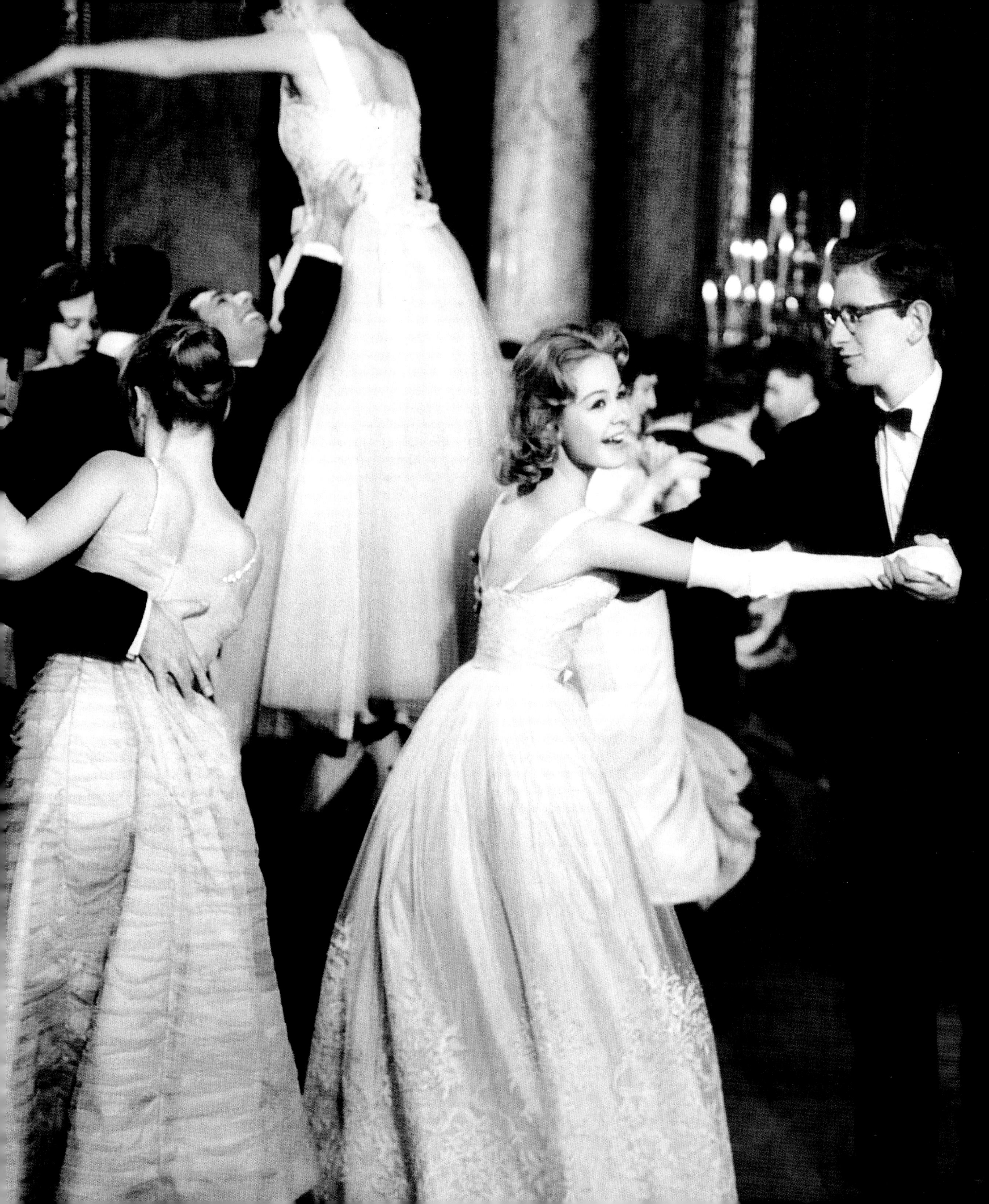

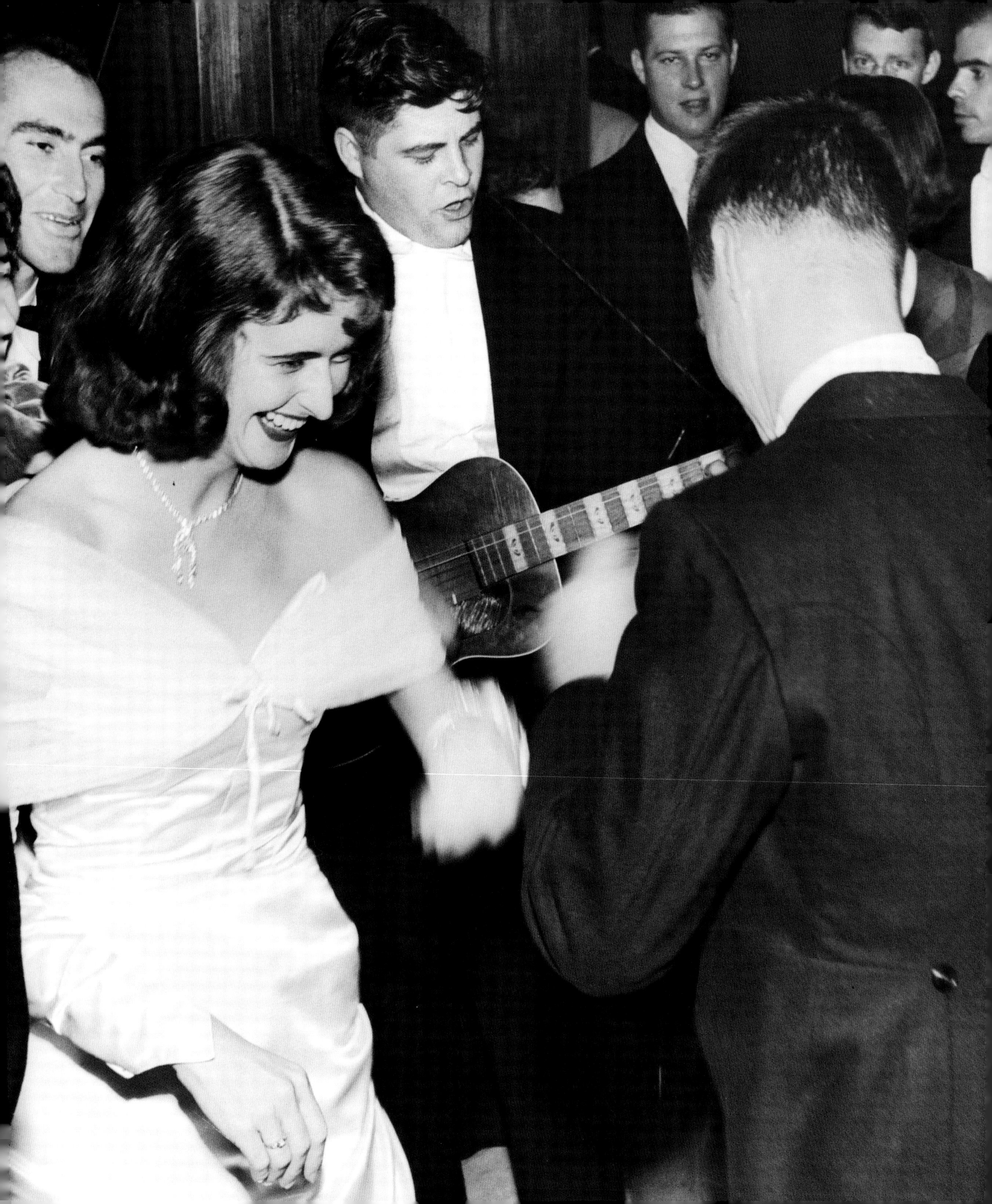

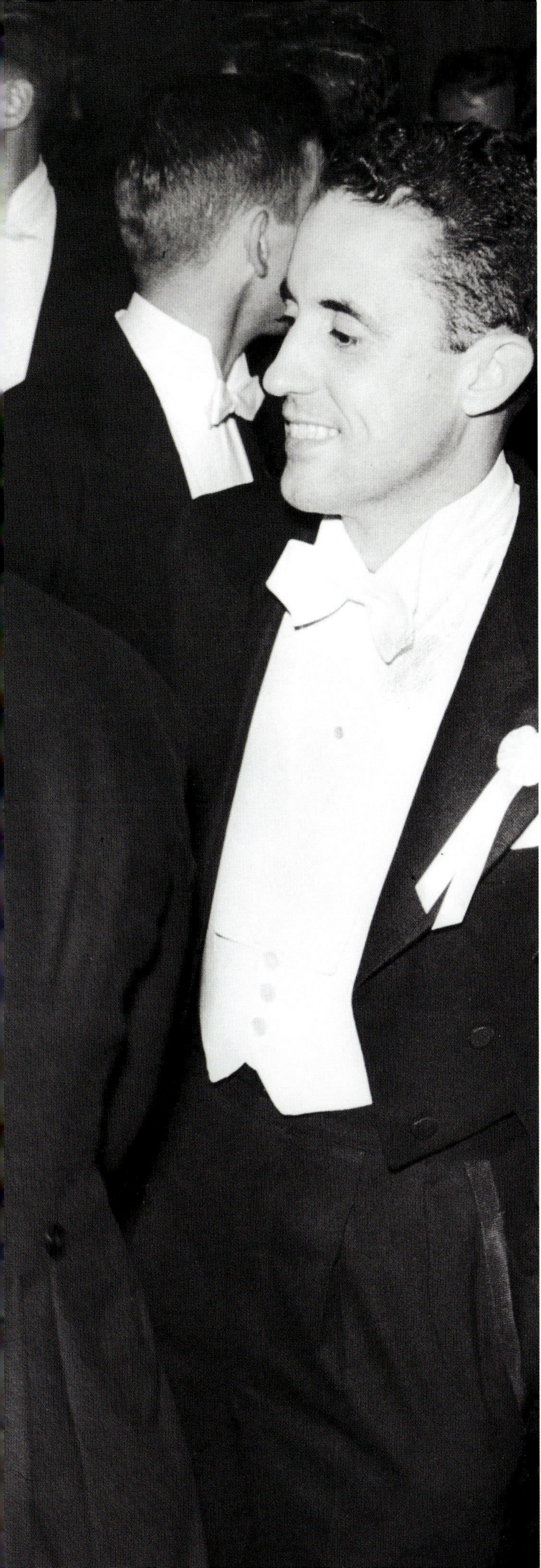

Gentleman's club the Terpsichorean Club of Raleigh, North Carolina has been host to debutantes since 1926. Debutante Betty Lou Merrill enjoys an impromptu dance for her coming out at the Terpsichorean Ball, 1949.

Lauren Bush with her escort at the Crillon Ball. Paris, 2002.

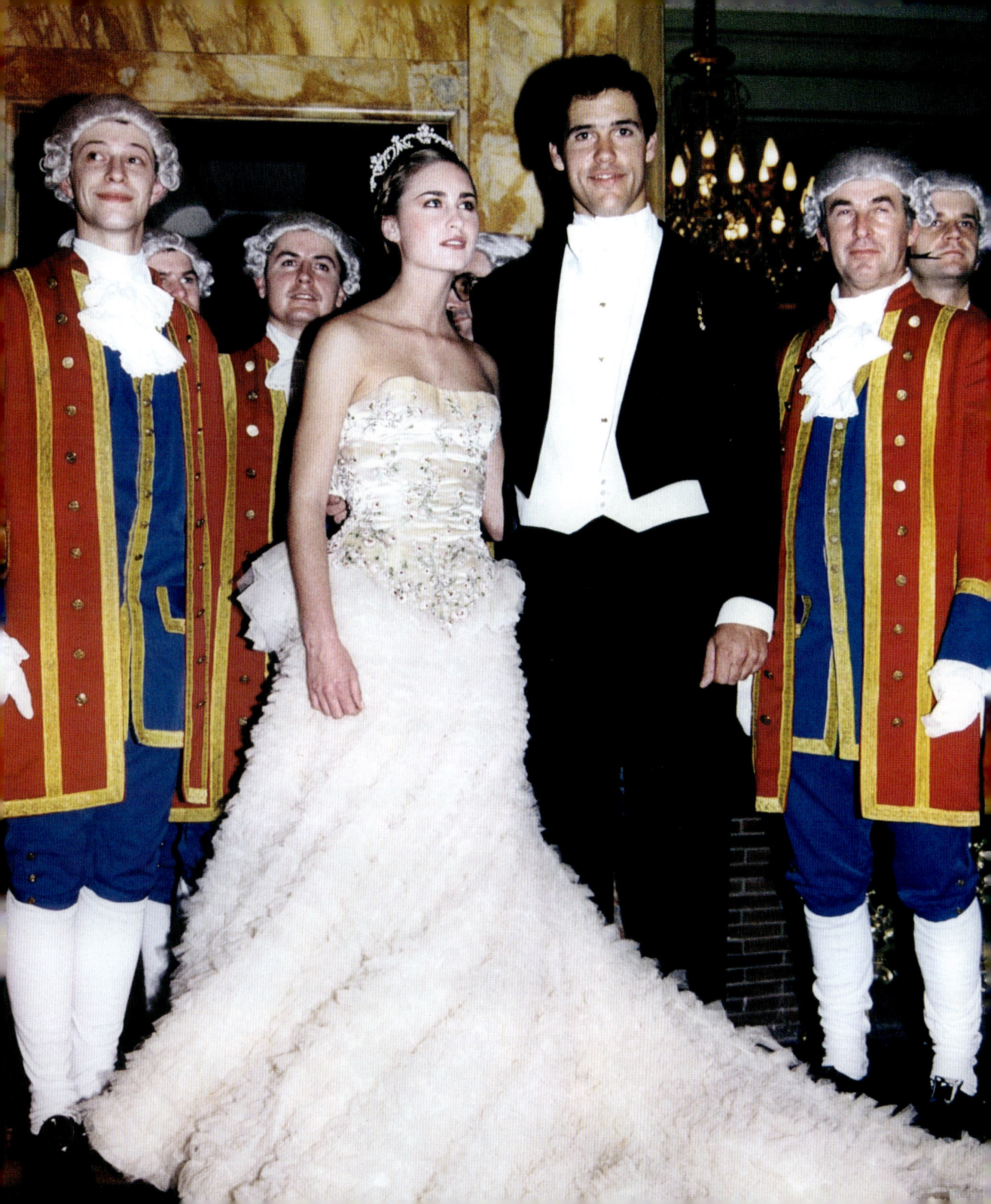

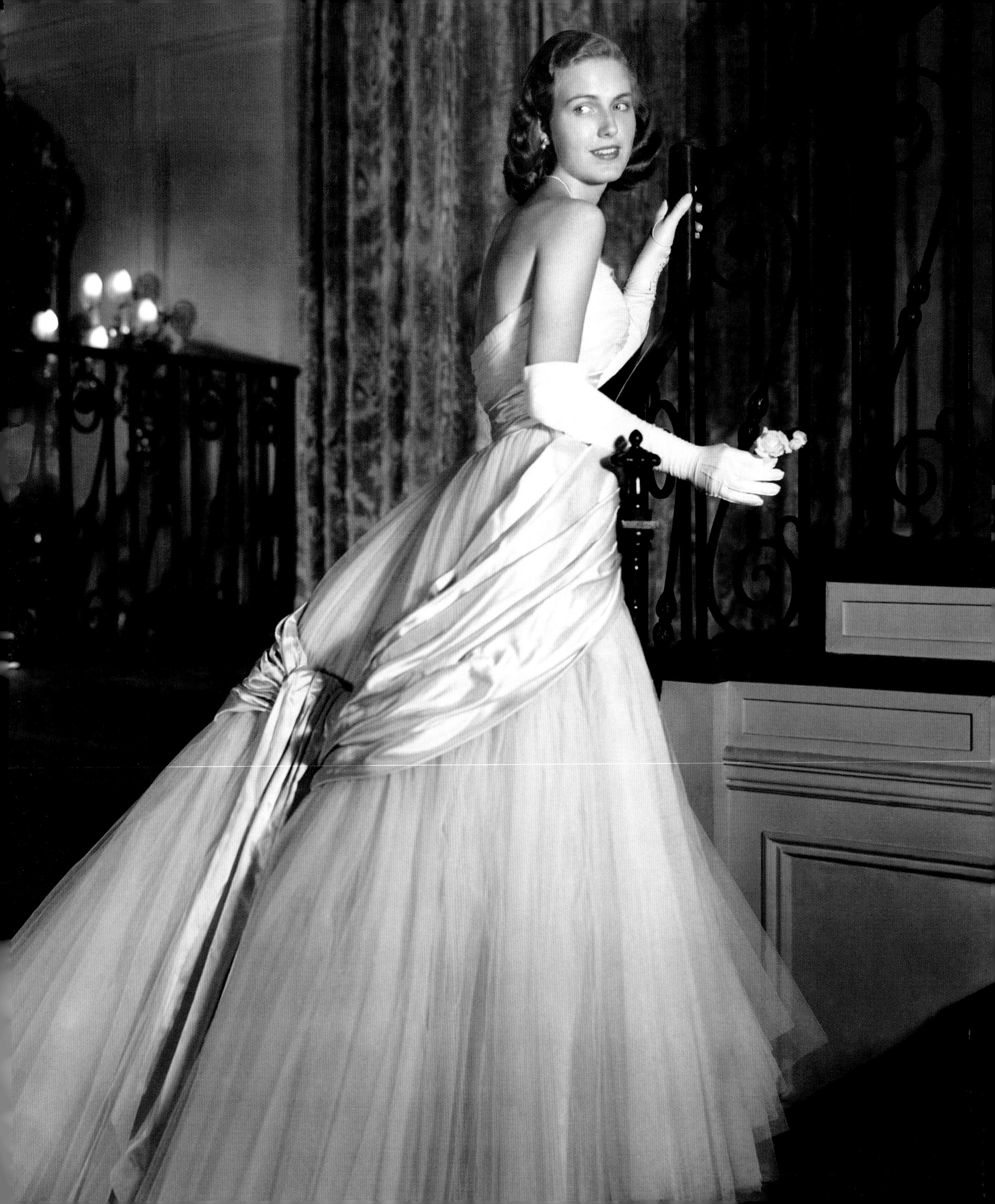

# GLITTER AND THE DRESS

*Look for the woman in the dress.*
*If there is no woman, there is no dress.*
—COCO CHANEL

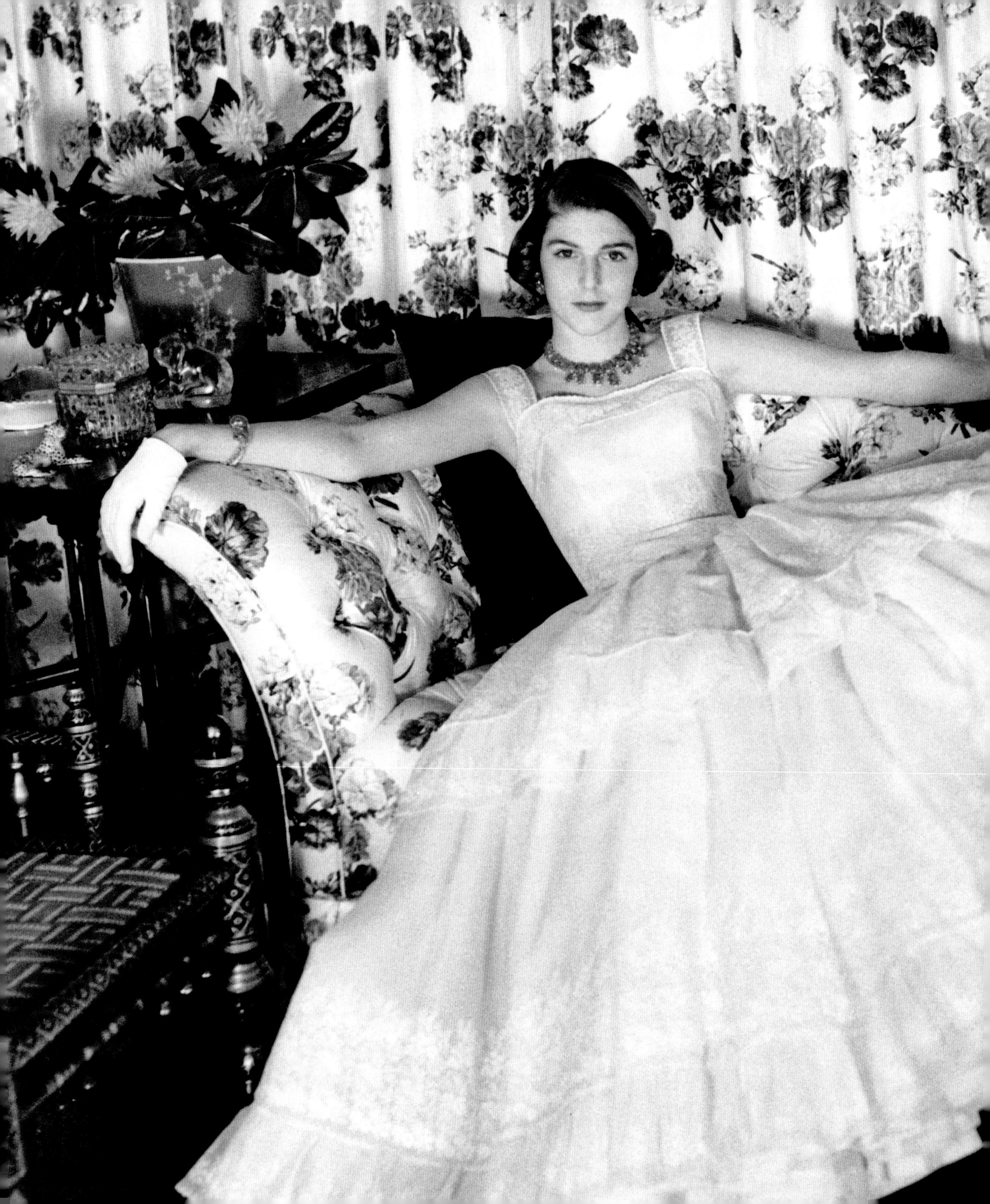

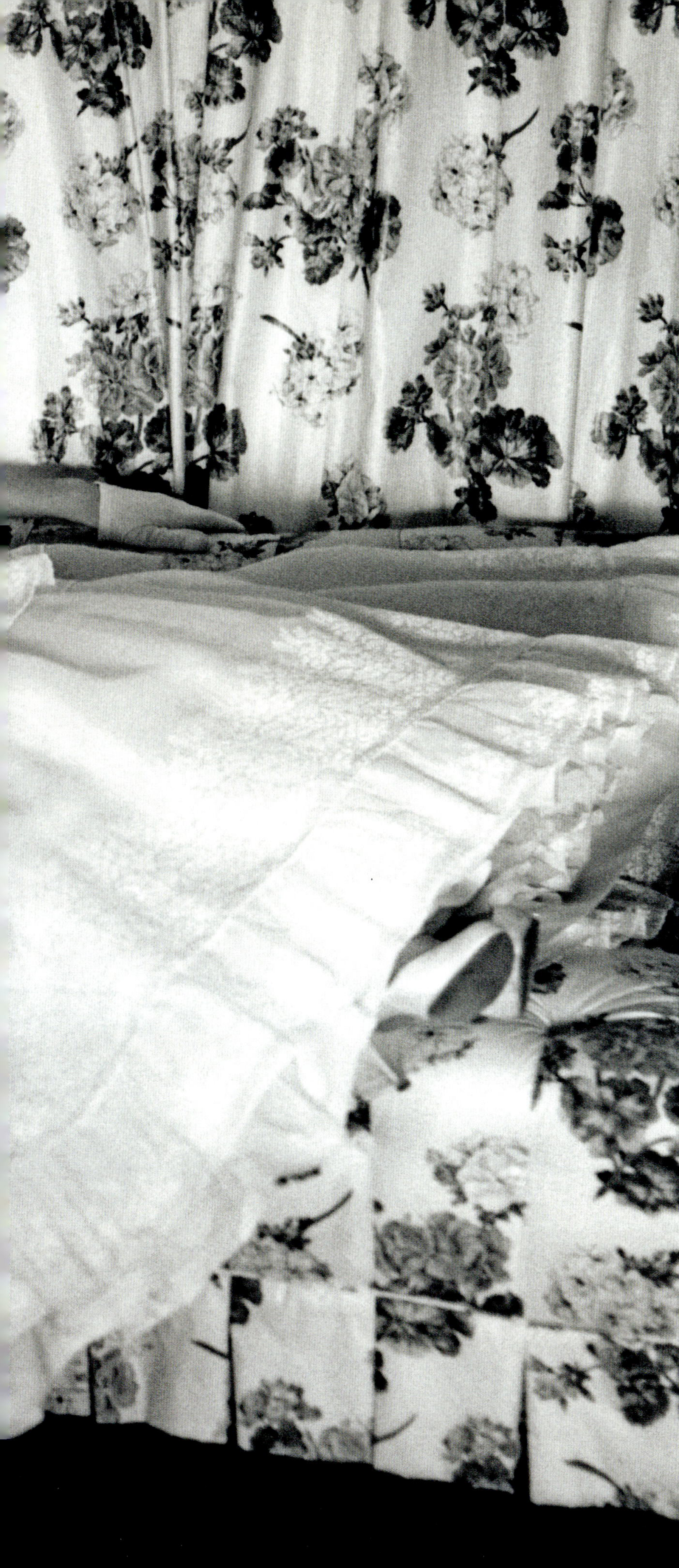

PREVIOUS PAGES

A master at creating shapes and silhouettes, Dior was known and sometimes even criticized for using over abundant amounts of fabric for just one dress. Chicago debutante Joan Peterkin stuns in a strapless tulle and white satin Dior with white satin gloves. Chicago, 1949. Photo by Horst P. Horst.

LEFT

Washington D.C. debutante Gwendolyn Rowan wears a flowing white organdy and lace Dior dress with a fitted bodice, complimented by a dazzling Indian diamond and emerald necklace, 1957.

FOLLOWING PAGES, LEFT

Marilyn Lowe attends Harlem's Debutante Cotillion wearing a dress of bird feathers made for her by her mother. Rockland Palace Ballroom, Harlem, New York, 1950.

FOLLOWING PAGES, RIGHT

Debutante Susan Y. Dear in a strapless gown. 1952.

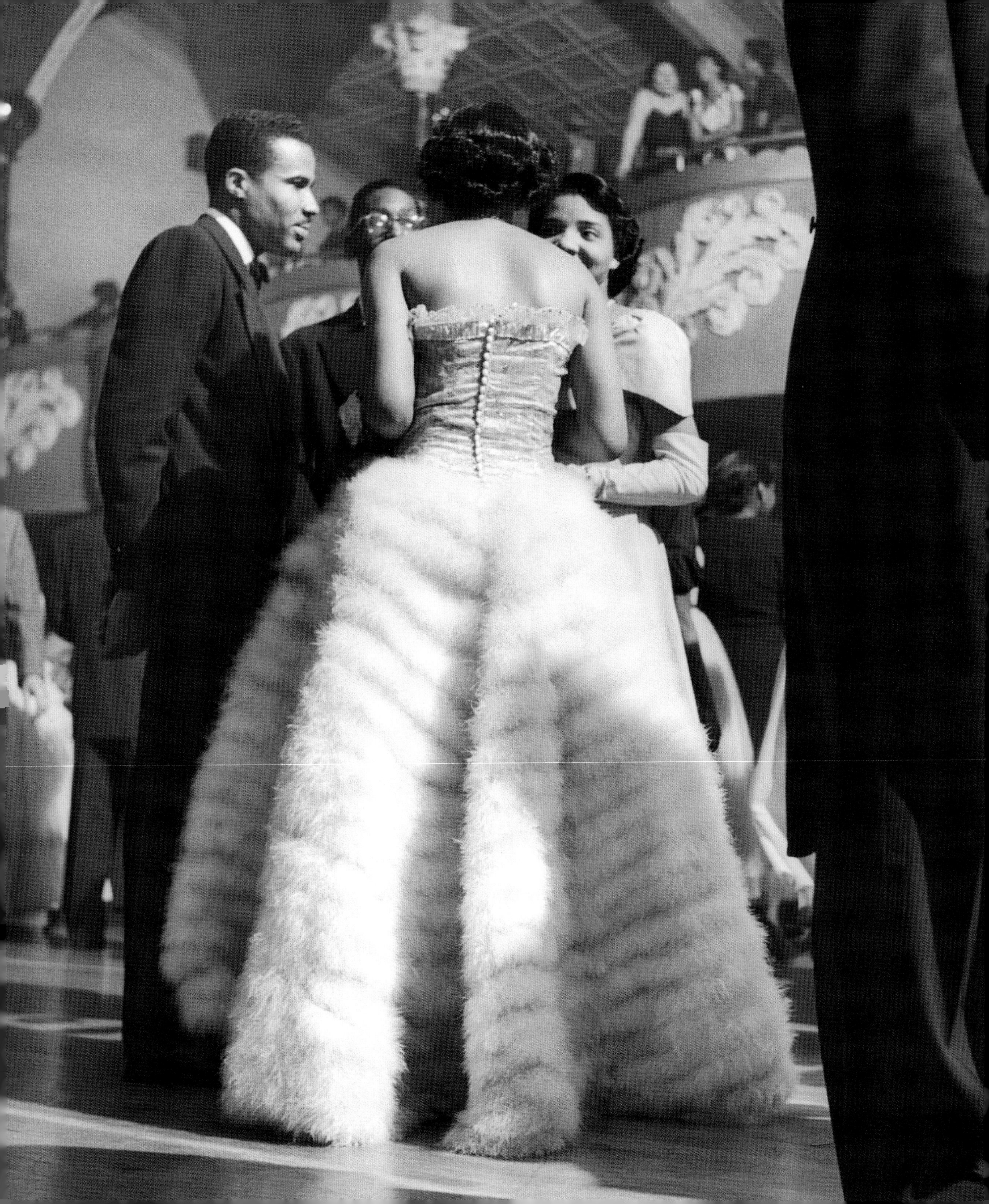

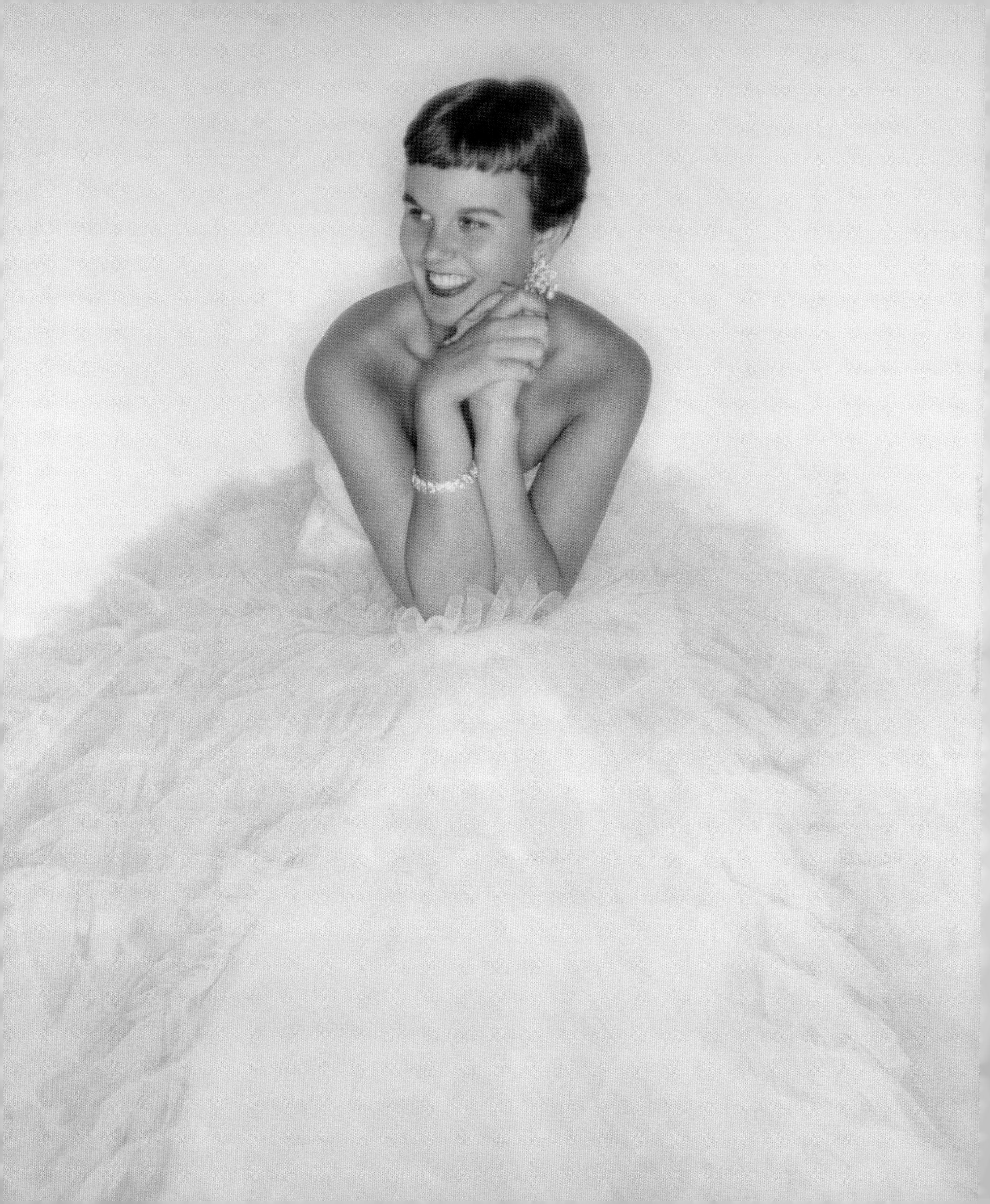

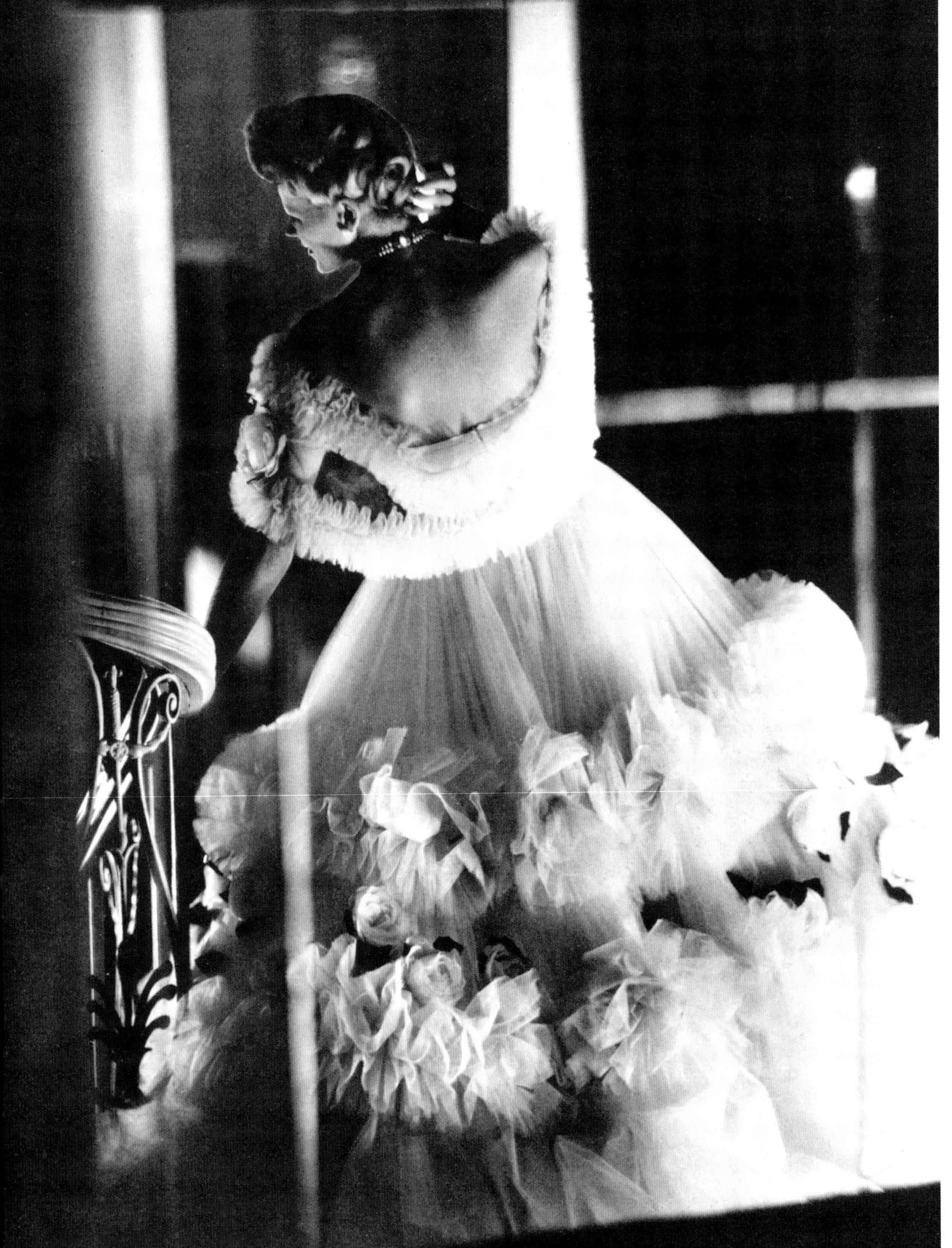

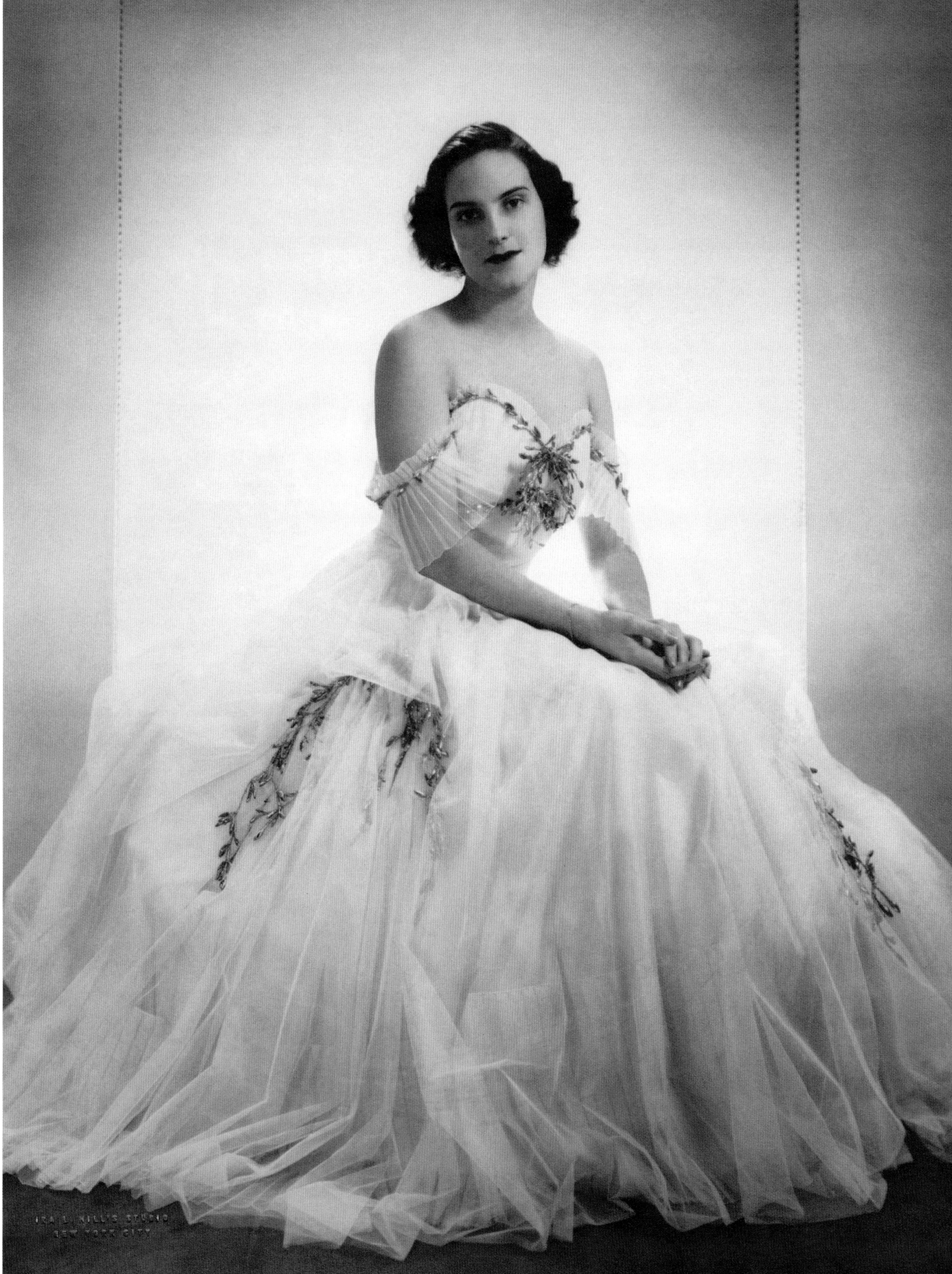
IRA L. HILL'S STUDIO
NEW YORK CITY

PREVIOUS PAGES, LEFT

Norman Hartnell glamour tulle dress, 1940. Hartnell was renowned for his romantic style dresses. White tulle roses and glossy green leaves are scattered between the ruches rising to the waistline of the crinoline skirt, a style particularly popular with Queen Elizabeth.

PREVIOUS PAGES, RIGHT

A belle of Alabama, Marion Oates ("Oatsie") in her coming out dress adorned with gold lamé oats as a nod towards her last name, 1938. Oatsie's grandfather was a Confederate commander in the Civil War and served seven terms in Congress before becoming governor of Alabama.

OPPOSITE

A debutante ball held at the Copley Plaza in Boston, 1958. Photo by Slim Aarons.

FOLLOWING PAGES, LEFT

Debutante Mazie Cox in a dress of her own design and which her mother made for her. New York, 1963.

FOLLOWING PAGES, RIGHT

Coco Chanel, Mainbocher, and Madeleine Vionnet were among the fashion designers to dominate haute couture in the 1930s. Silk brocade fabrics, lace bodices (as Chanel was noted for), and white satin gloves and feathers—whether in a boa or a headpiece—added dramatic flair and movement. Debutante Eleanor Frothingham wears a white net dress with silver sequins by Chanel, 1939. Photo by Horst. P. Horst.

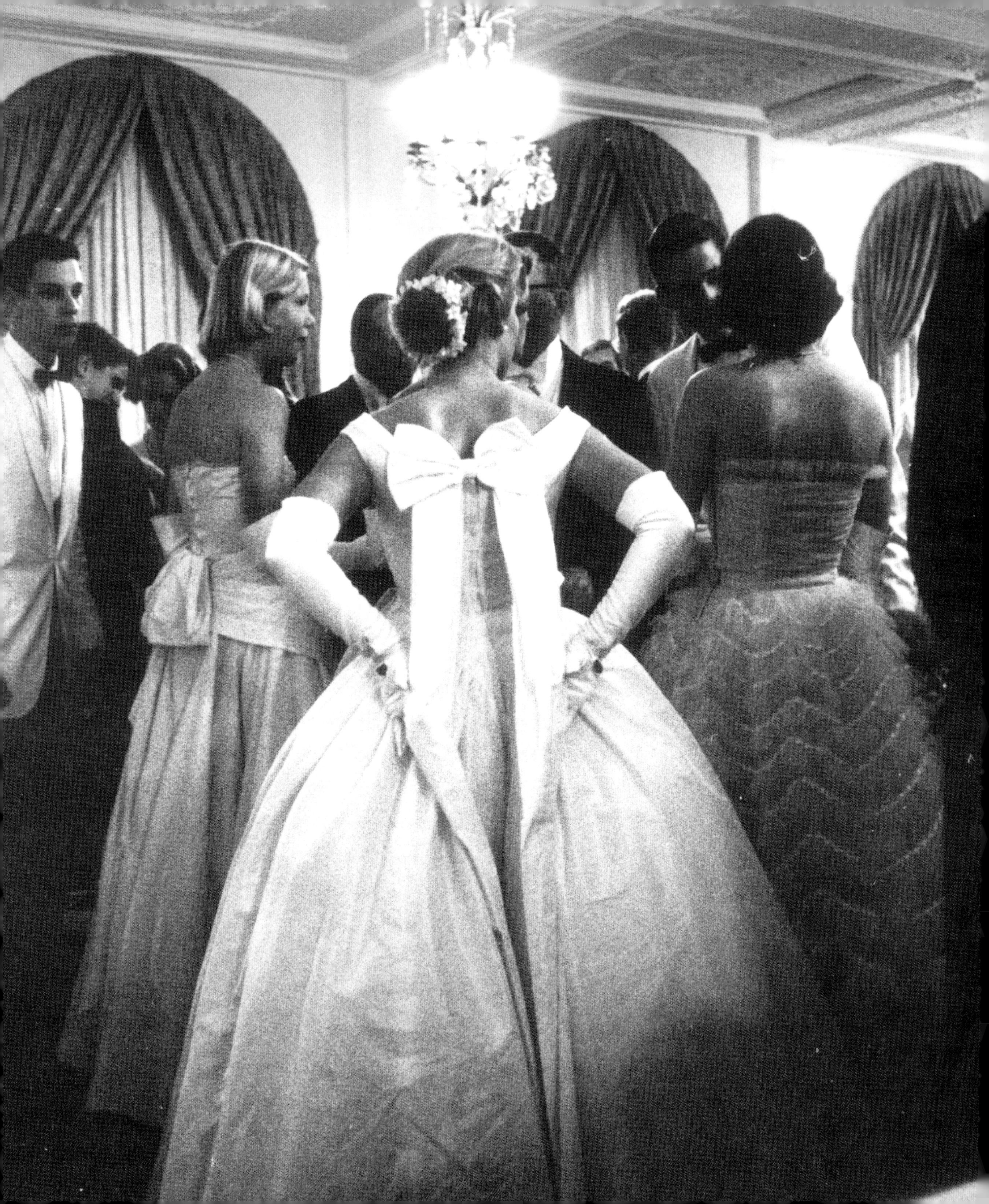

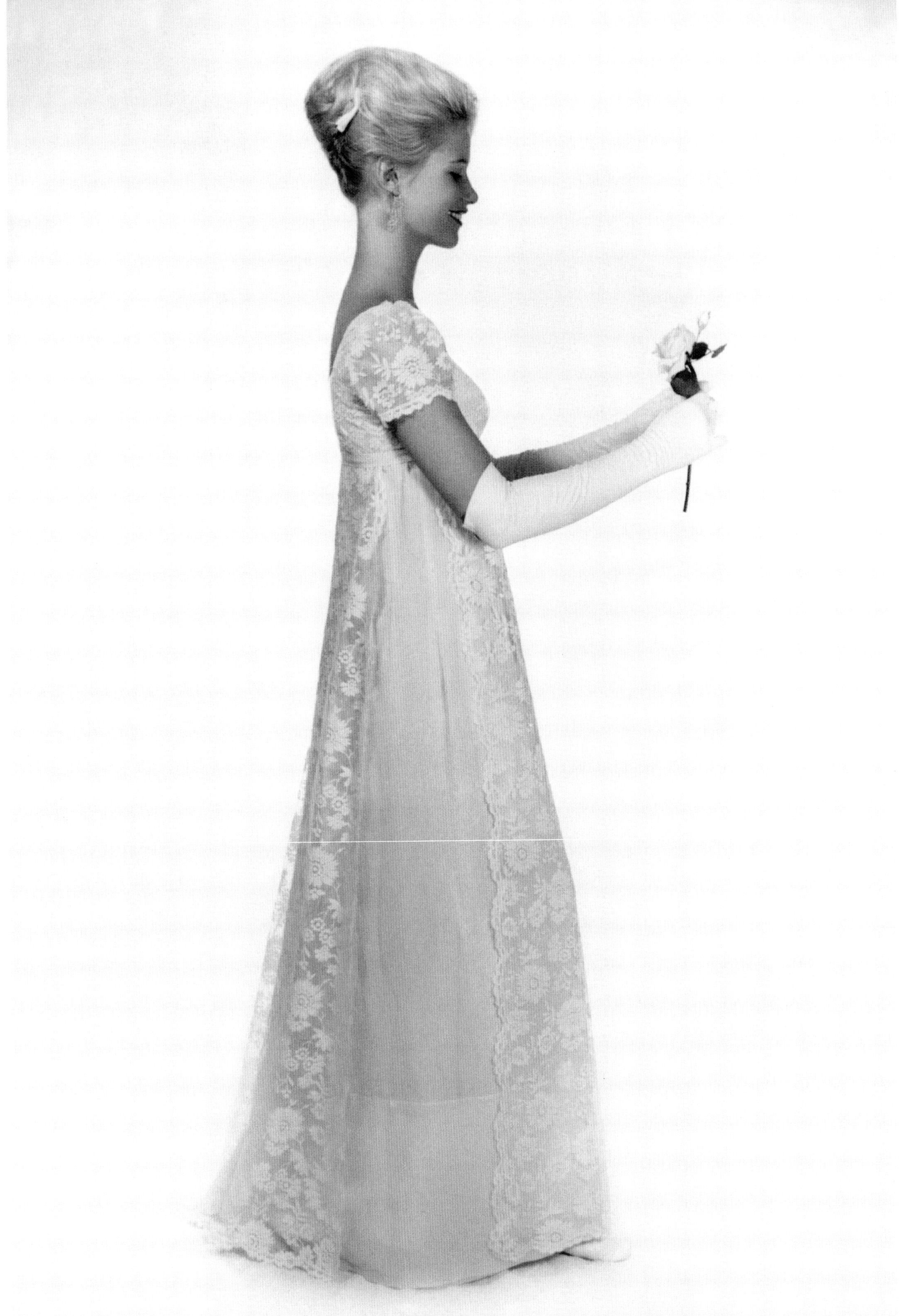

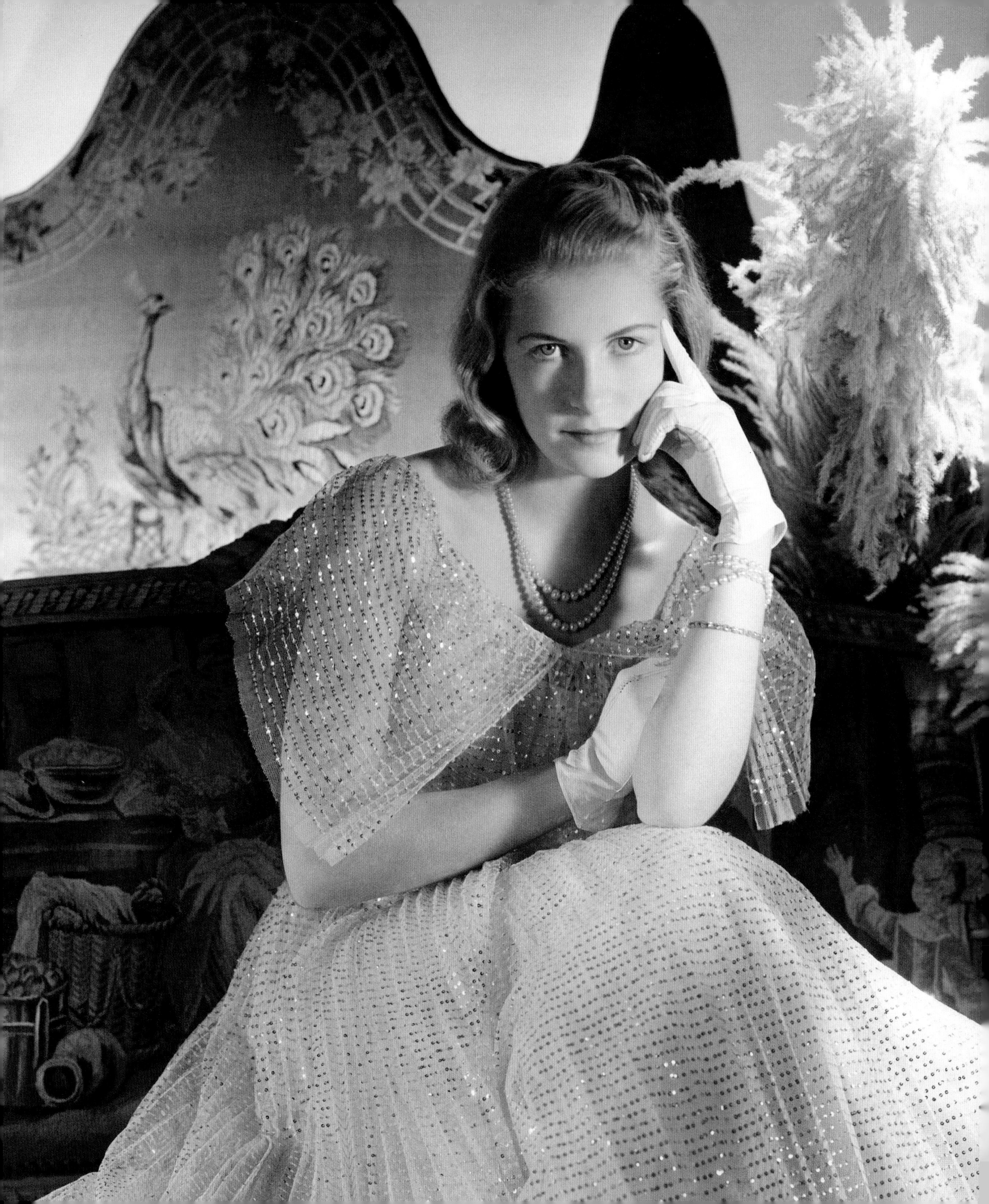

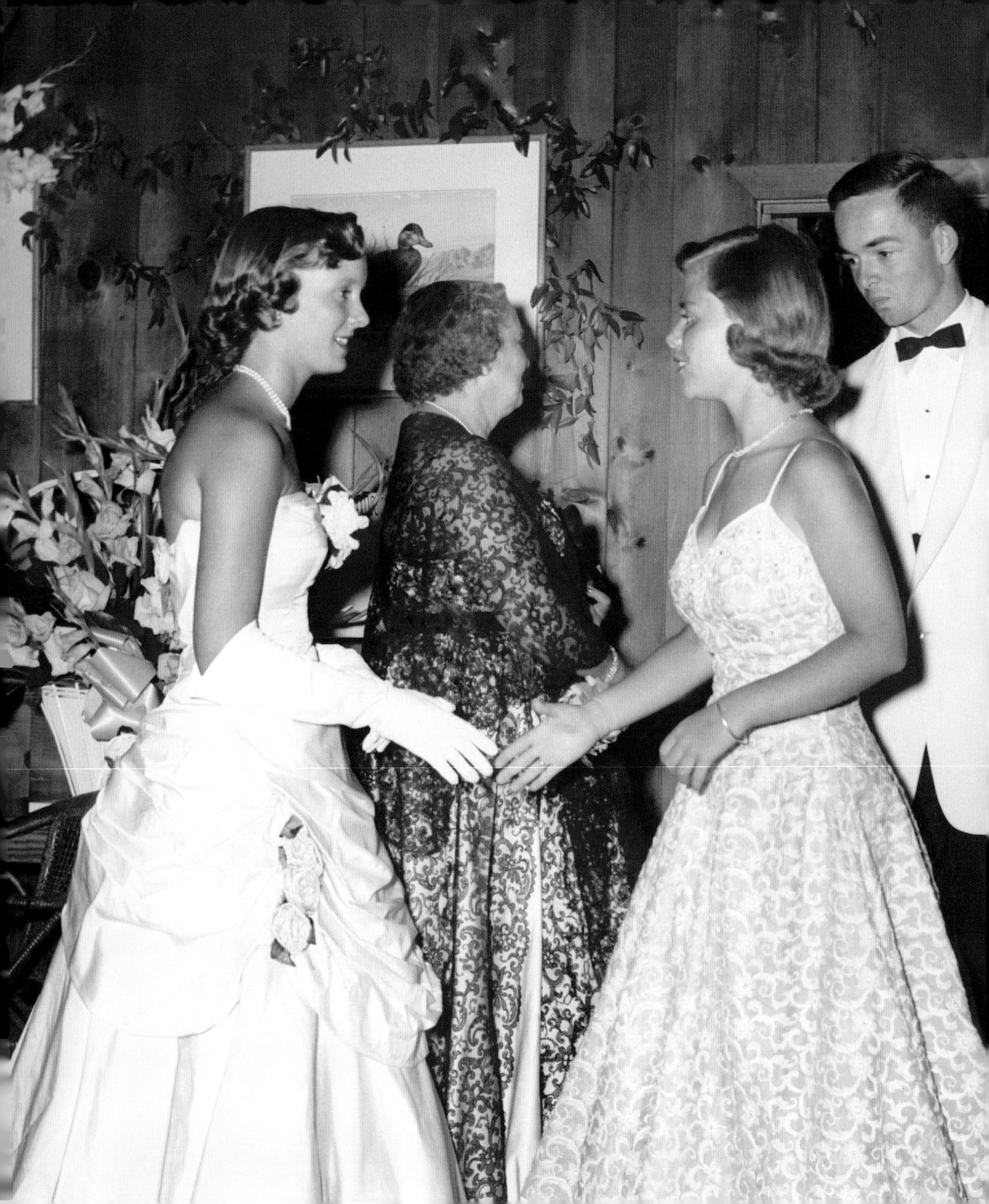

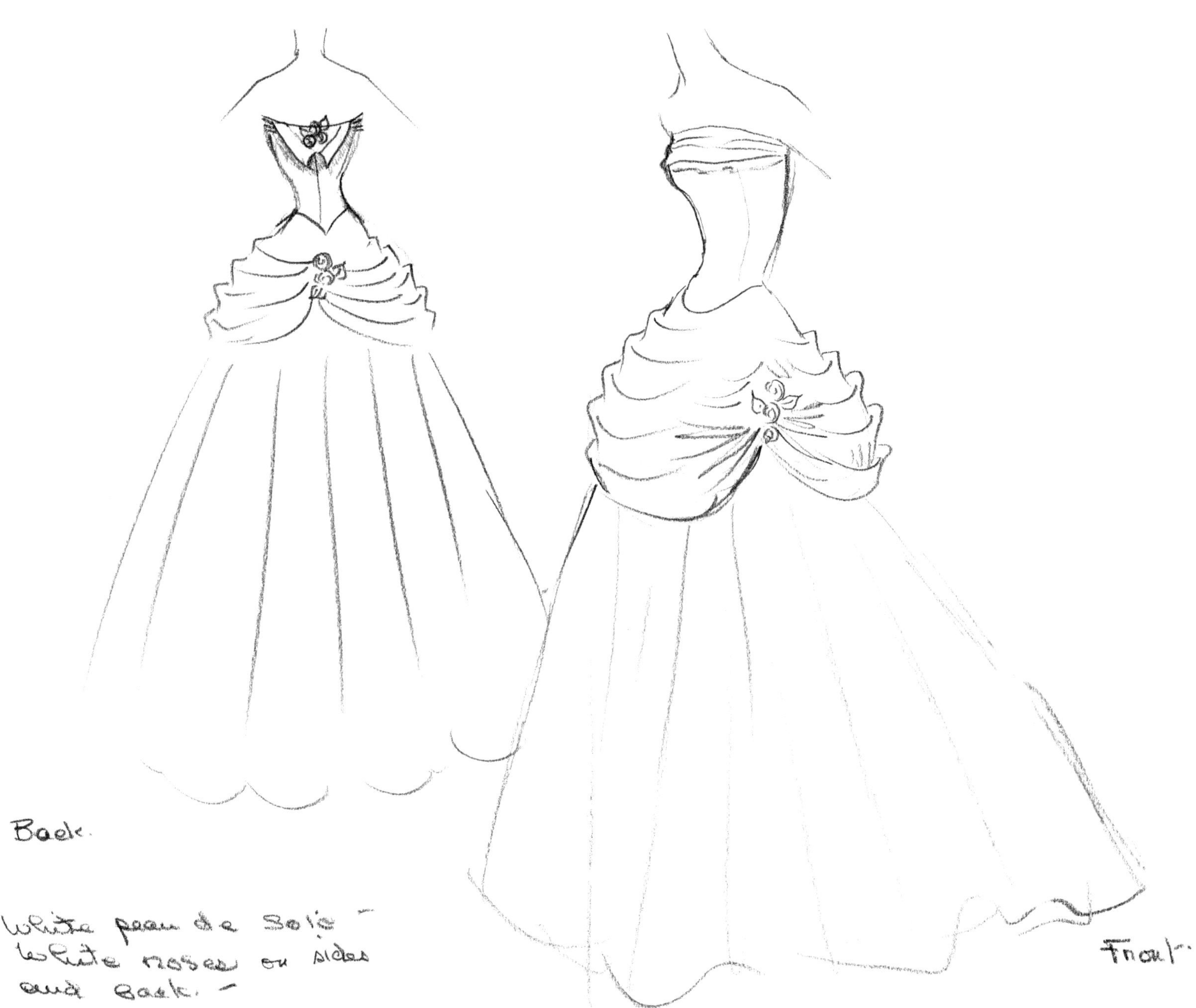
Back.
White peau de soie -
White roses on sides
and back. -
Front.

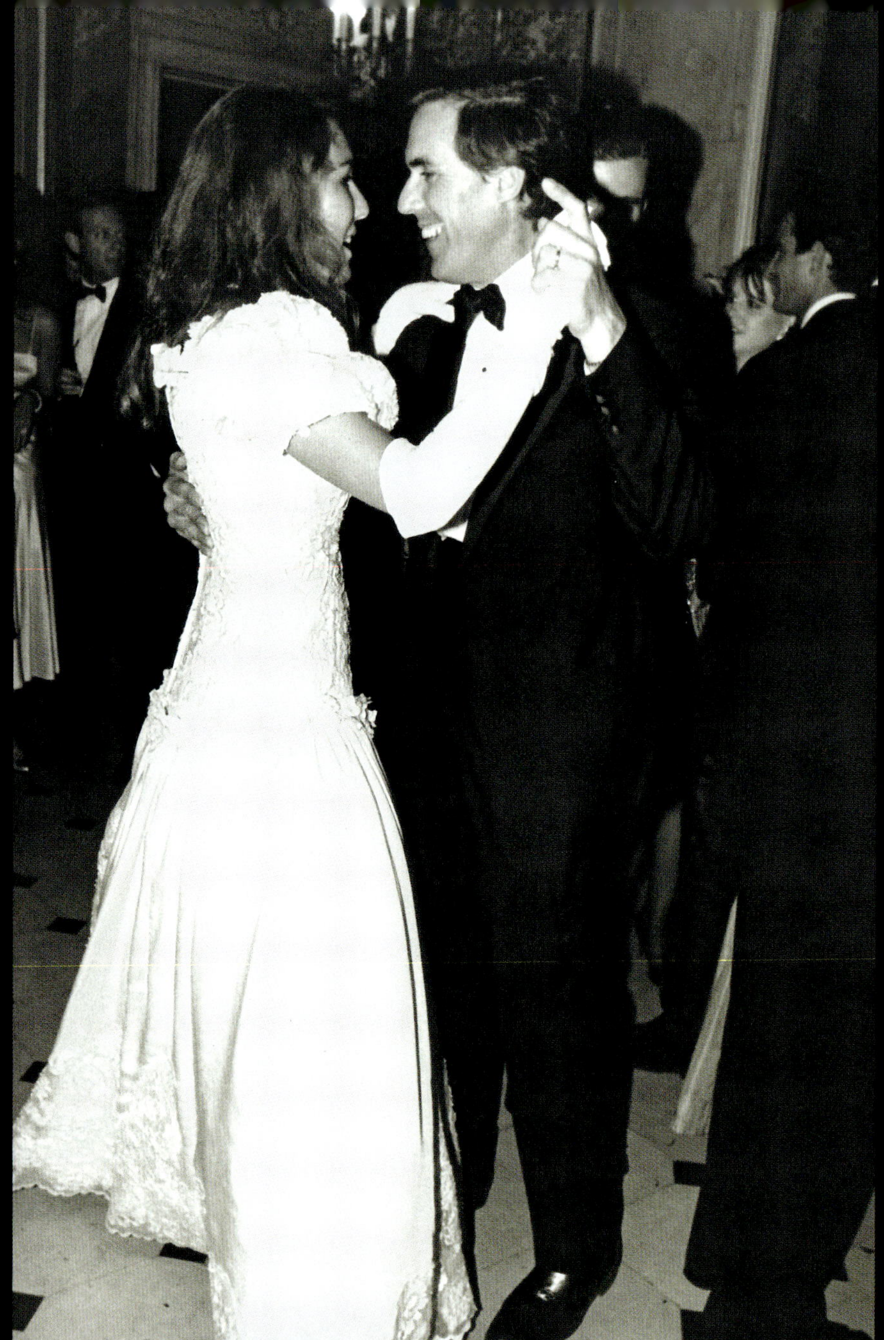

**PREVIOUS PAGES, LEFT**
Sheila Ryan greets guests at her debut, 1957.

**PREVIOUS PAGES, RIGHT**
Preliminary sketches of Sheila Ryan's Hattie Carnegie evening dress. Born Henrietta Kanengeiser in Vienna, Austria, Hattie immigrated to America in 1900 at age 11. Folklore has it that while on the ship she asked a fellow passenger who the richest and most prosperous people in America were. The answer: "Andrew Carnegie." According to the story, young Hattie changed her last name to Carnegie and went on tobecome one of the more elegant designers of the day—first known for her hats, then later for her chic, sophisticated dresses.

**LEFT**
Debutante Sophie Trevor dances with her brother John in the marble ballroom of their grandmother Eileen Slocum's house. Eileen Slocum, a descendant of the Brown family of Rhode Island, was often referred to as the "grand dame" of Newport. Having been a debutante herself in 1933 in New York, Eileen reveled in hosting wonderful summer coming out parties for all of her granddaughters. Newport, Long Island, 1992.

**OPPOSITE**
Debutante Pamela O'Connor enjoys a dance with Tiffany's chairman Harry Platt. New York, 1980. Photo by Bill Cunningham.

**FOLLOWING PAGES**
Debutante party at the Everglades Club. Palm Beach, Florida, circa 1955.

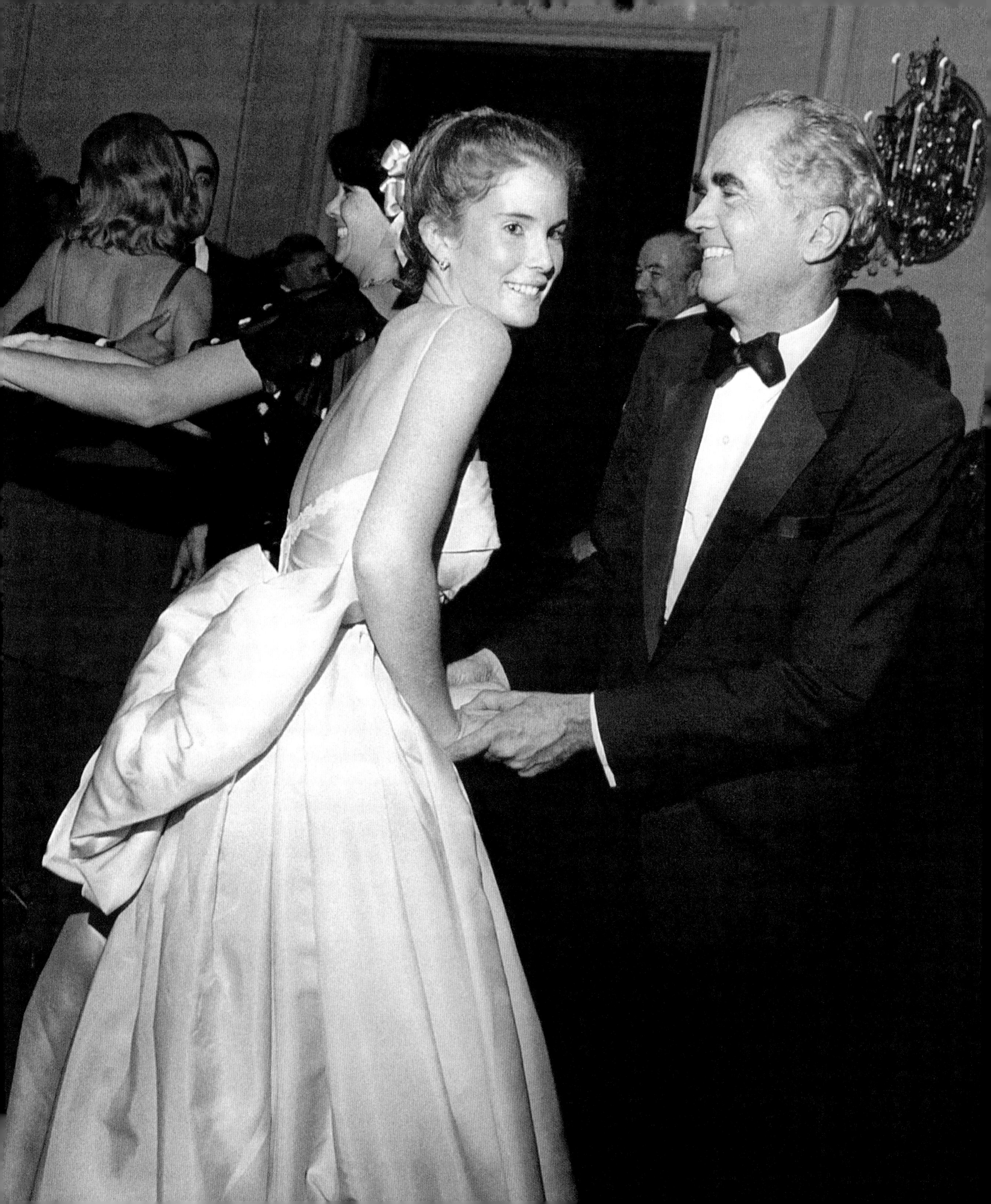

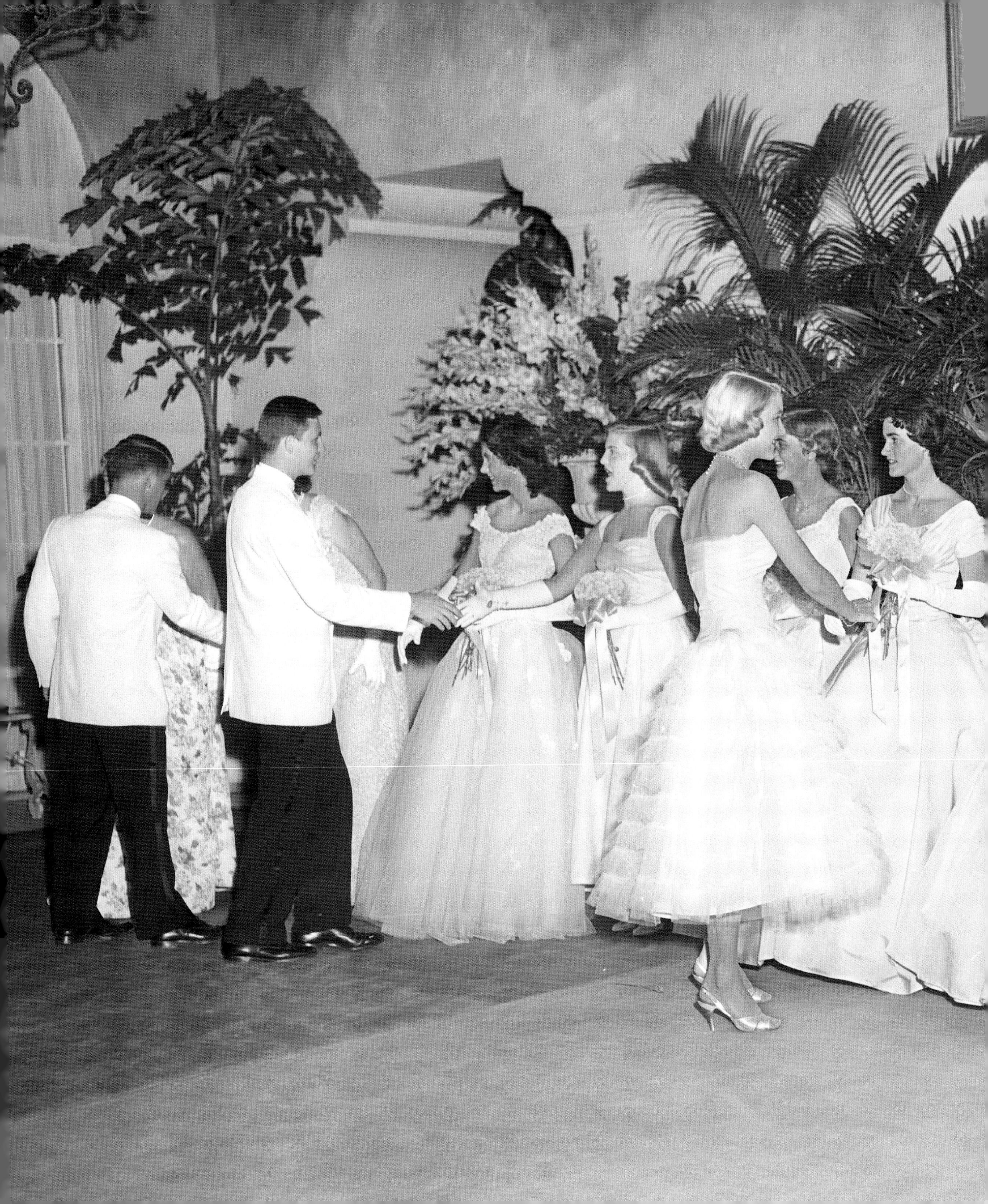

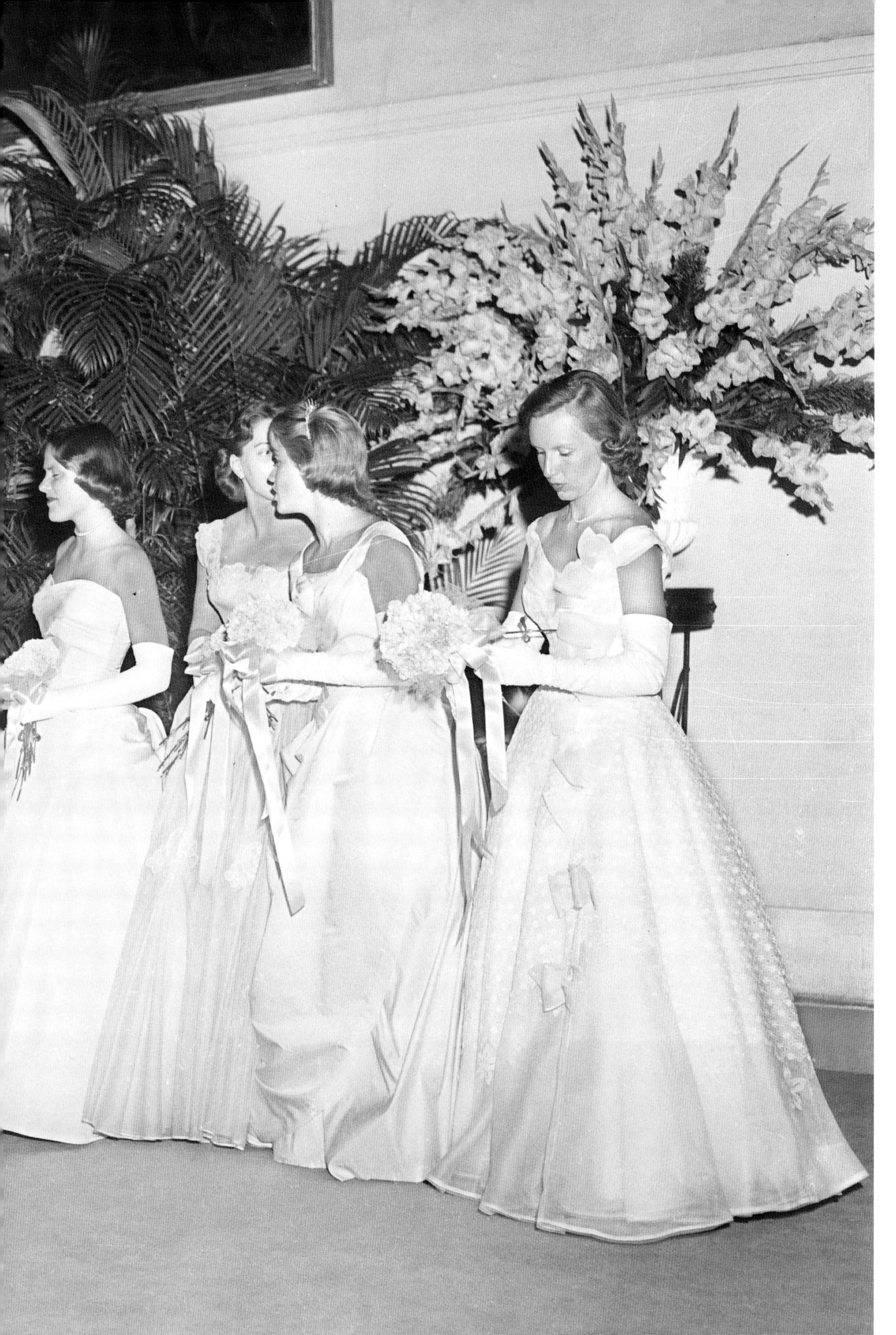

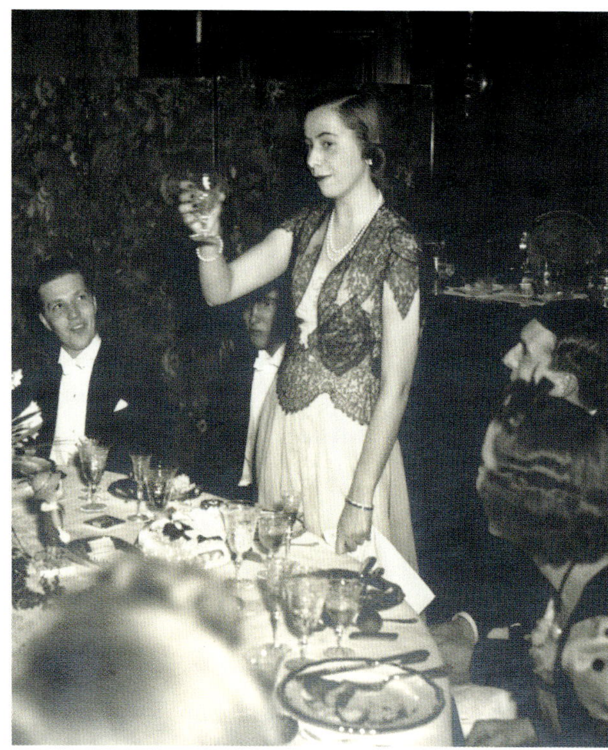

The coming out dinner for Helen Michalis at the St Regis Hotel. New York, 1938.

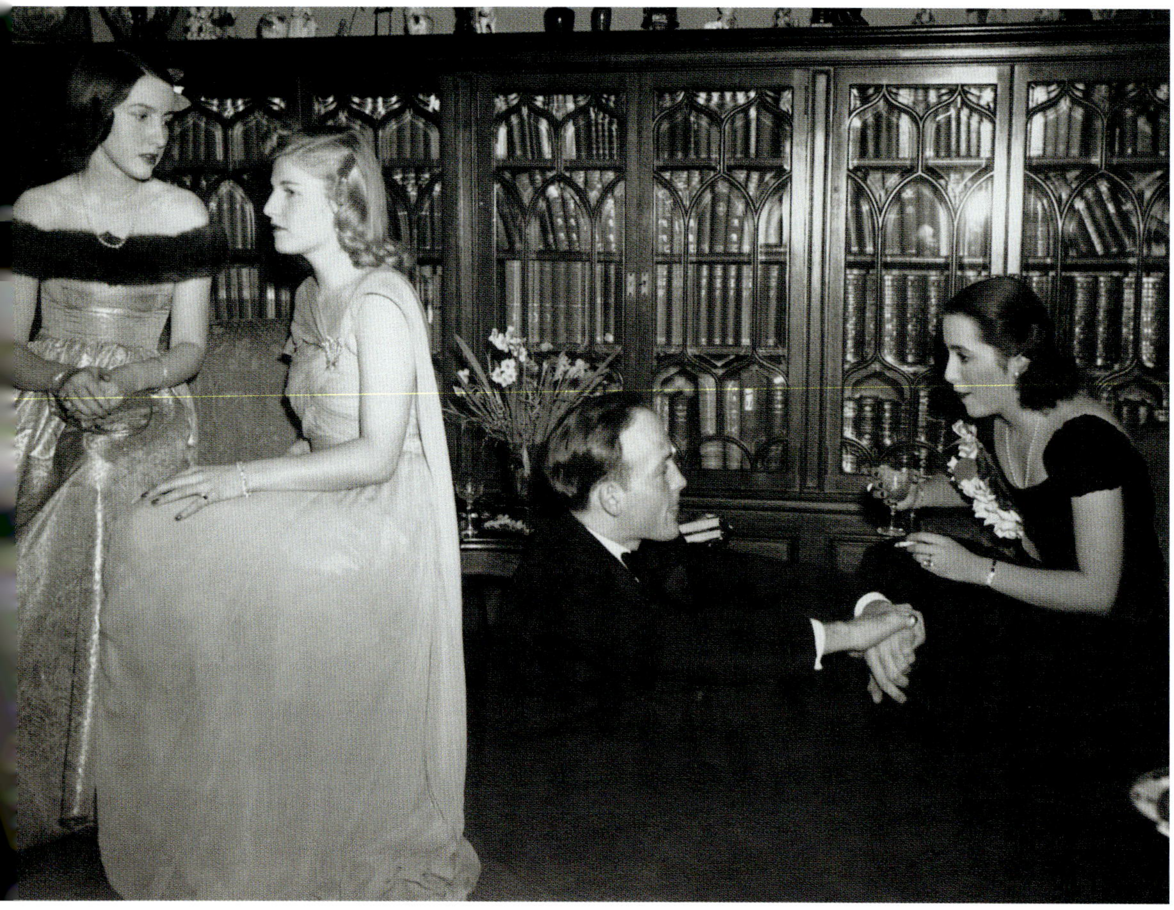

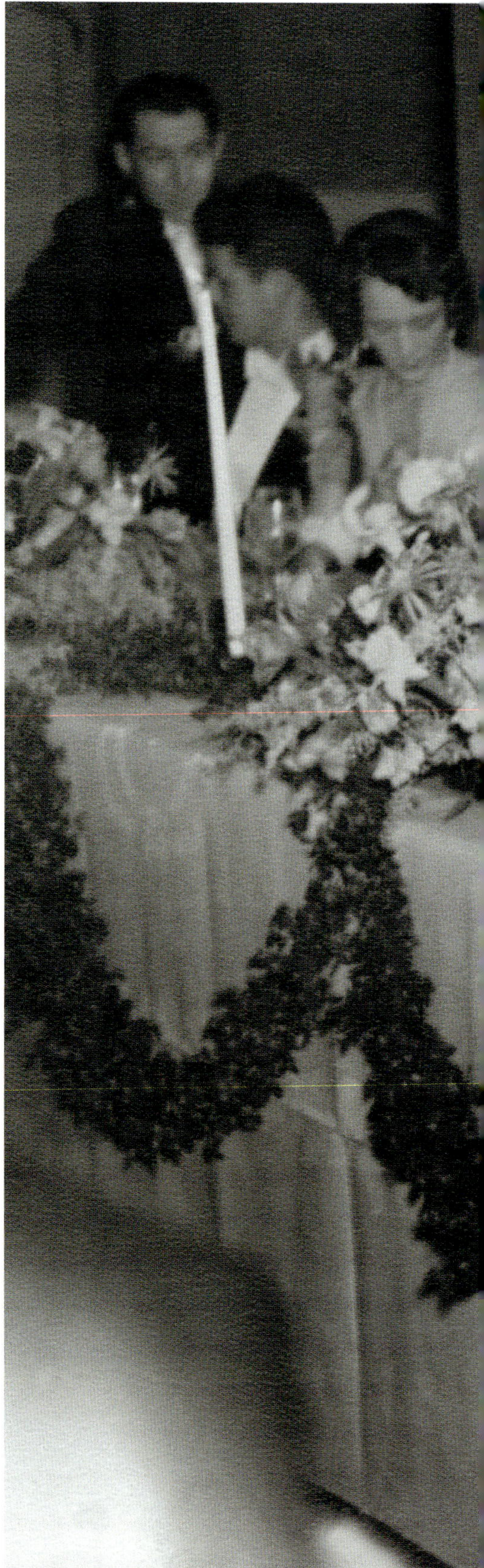

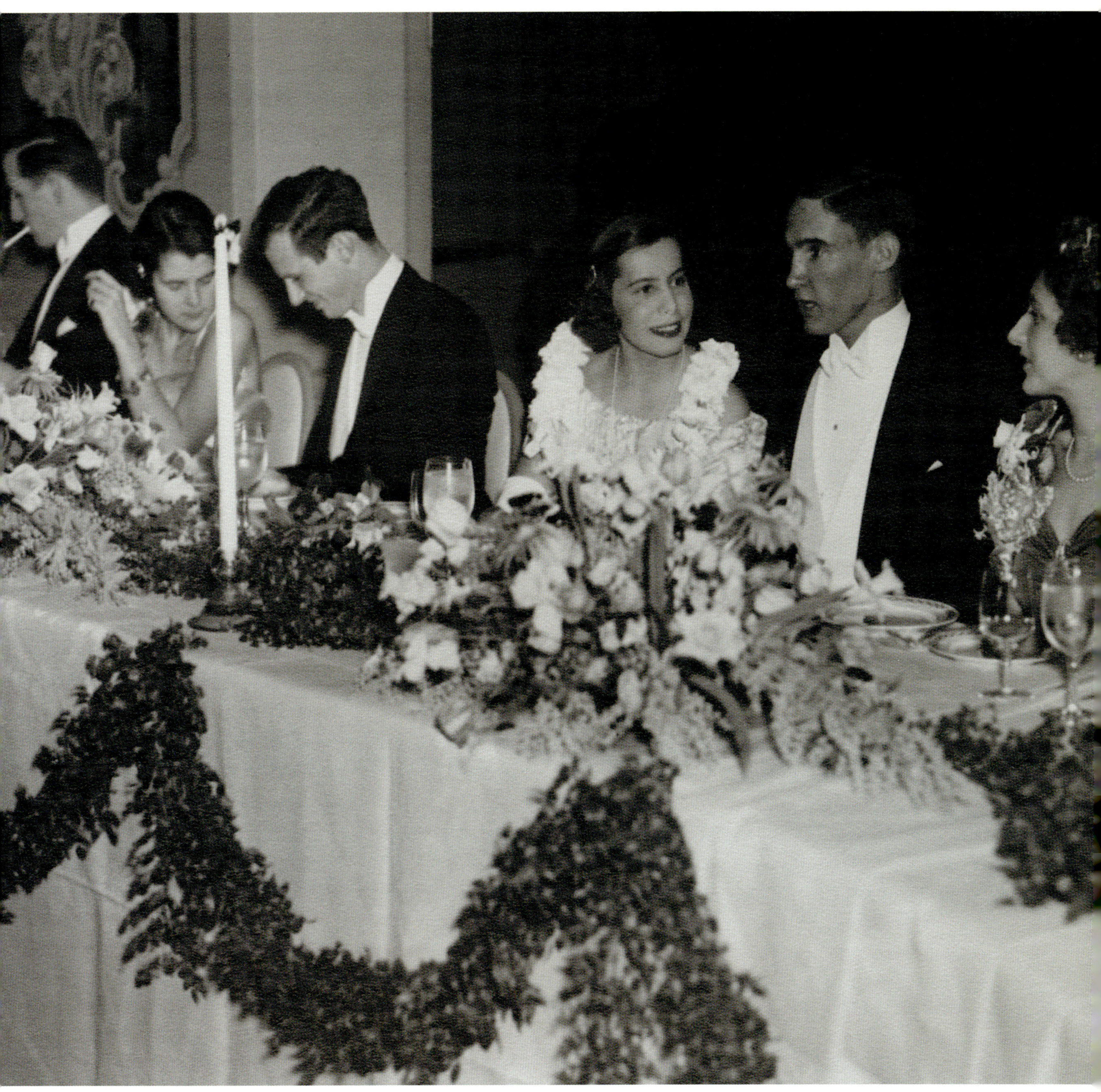

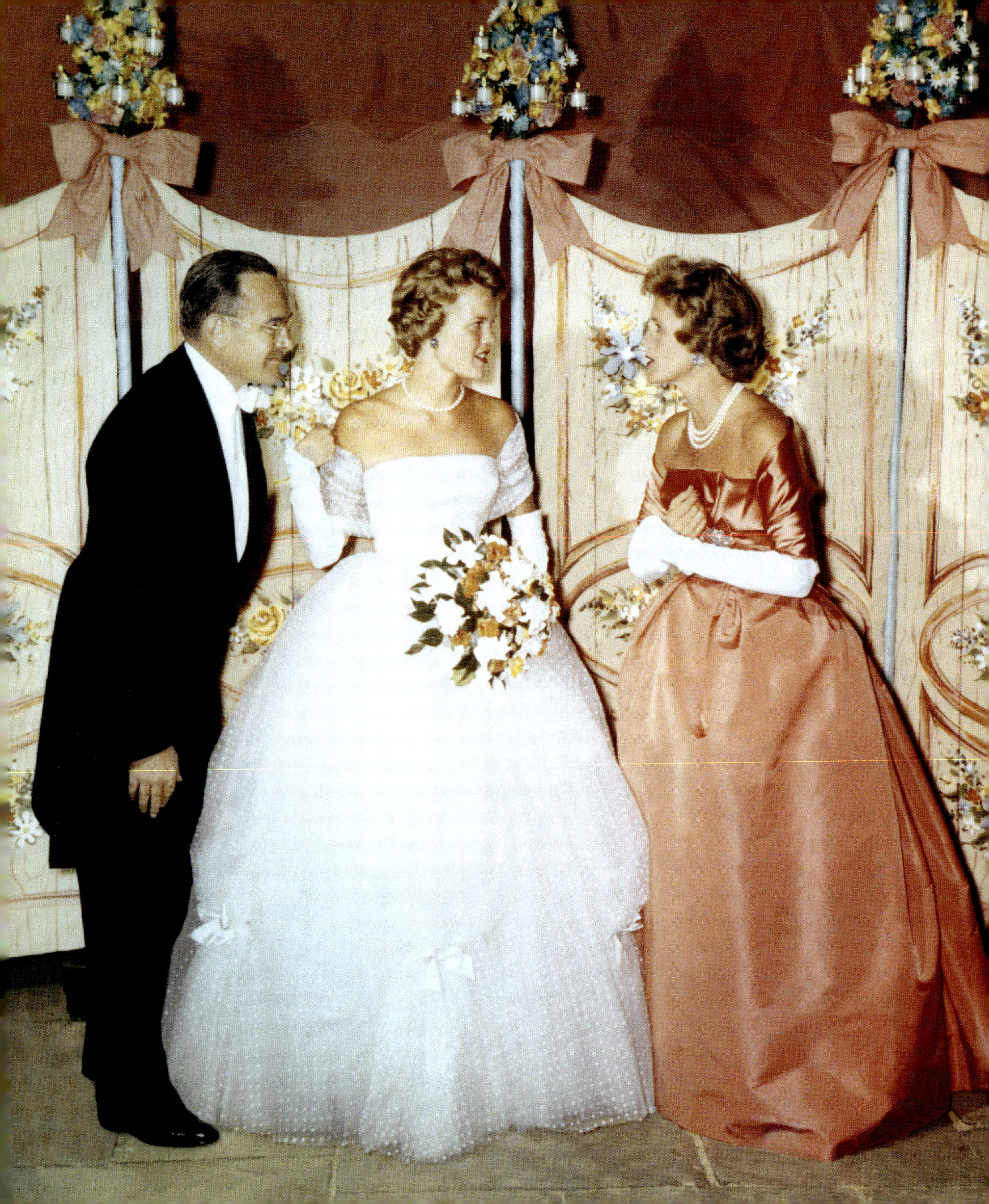

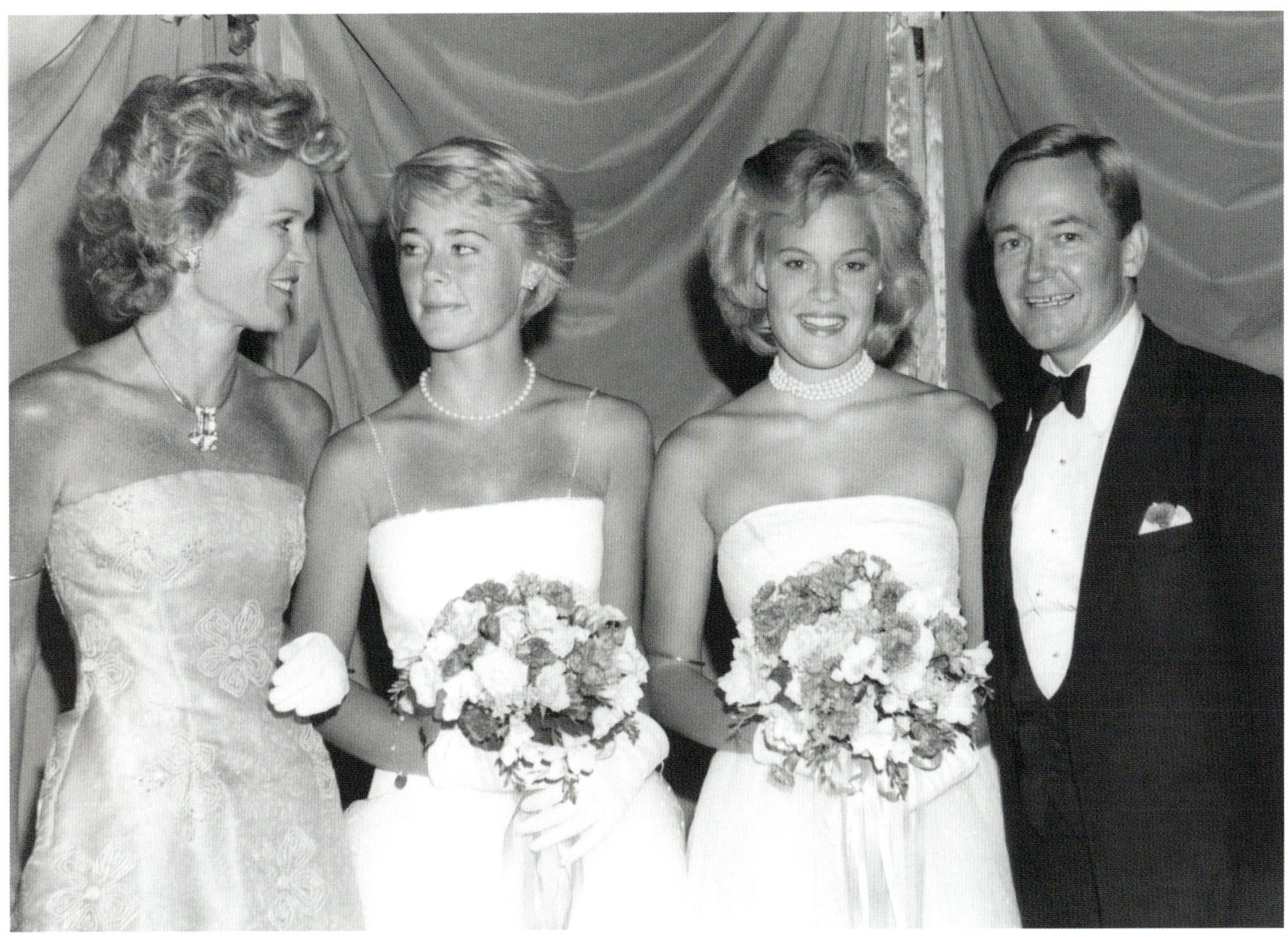

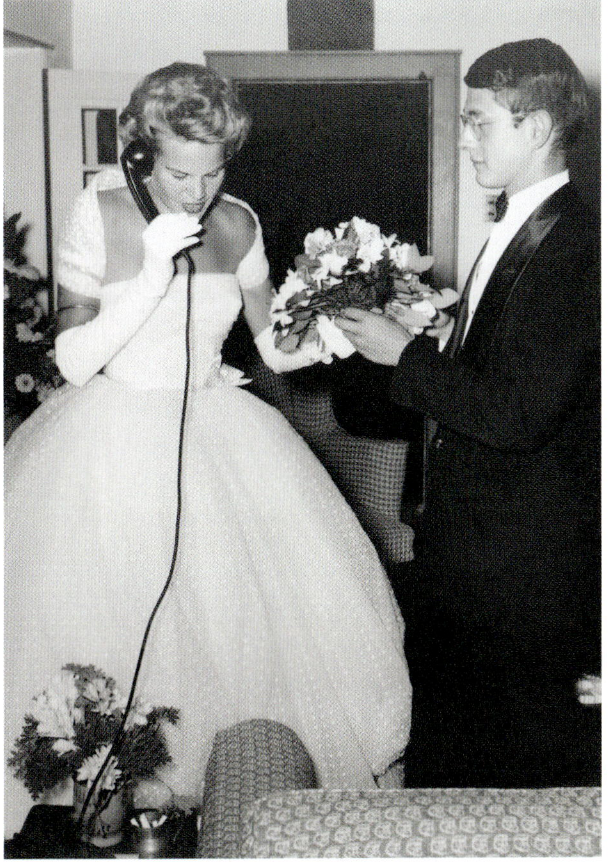

ABOVE

Nicole du Pont Limbocker and Derek Limbocker with their two debutante daughters, Hilary Dick and Ridgley Brode. New York, 1984.

LEFT

Debutante Nicole du Pont at her dinner dance in Wilmington Delaware, 1959.

OPPOSITE

Nicole du Pont at her dinner dance with her parents, Mr. and Mrs. Nicholas du Pont. Wilmington, Delaware, 1959.

BELOW

Gentleman guests attend debutante Ginny Wright's dinner dance, where Lester Lanin played into the night. Mayflower Hotel, Washington, D.C., 1959.

OPPOSITE

Debutante Ginny Wright with her escort, midshipman Don Uehling. Mayflower Hotel, Washington, D.C., 1959.

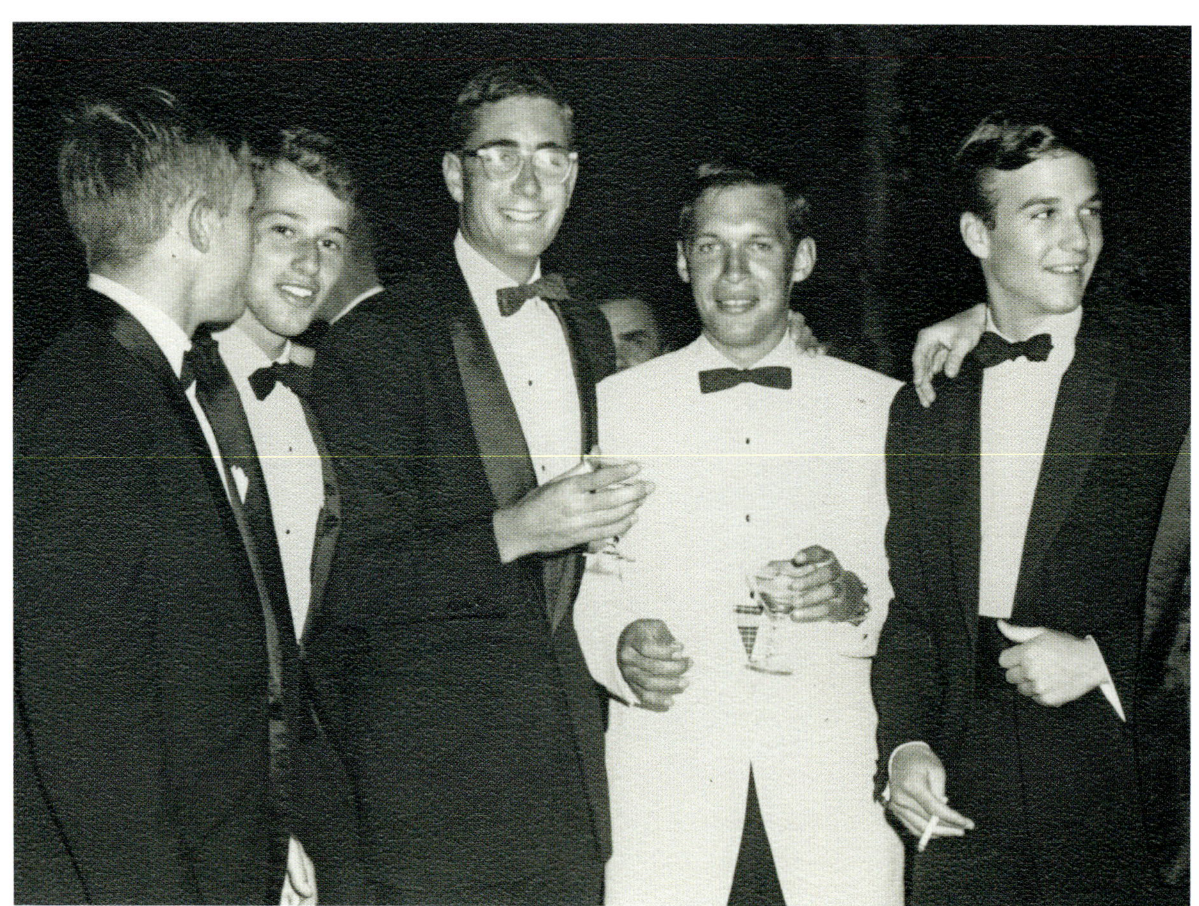

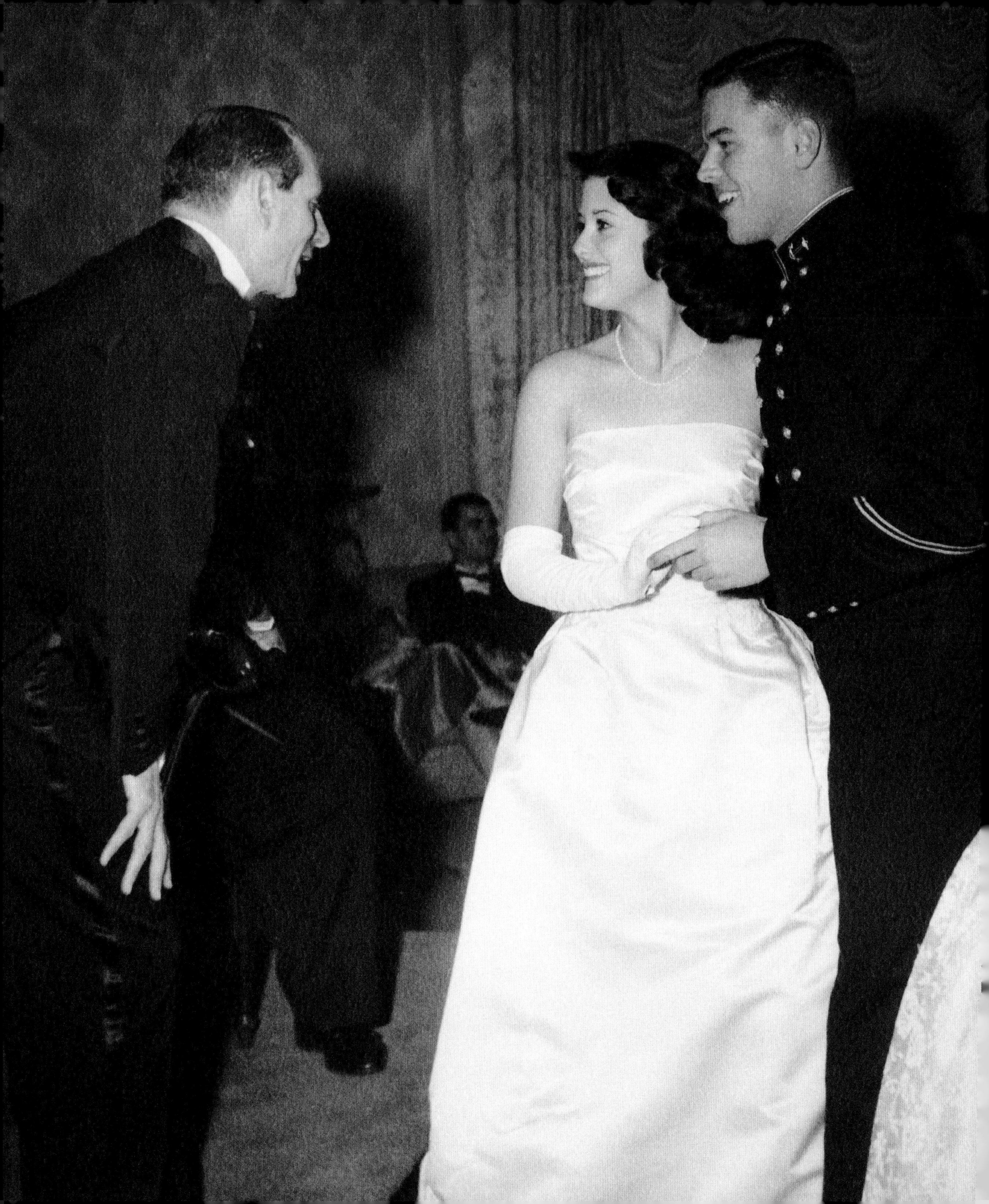

Mr. and Mrs. Ernest Henderson

request the pleasure of your company

at a small dance

in honour of their daughter

Miss Mary Stephens-Caldwell Henderson

on Tuesday the ninth of June

leaving at half after nine o'clock

Boston Belle

Nine Rowes Wharf Boston

8A Louisburg Square
Boston

Please reply

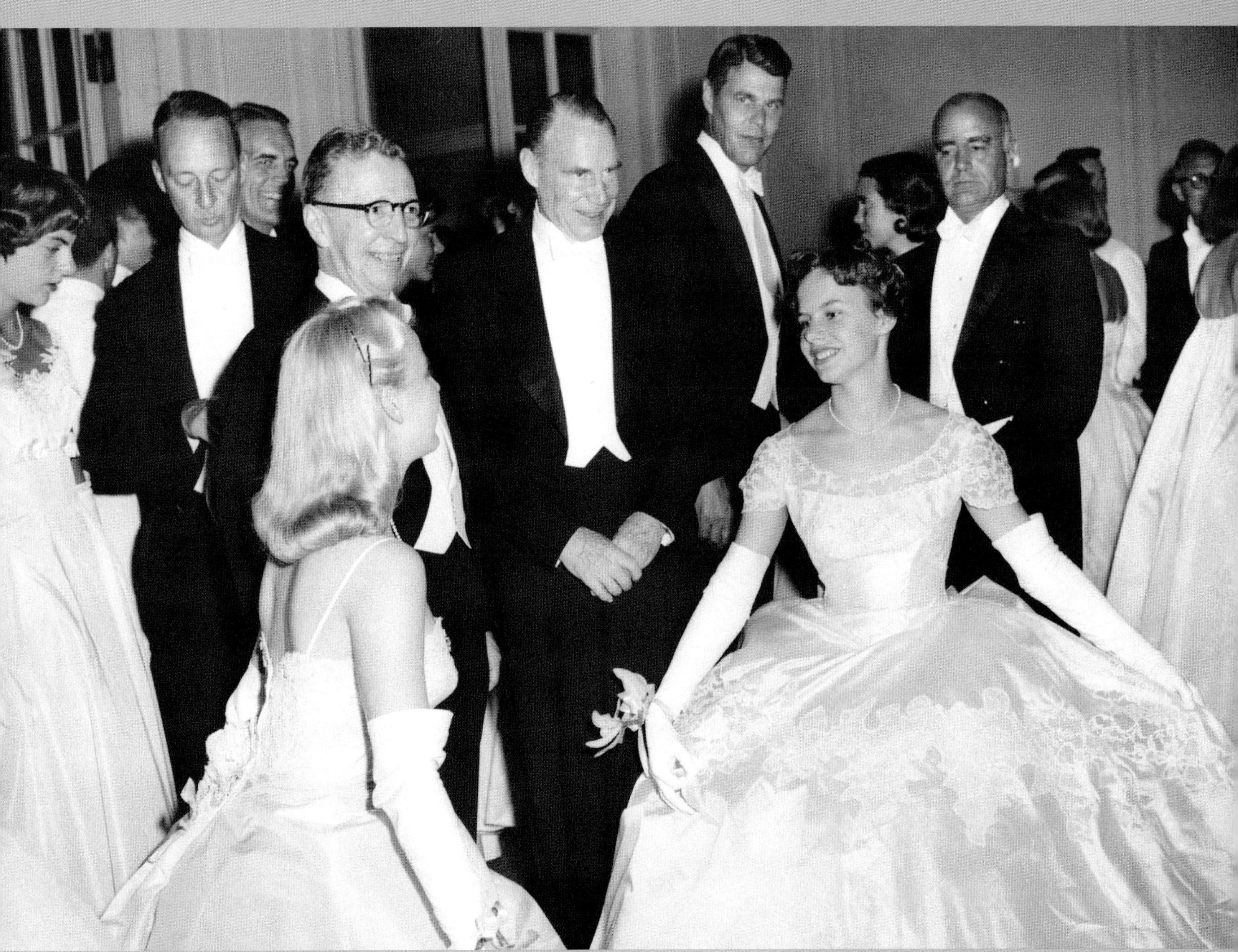

ABOVE
Debutante Mary Henderson takes a curtsey at her coming out party. Boston, 1959. Mary (Mitzie) later became the wife of Mr. Frank Purdue.

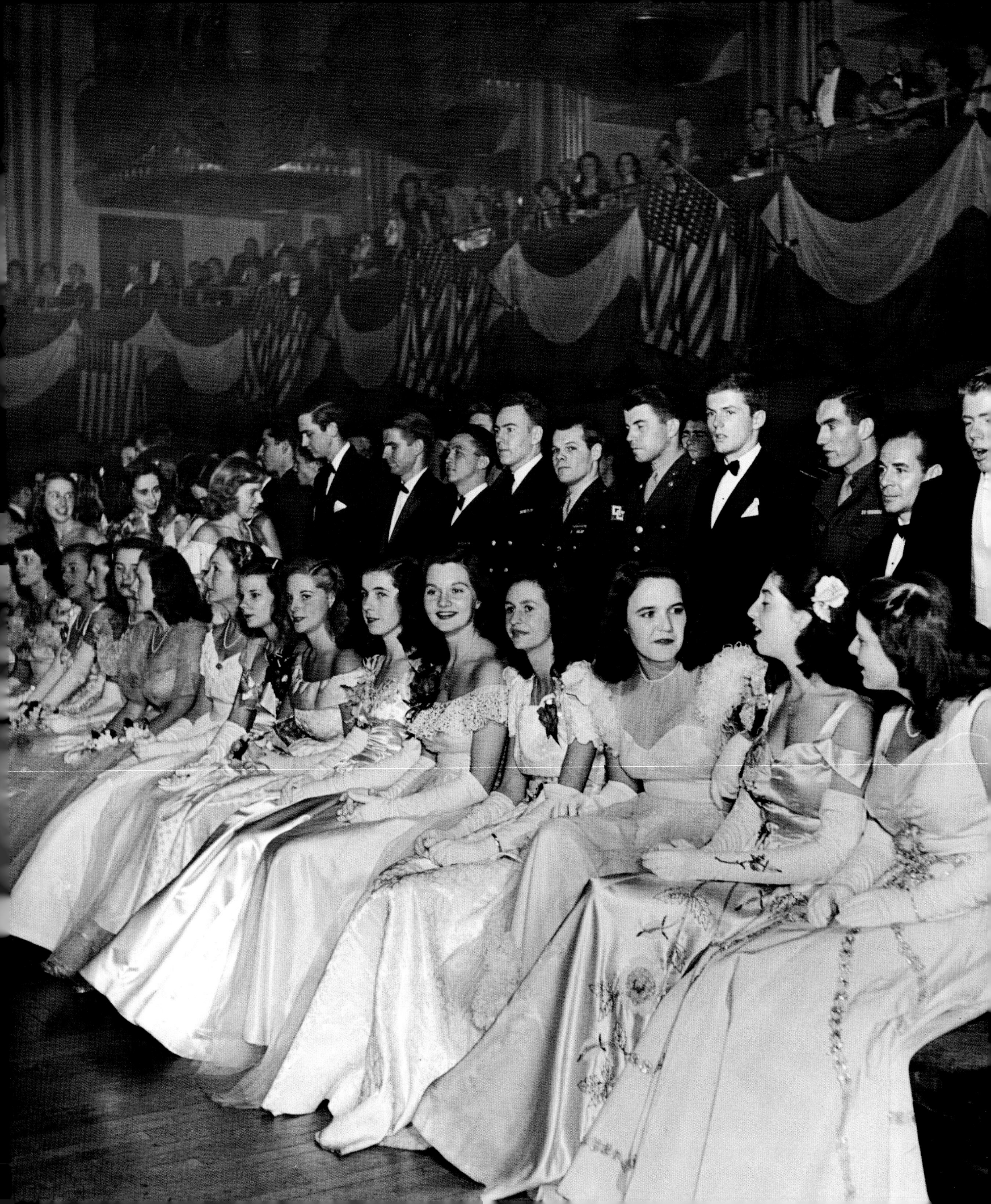

# THE GRANDIOSE

*I like large parties. They're so intimate. At small parties there isn't any privacy.*

—F. SCOTT FITZGERALD, *THE GREAT GATSBY*

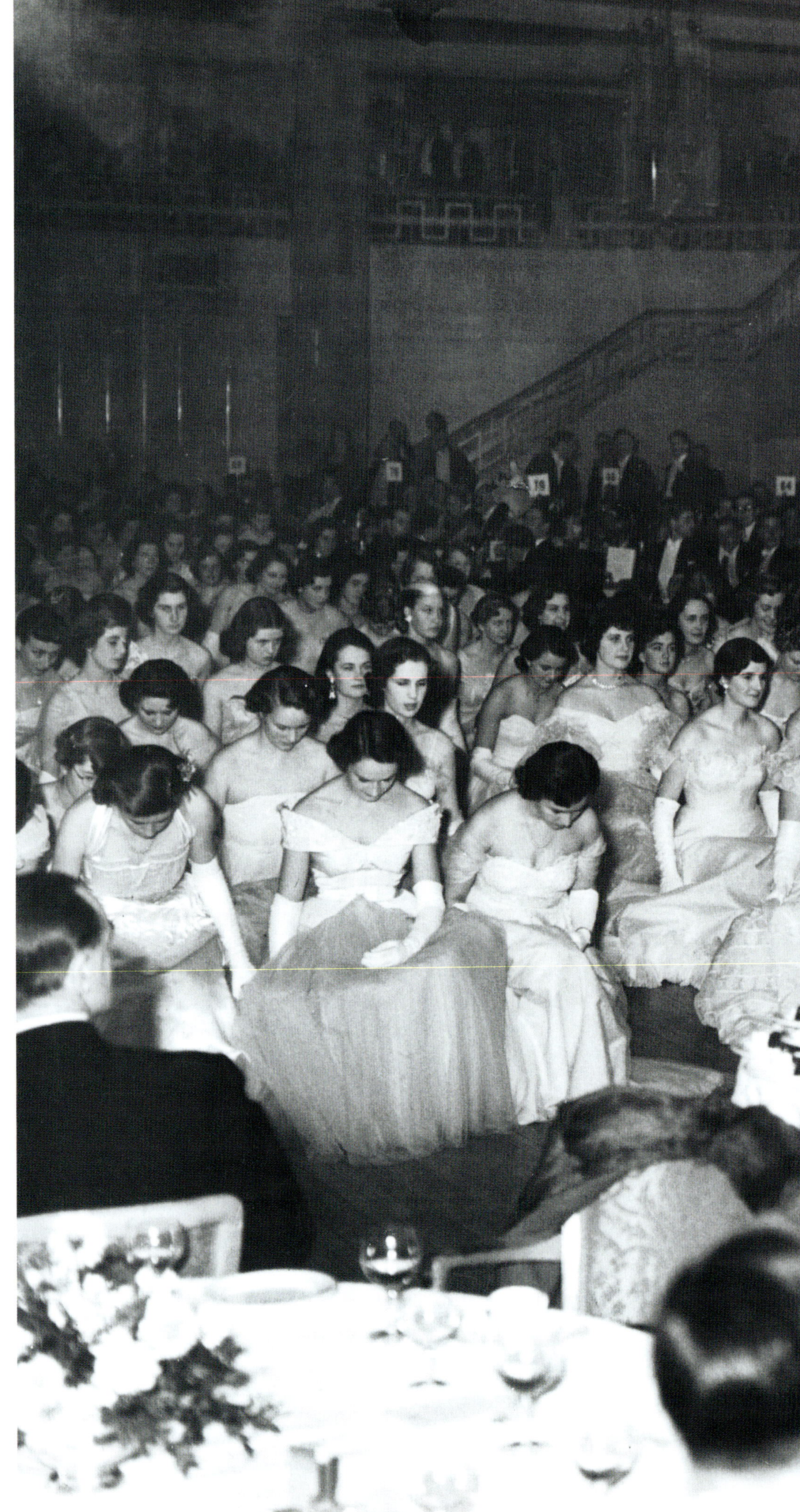

PREVIOUS PAGES

Debutants sit around the dance floor as men stand behind them awaiting the polka dance at the Allied Flag Ball at the Waldorf-Astoria Hotel. New York, 1944.

OPPOSITE

A host of debutantes perform a solemn curtsey while the Duchess of Roxburghe cuts a giant birthday cake with 208 candles, during the Queen Charlotte Ball at Grosvenor House. London, 1952.

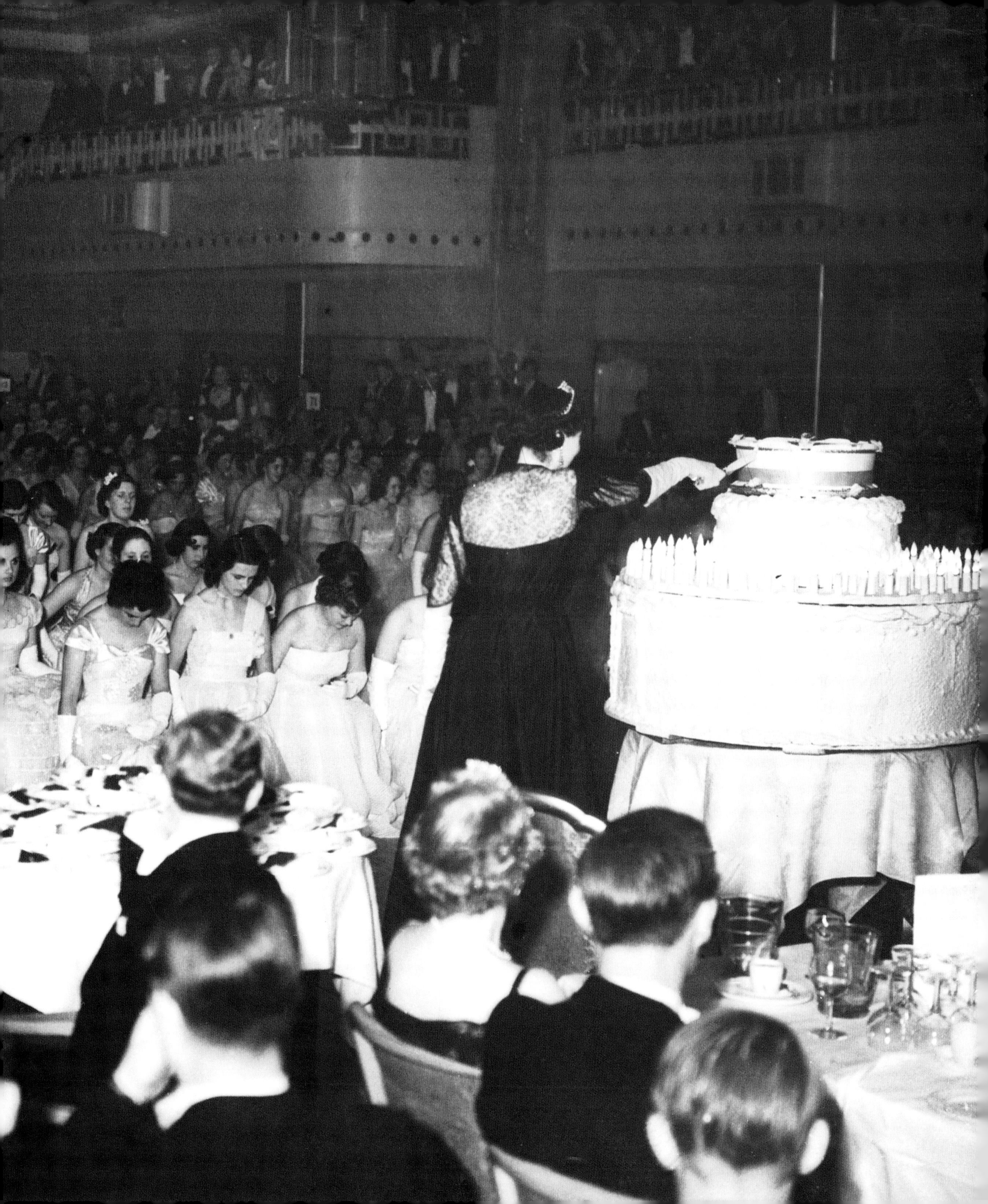

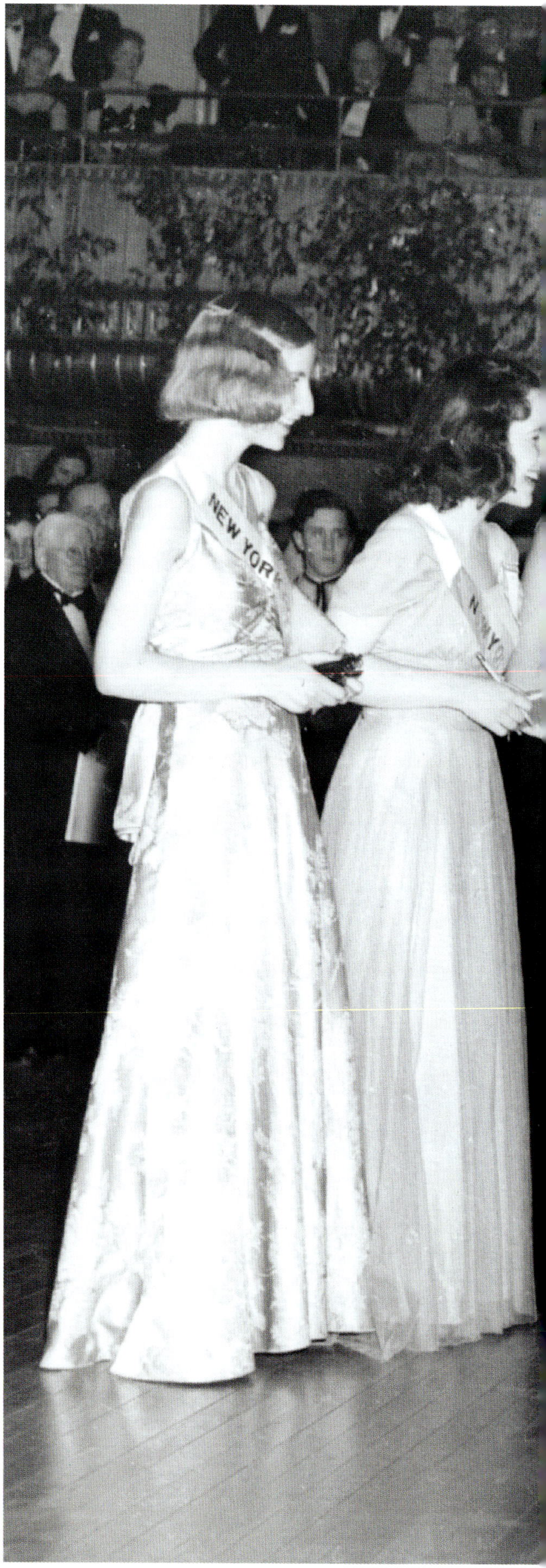

New York City debutantes at the Annual Grand Ball of the Republican Party, complete with a live elephant mascot, which has symbolized the Republican party since it was depicted in 1874 in a political cartoon in *Harper's Weekly*. The Waldorf-Astoria Hotel, New York, 1940.

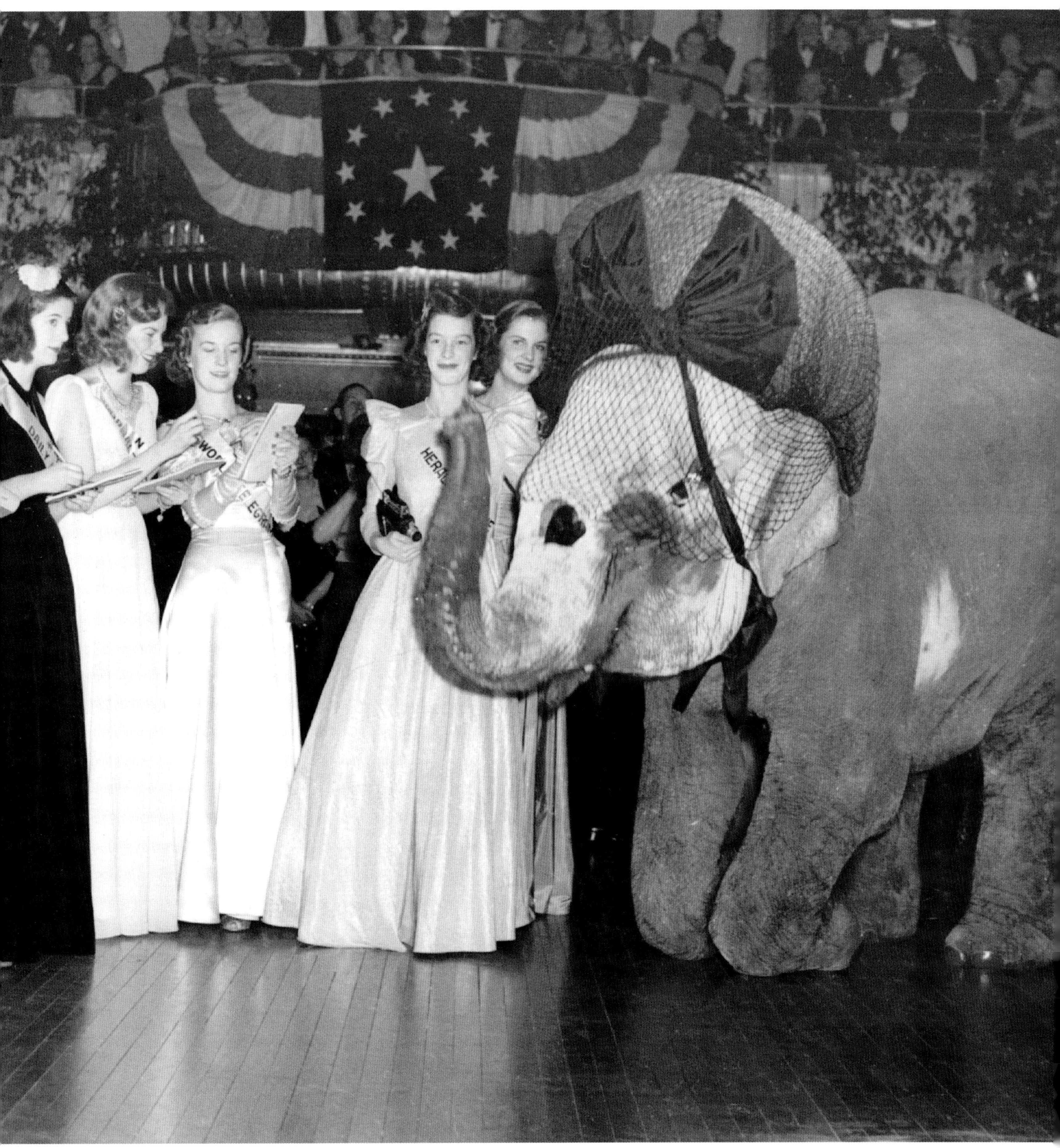

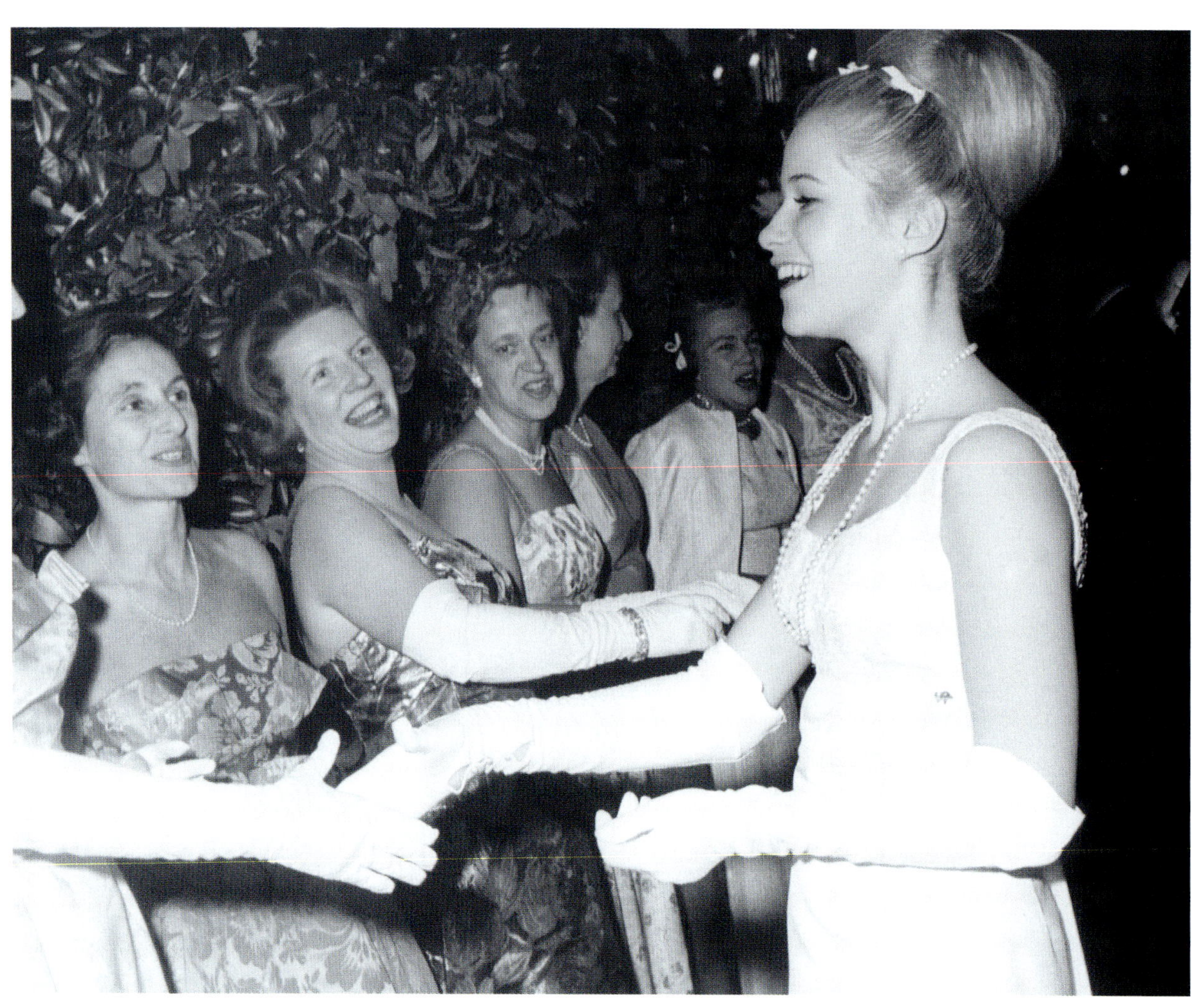

ABOVE, OPPOSITE AND FOLLOWING PAGES
Mazie Cox makes her debut at the Waldorf-Astoria Hotel. New York, 1963.

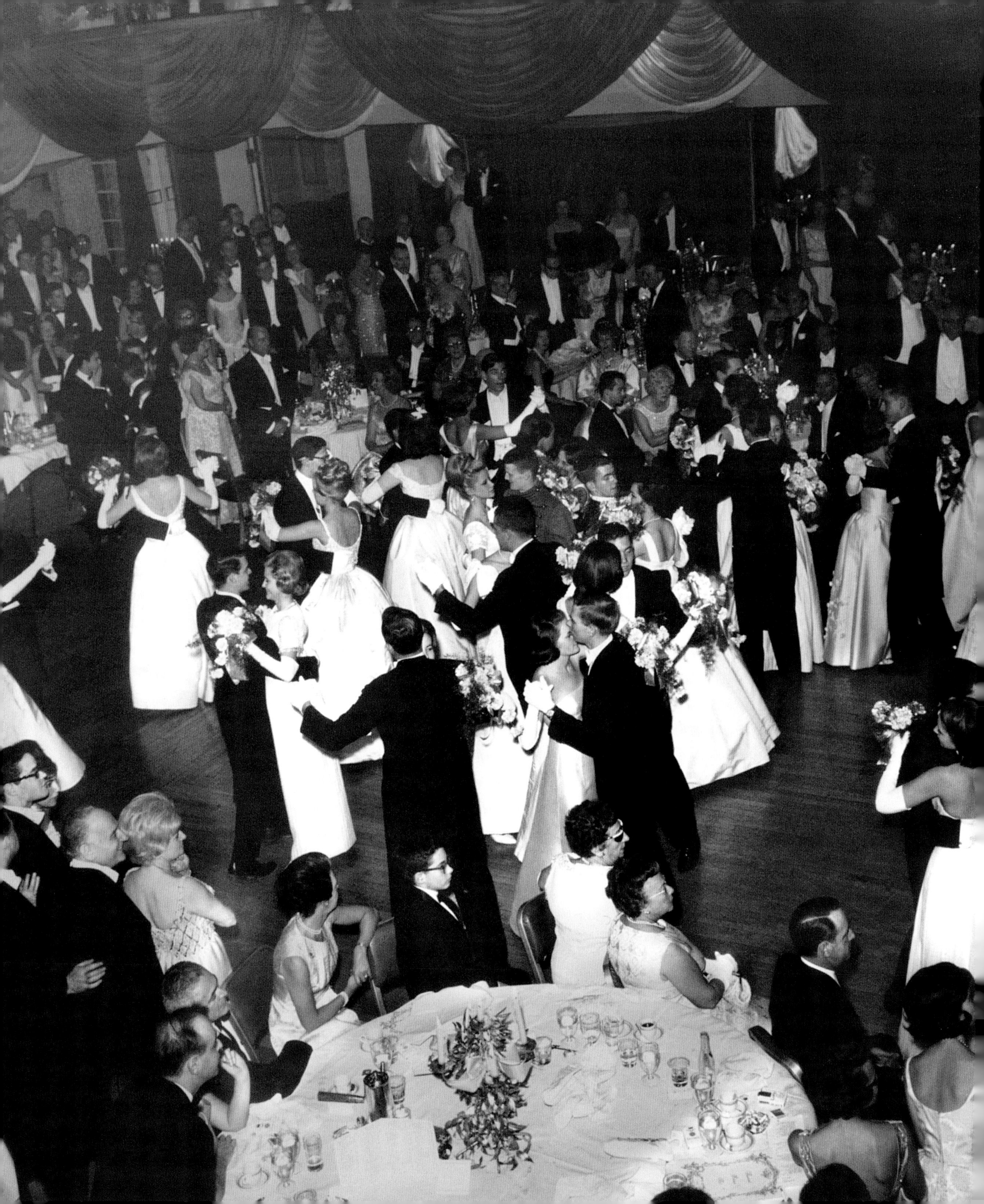

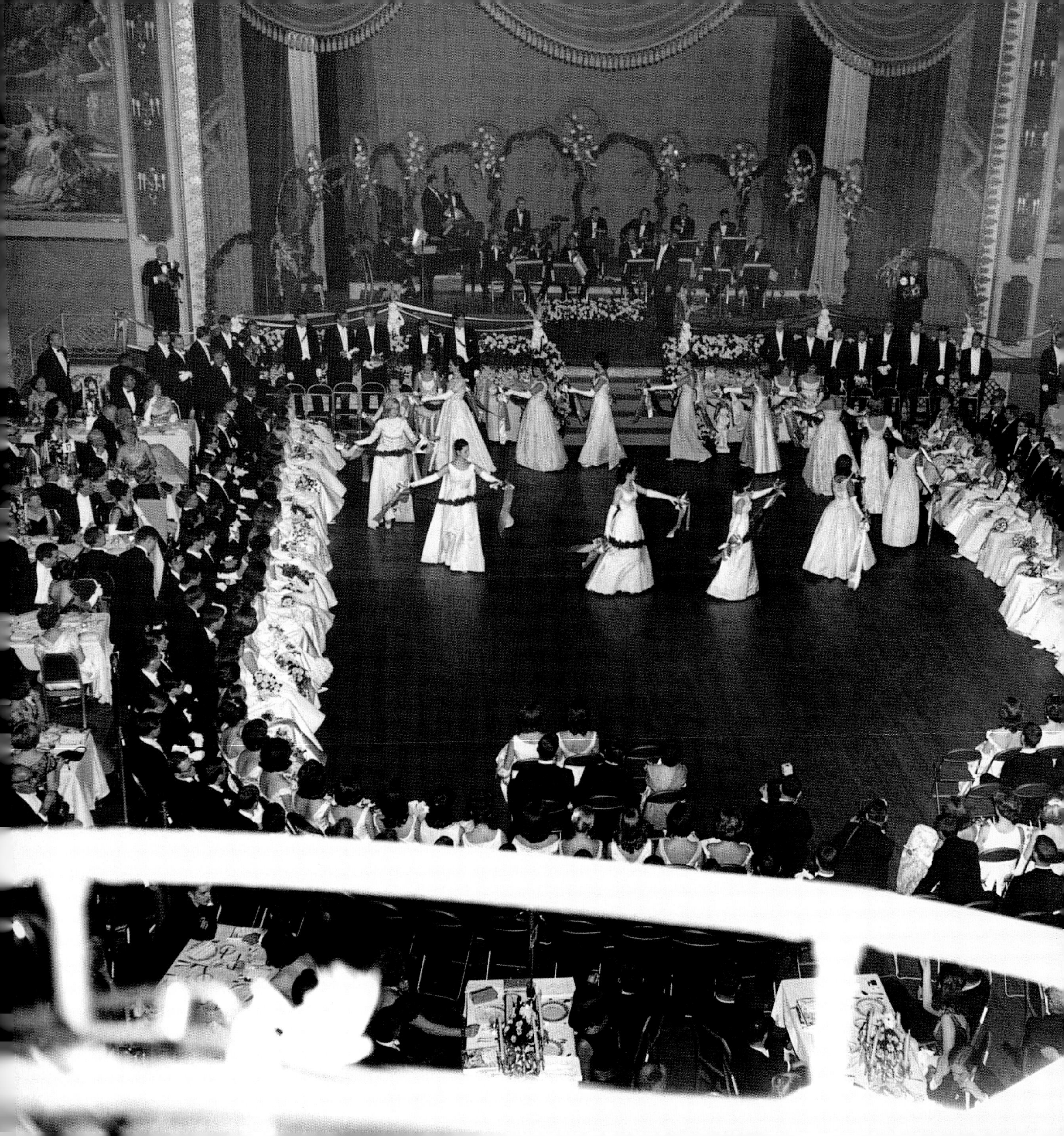

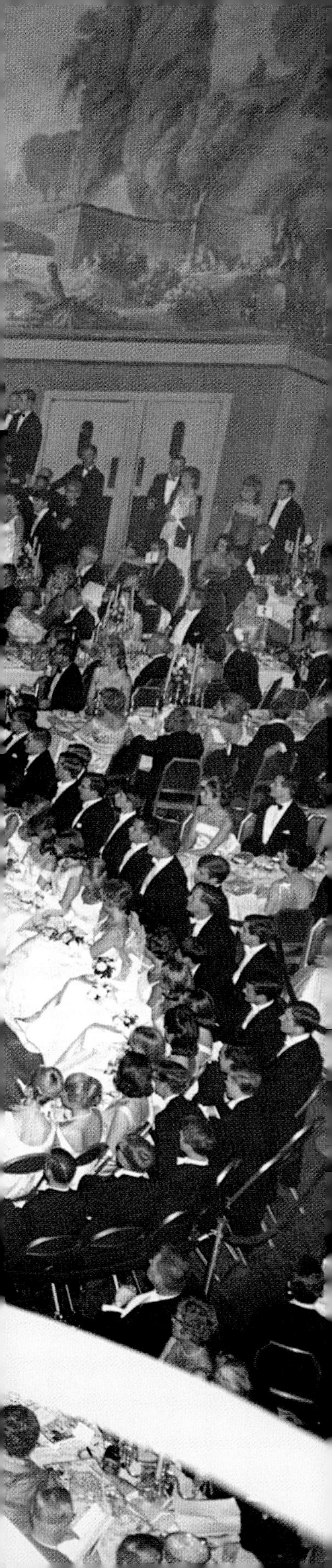

One hundred and twenty young ladies will make their bow on December twenty-first at the 1951 Debutante Cotillion and Christmas Ball to be held at the Waldorf-Astoria for the benefit of the New York Infirmary and sponsored by Kayser. Among them will be Mona Ann Waters, the daughter of Mr. and Mrs. James J. Waters, shown at the right in palest satin, from the custom atelier of Madame Claras. The clever two-piece gloves, made especially for the occasion, are Kayser's. Kramer rhinestones. Below right: Leonora Blount Horgan, debutante daughter of Mr. and Mrs. Everett Horgan, in holiday gala of tissue satin, topped with a bandmaster bolero. A Wilson Folmar design for Ben Gam, at Bergdorf Goodman; Garfinckel's; Balliet's. Jewelry by Ciner. Far right: Not even a mouse stirs as Kyra Hawkins, daughter of Mr. and Mrs. Ashton William Hawkins, poses in Bianchini's pristine chiffon. A Jean Dessès design for Nanty, at Bergdorf Goodman; John Wanamaker's Tribout Shop, Philadelphia; Montaldo's; I. Magnin. The diamonds are by Cartier. Christmas trees on both pages from Ellen Lehman McCluskey

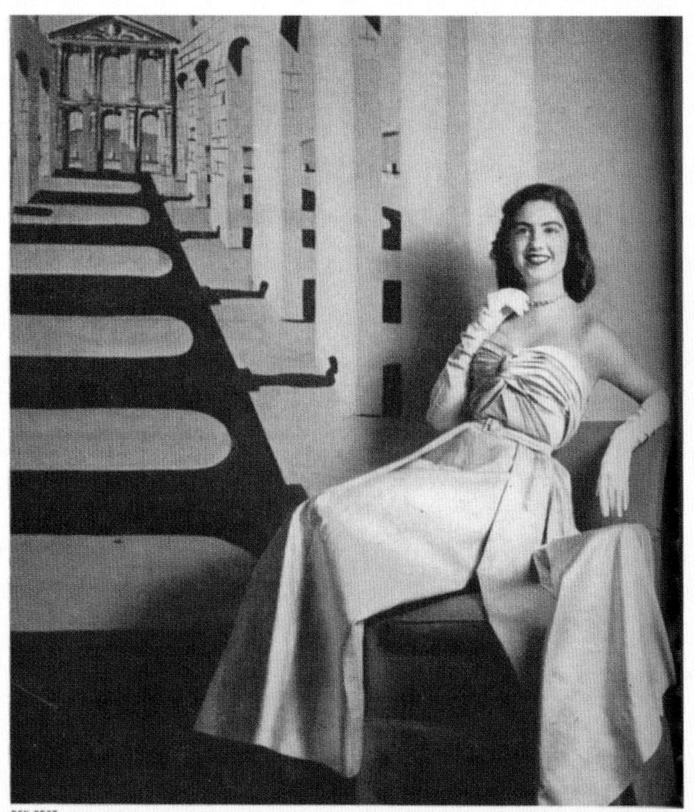

BEN ROSE

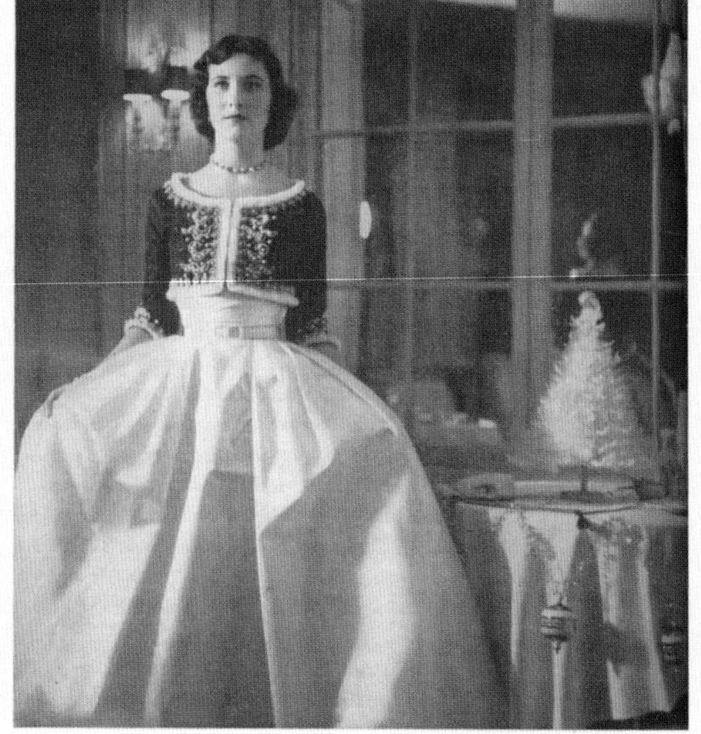

JAMES ABBE, JR.

# SUNDOWN SERENADES

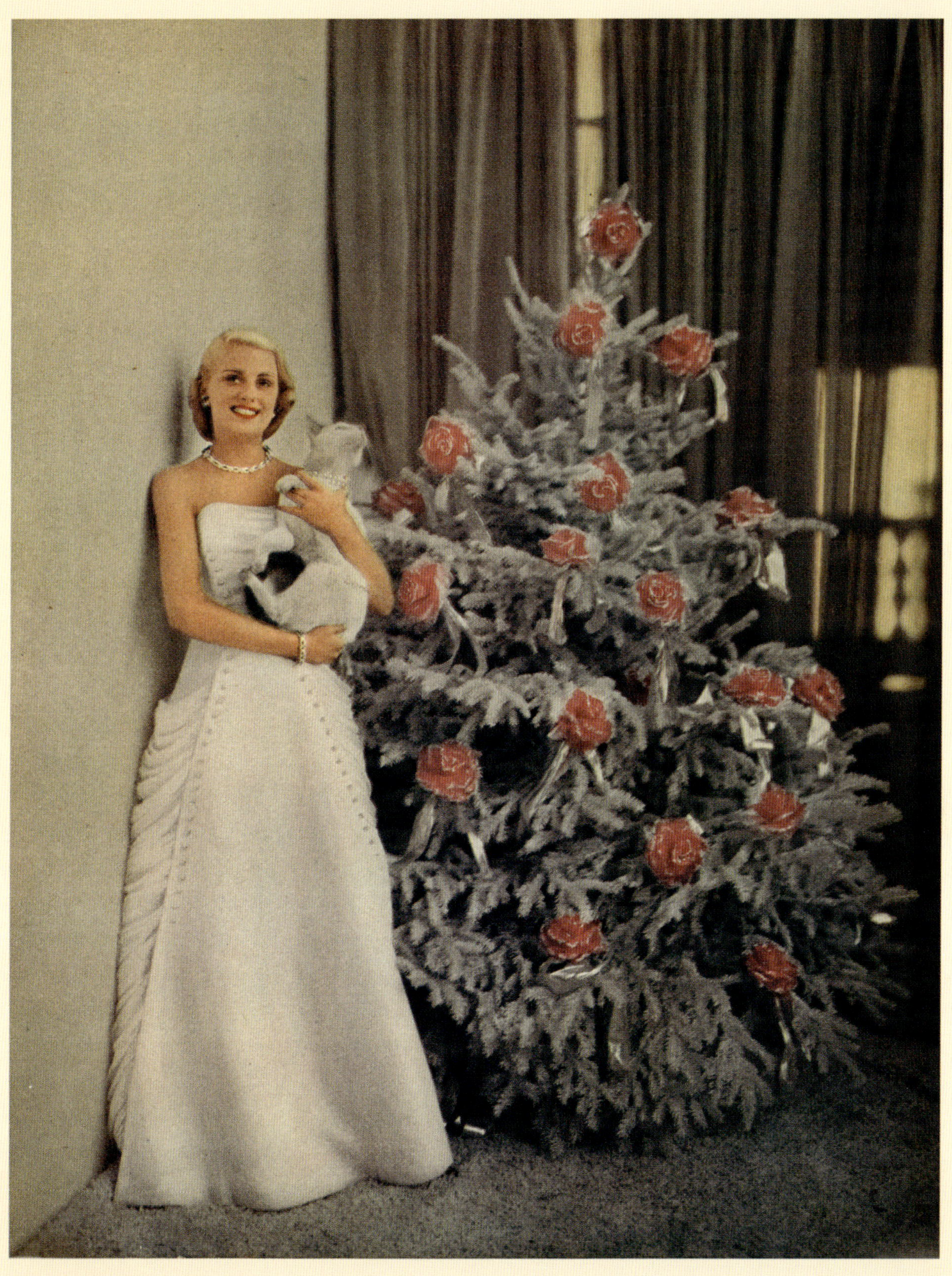

"'TWAS THE NIGHT BEFORE CHRISTMAS, WHEN..."

Cartier diamonds. As seen in *Town & Country*, 1951.

BELOW AND OPPOSITE

The first United States debutante ball held at Versailles Palace, 1958.

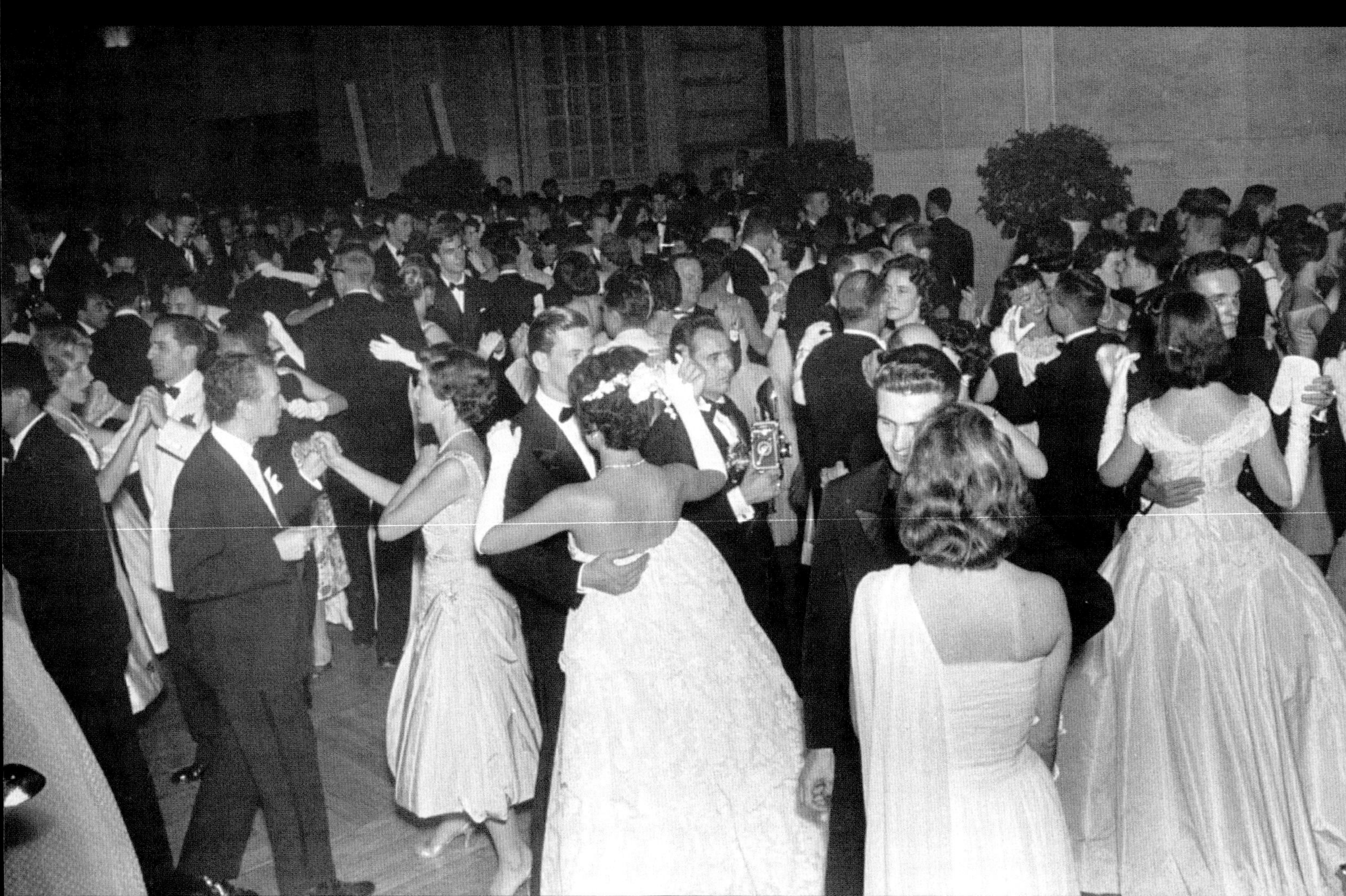

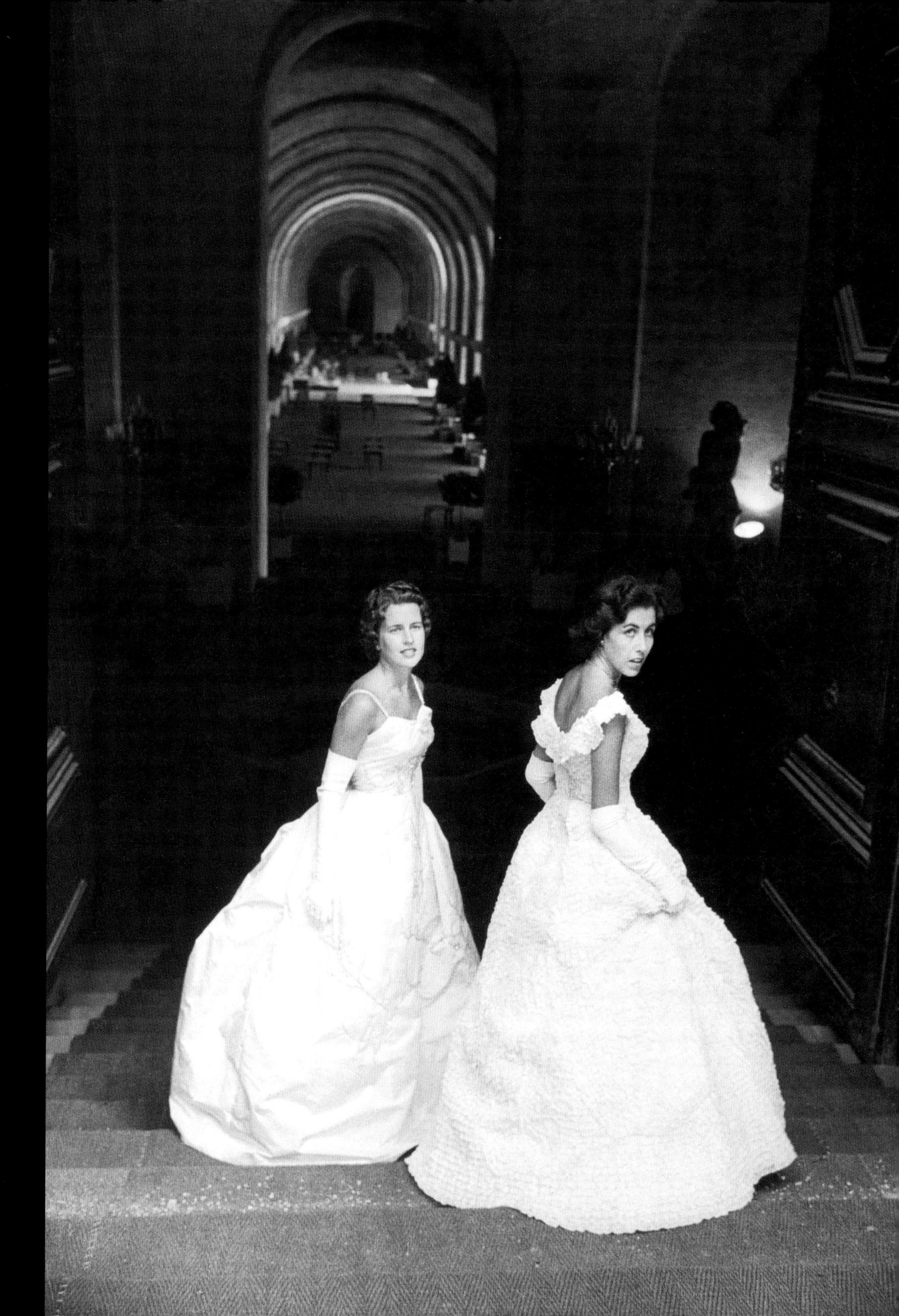

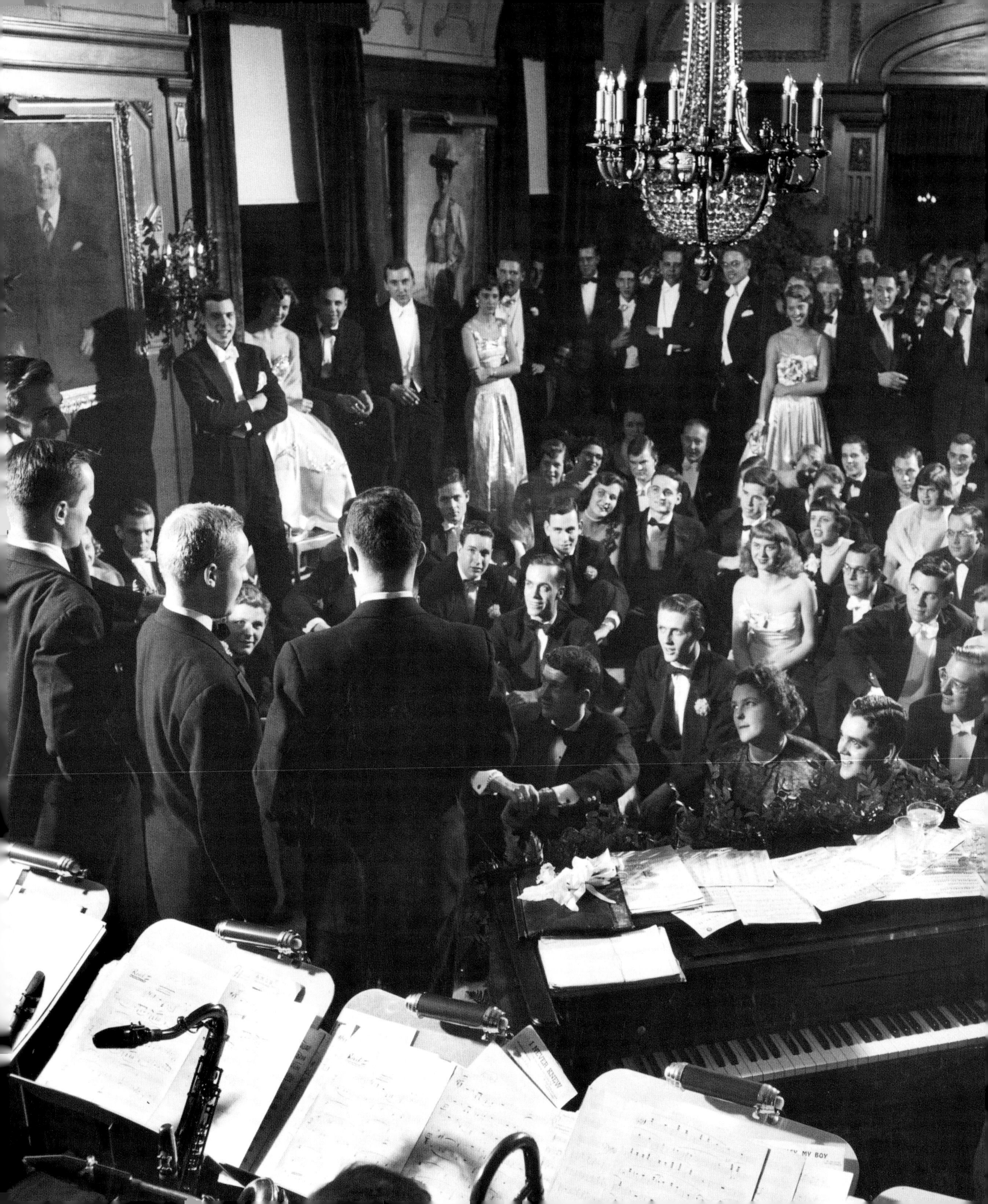
I NEVER KNEW

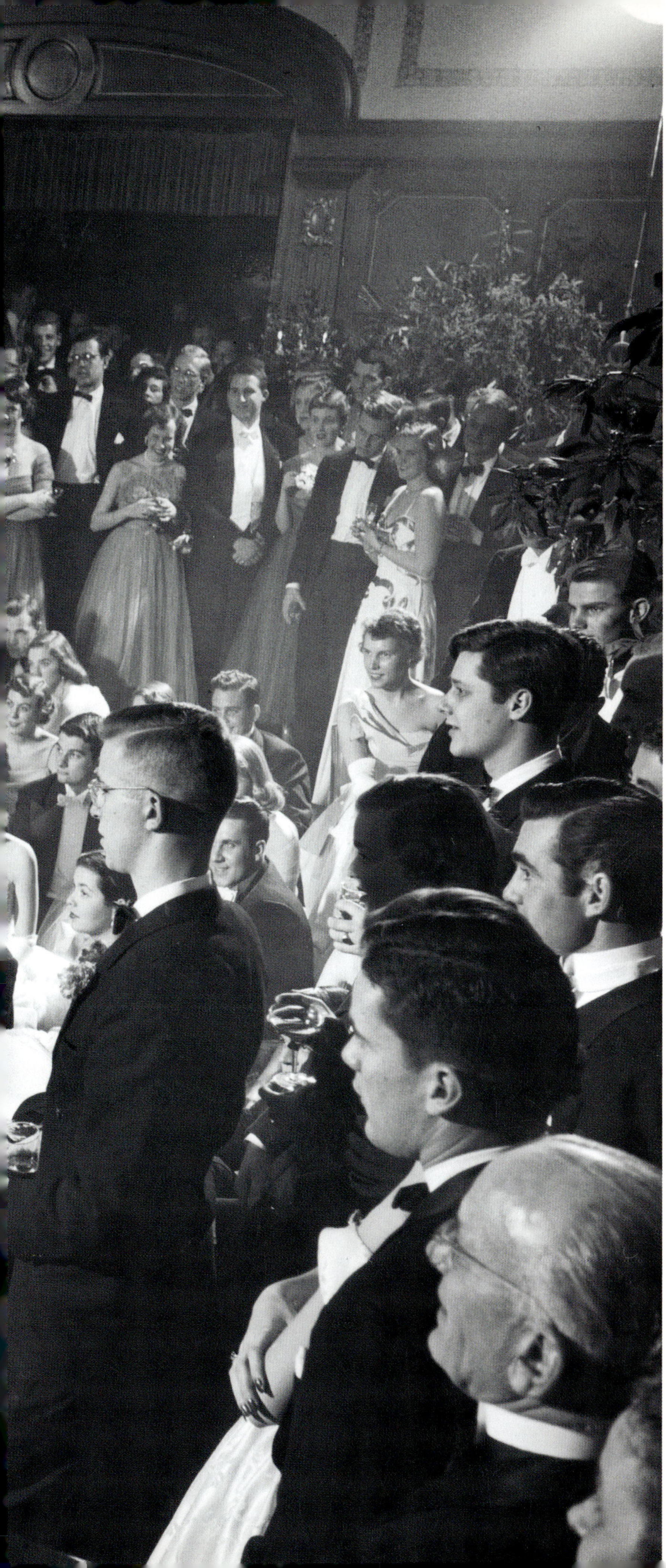

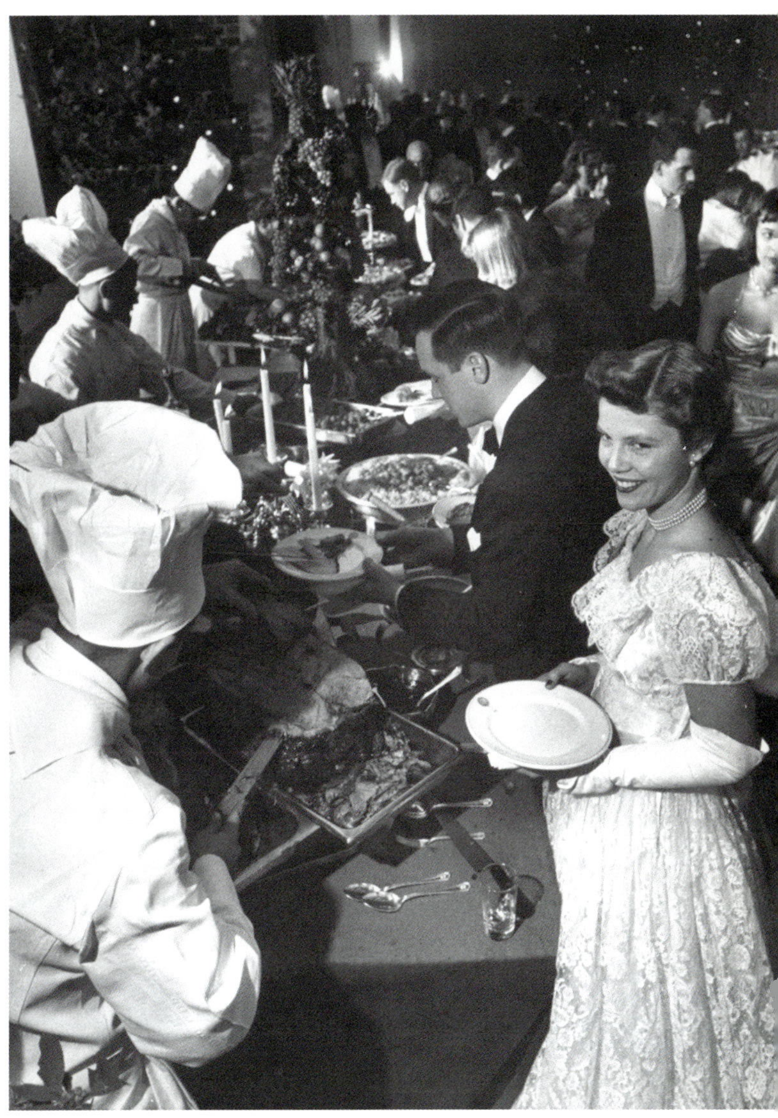

ABOVE AND OPPOSITE

St. Louis debutante Sallie Marie Busch, of the Anheuser-Busch family, received one of the most celebrated and talked about debutante parties of her generation. Entertainment was provided by the Princeton Triangle Club, the oldest touring collegiate musical troupe in the United States. A total of forty-five stewards and bartenders tended to guests every need well in to the early morning hours. St Louis, Missouri, 1950.

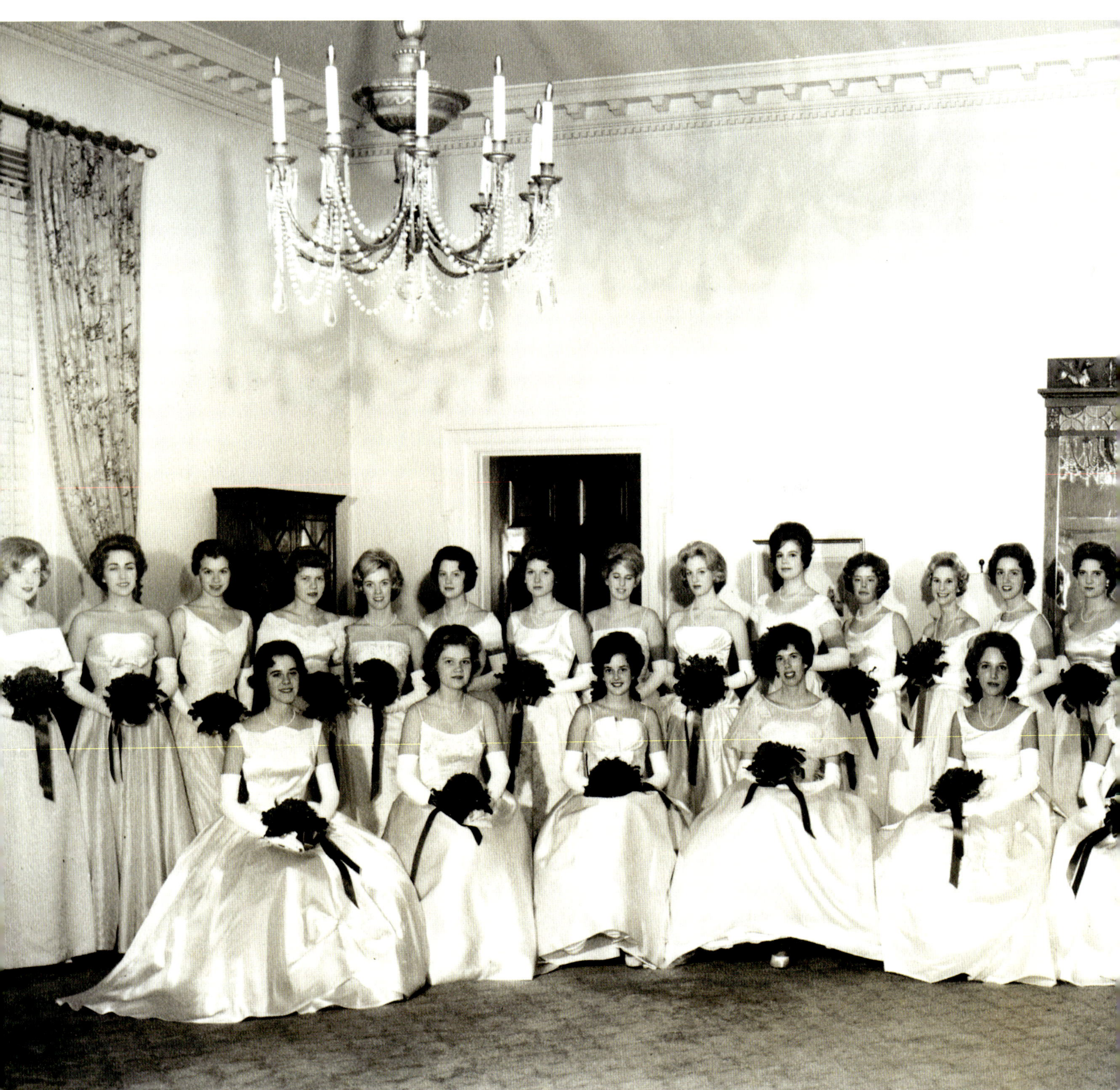

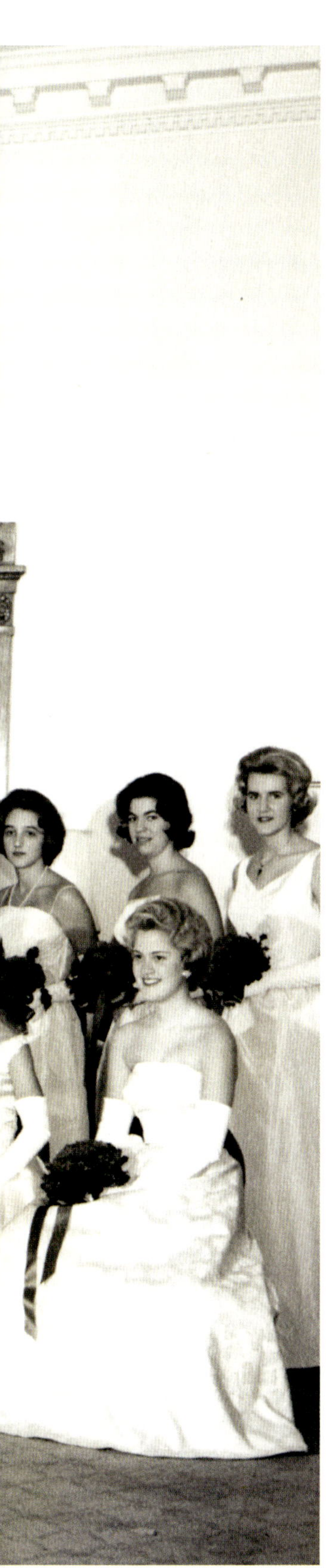

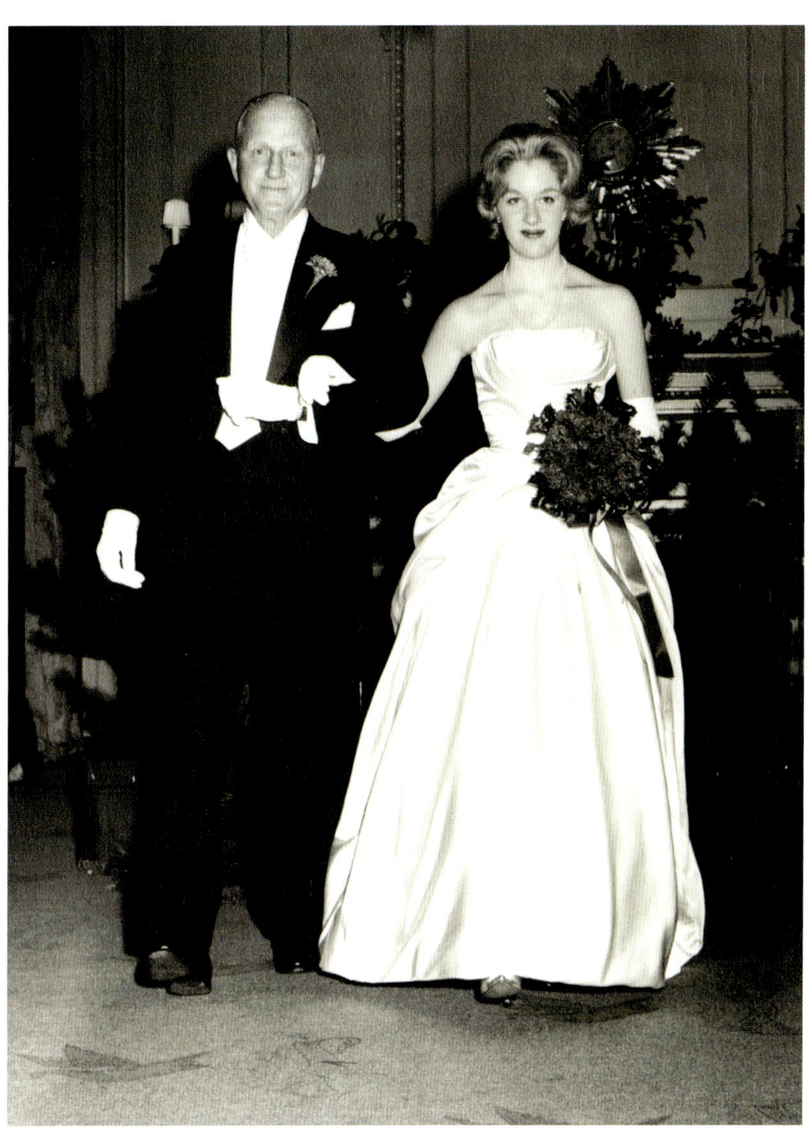

ABOVE

Mr. William Cutchins presents his daughter Alexandra Cutchins in a Ceil Chapman dress at the Pendennis Club Bachelor's Ball. Louisville, Kentucky, 1961.

OPPOSITE

Debs of the season gather at the Pendennis Club Bachelor's Ball. Louisville, Kentucky, 1961.

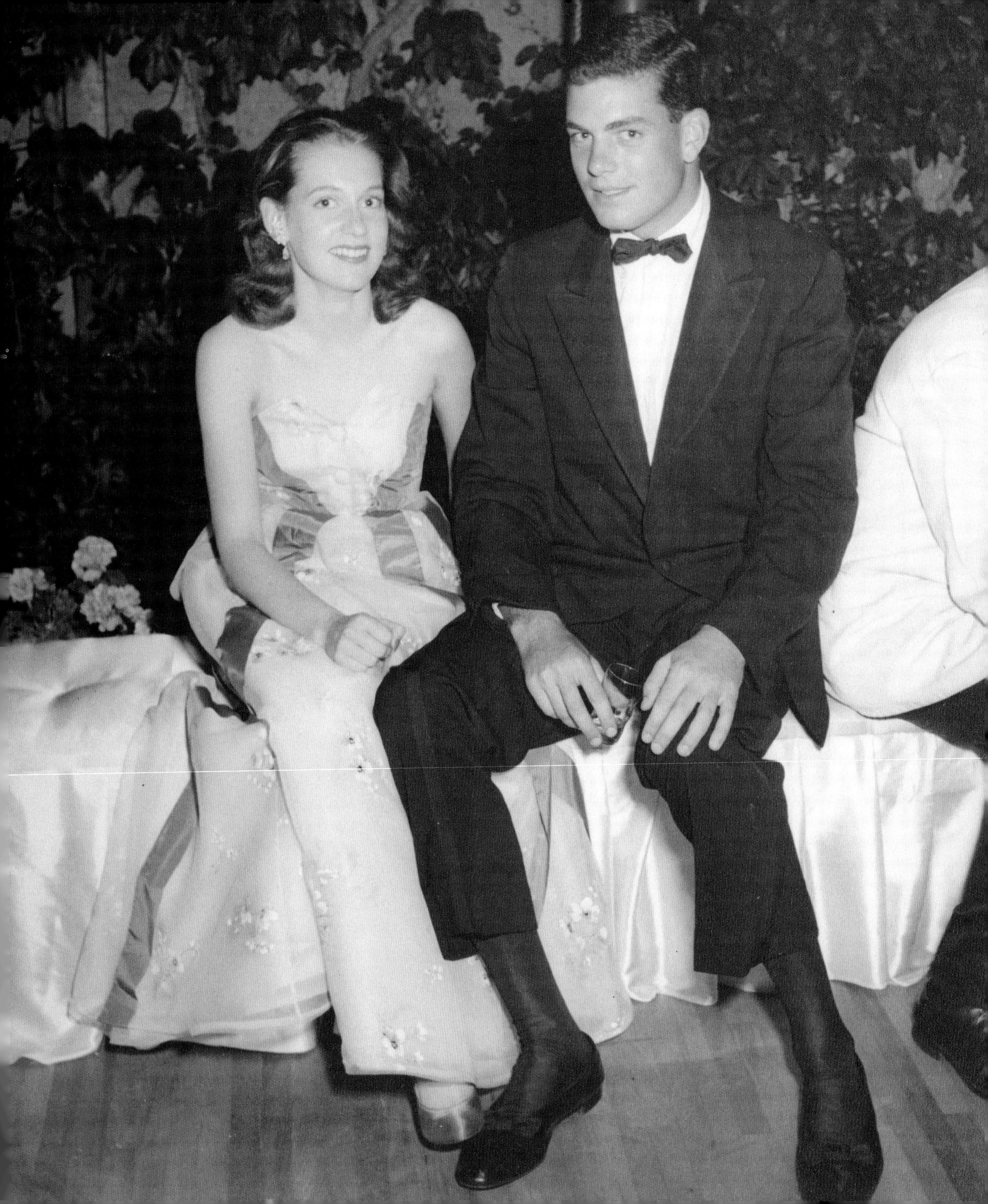

# SUMMER SOIRÉES

*I've been to a marvelous party/ I must say the fun was intense:/ We all had to do/ What the people we knew/ Might be doing a hundred years hence . . .*

—NOËL COWARD, "I'VE BEEN TO A MARVELLOUS PARTY"

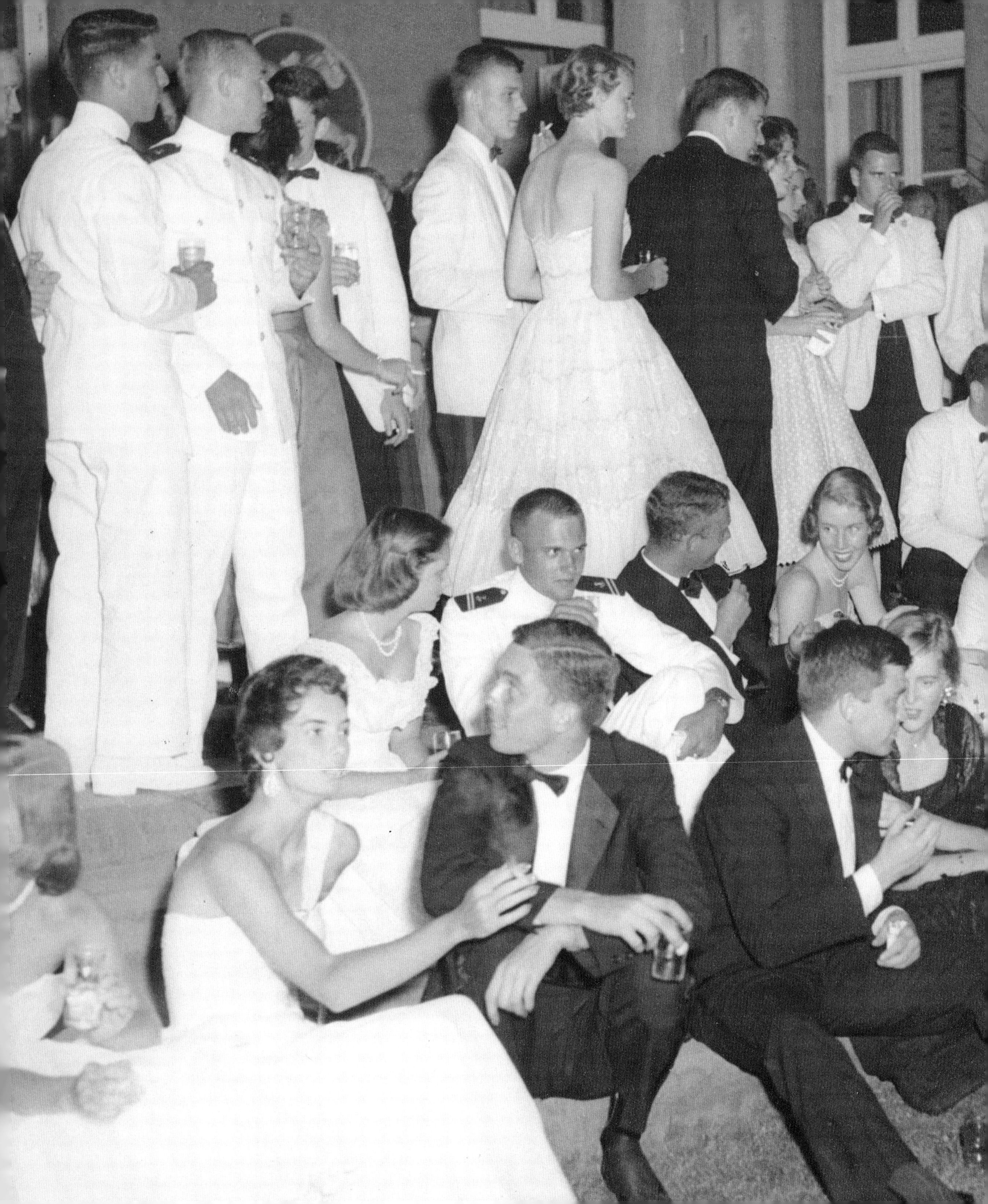

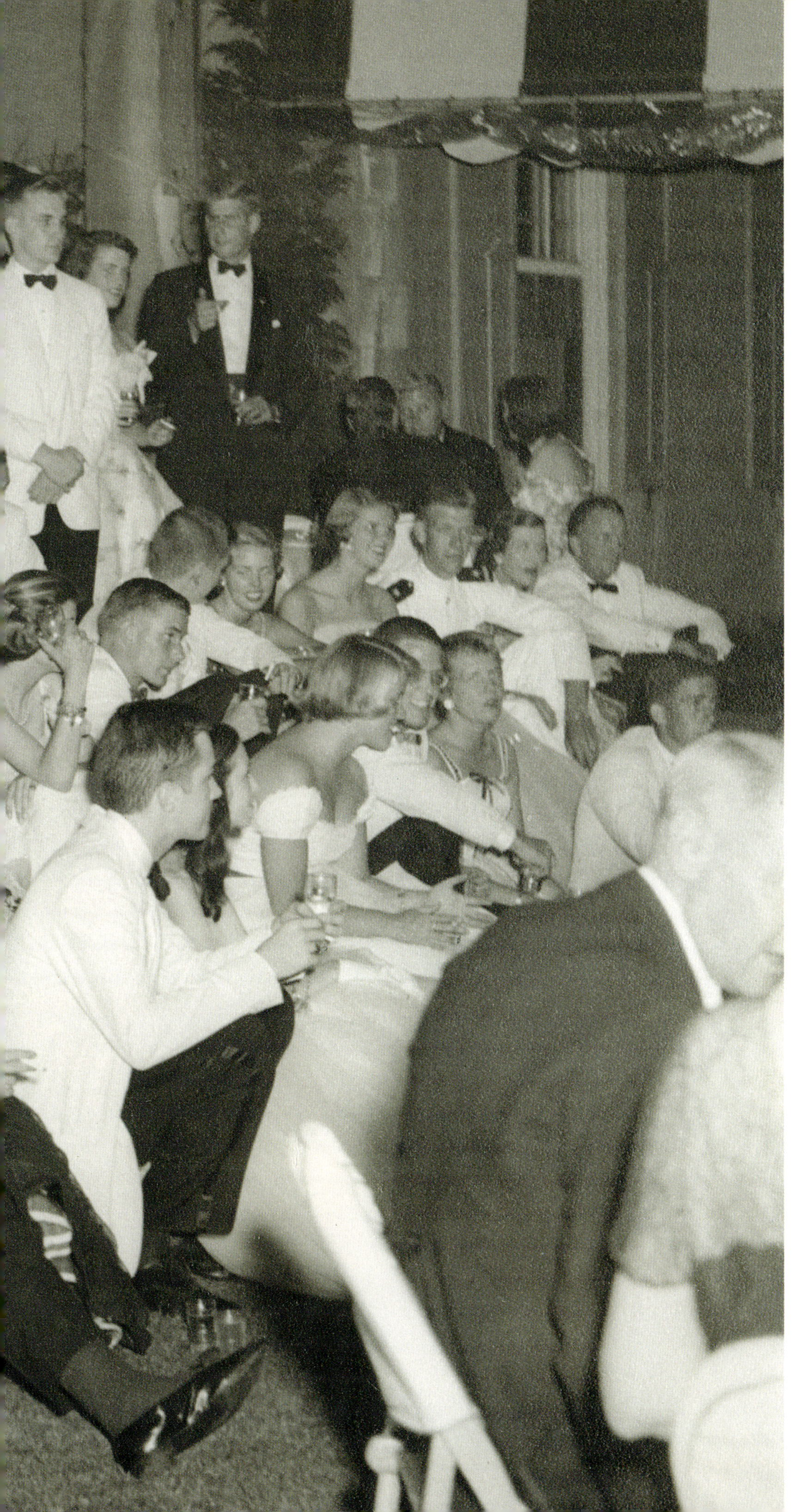

PREVIOUS PAGES

Mary McFadden and Andy Burden steal a moment at Angela Brown's coming out party. Newport, Rhode Island, 1957.

OPPOSITE

Natalie and Freddy Cushing (forefront) enjoy front row status as the band strikes up for the next chapter of the evening at Angela Brown's coming out party at the Brown's summer house, Harbour Court (now home to the New York Yacht Club). Newport, Rhode Island, 1957.

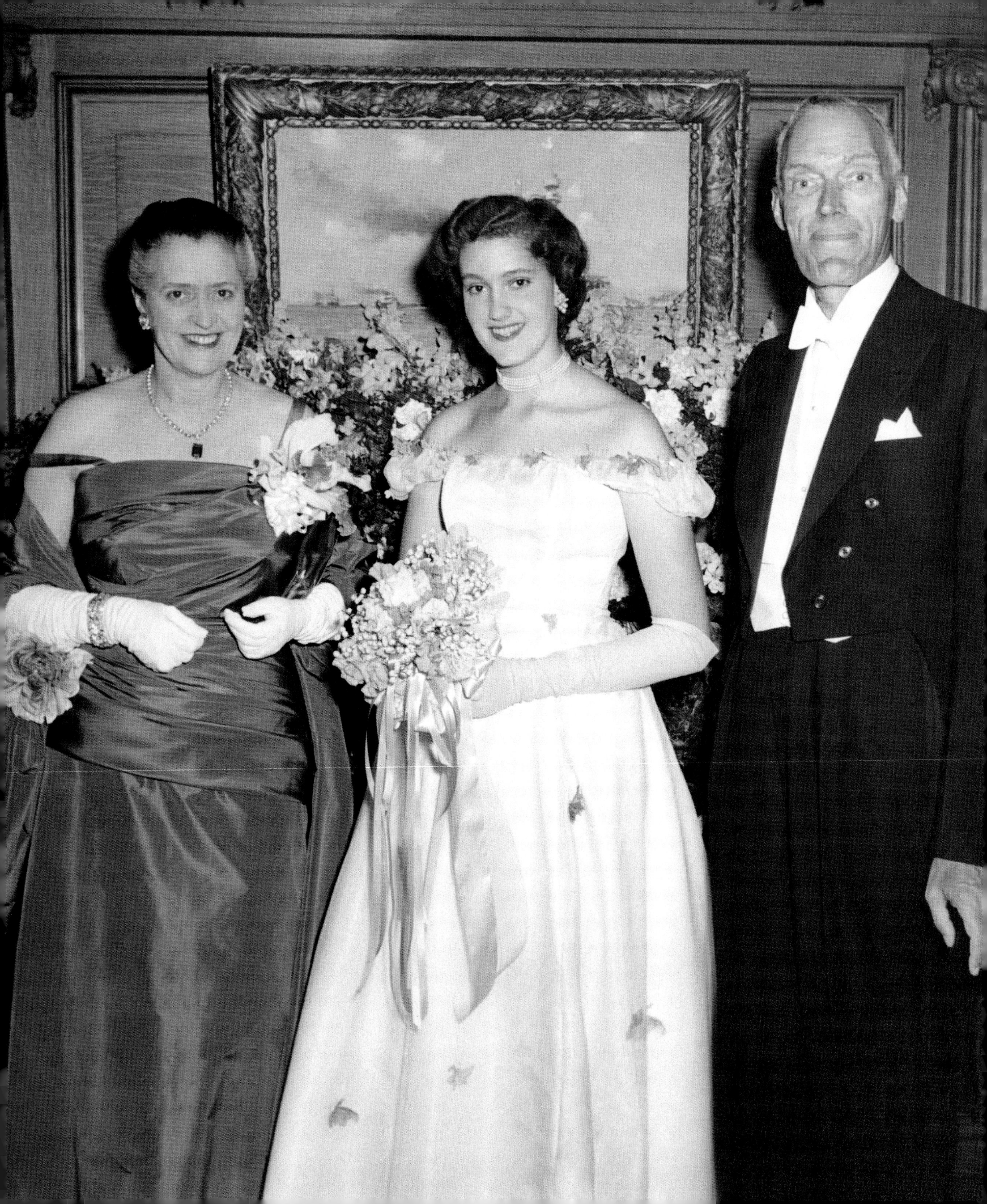

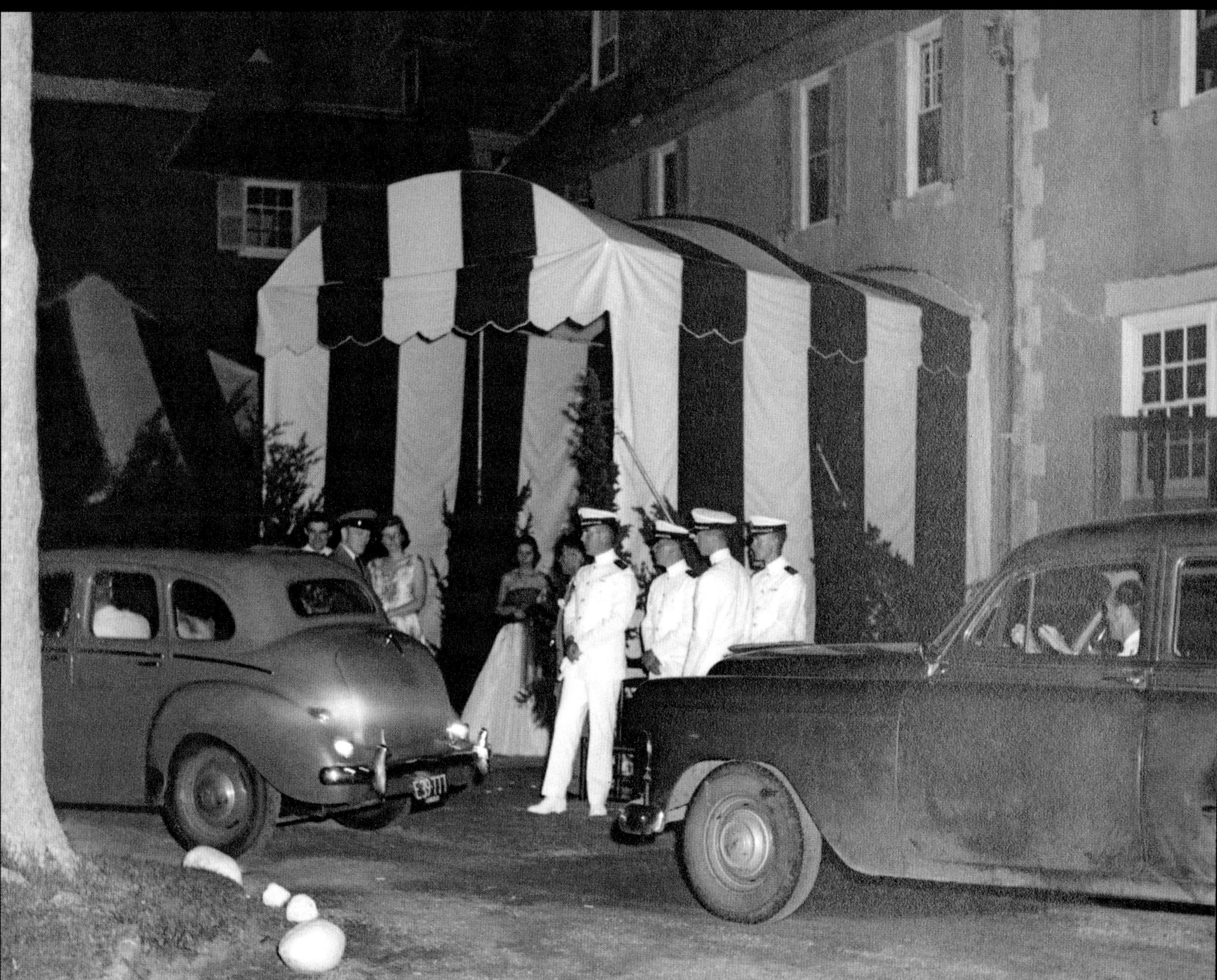

OPPOSITE

Debutante Angela Brown with her parents, Mr. and Mrs. John Nicholas Brown II. John Nicholas Brown II was the United States Assistant Secretary of the Navy and a member of the illustrious Brown family who were early benefactors of Brown University. Newport, Rhode Island, 1957.

ABOVE

Uniformed Navy gentlemen wait near the entrance to Harbour Court during Angela Brown's party. Since Newport is home to the Naval War College, young Navy men were often happy to step in to the social whirl when there was a lack of eligible escorts and dancing partners. Newport, Rhode Island, 1957.

FOLLOWING PAGES

Guests mingle under the awning at the Brown residence. Newport, Rhode Island, 1957.

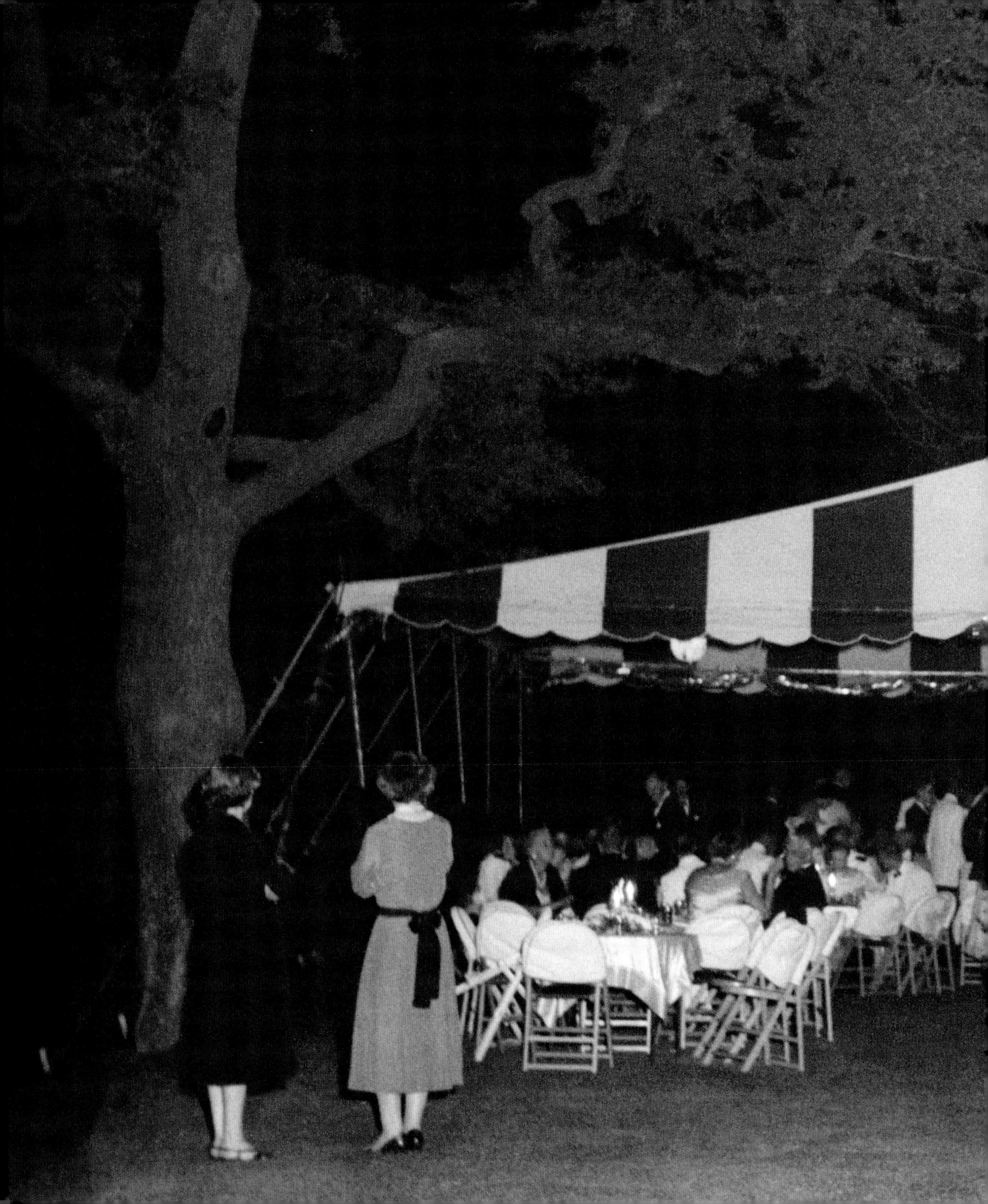

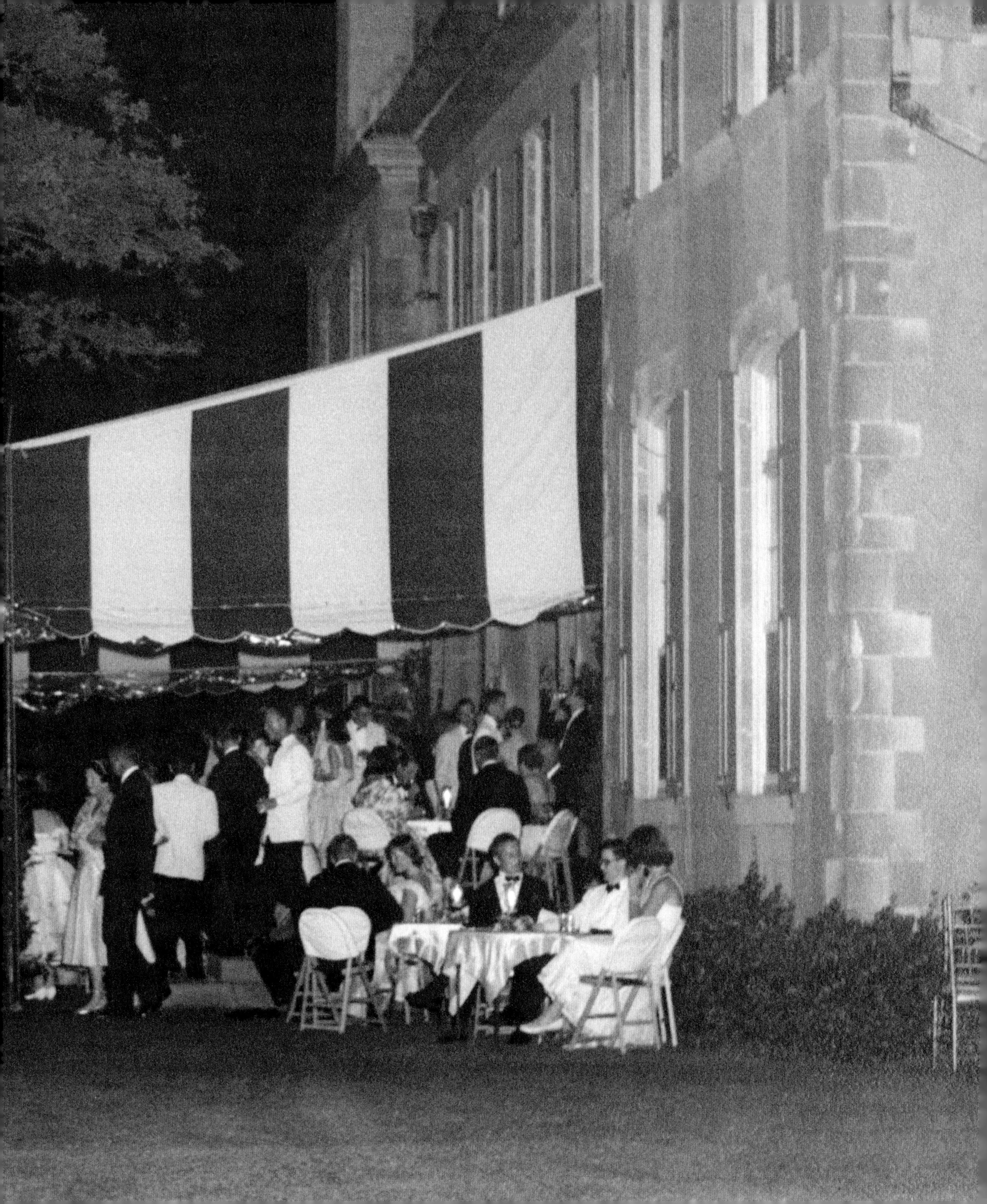

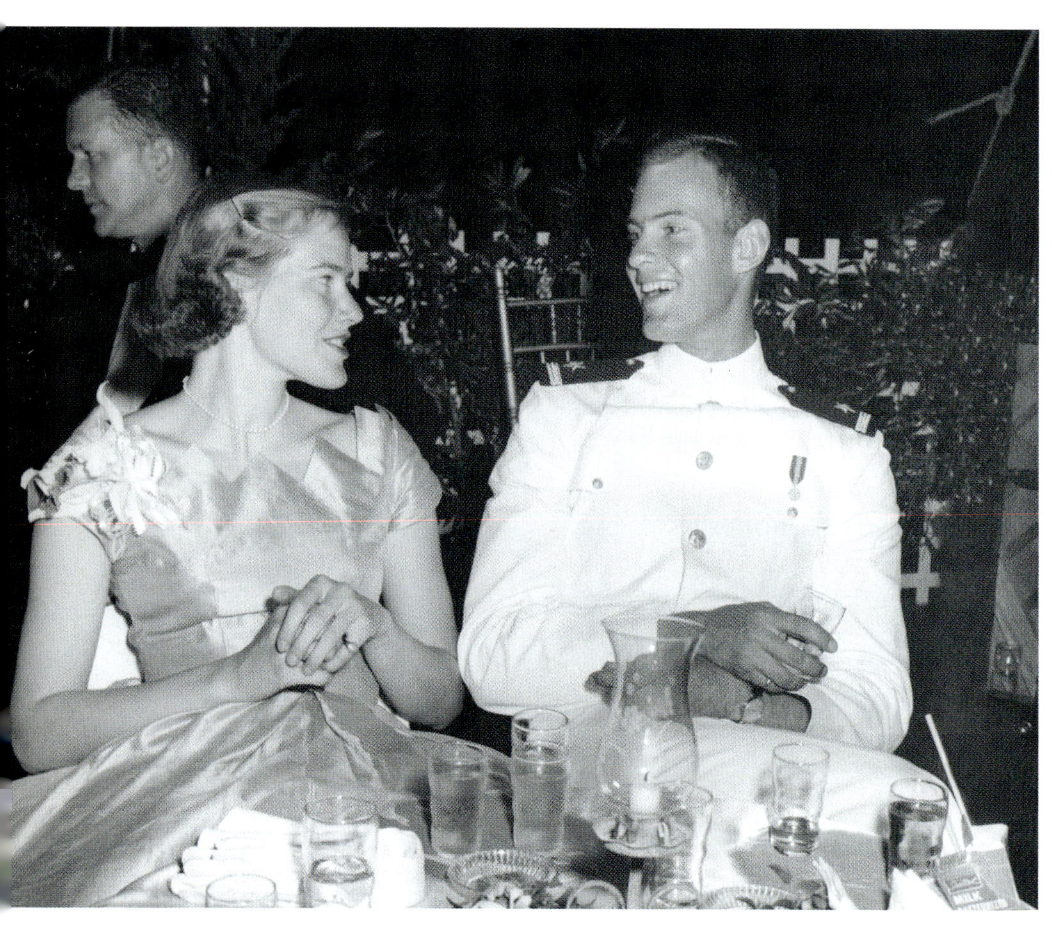

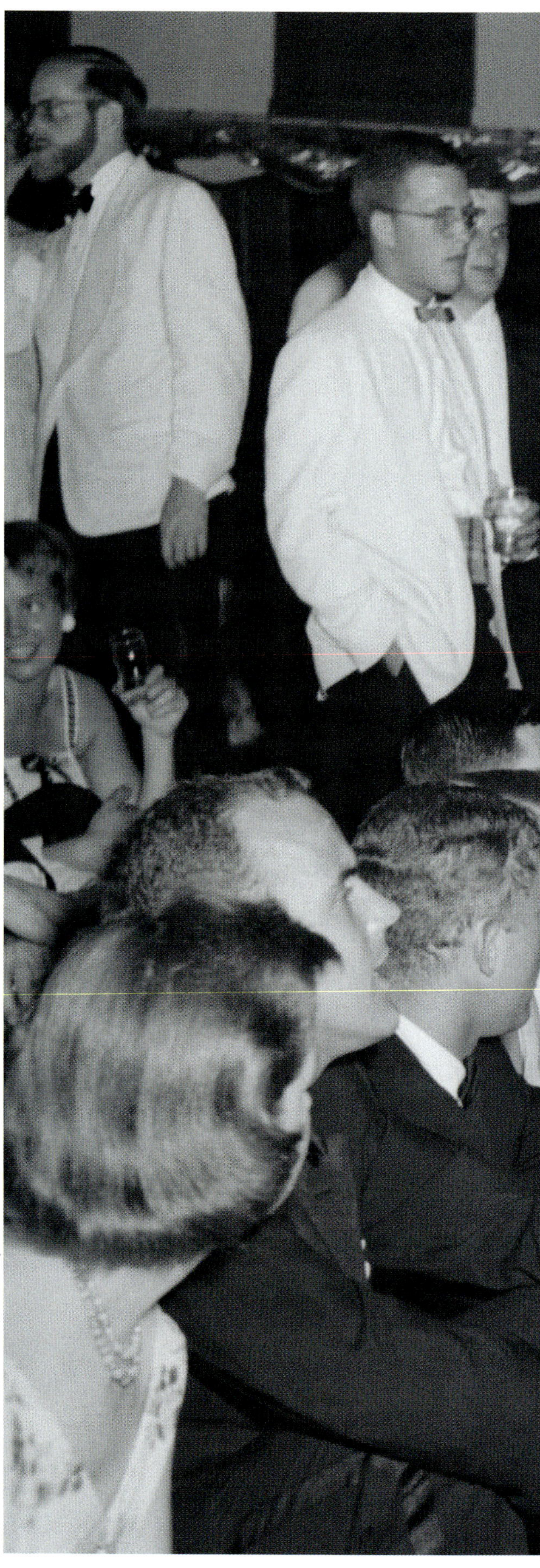

ABOVE

Angela Brown's cousin, Rosalie Sellar, strikes up an engaging conversation with her dinner partner. Newport, Rhode Island, 1957.

RIGHT

The Meyer Davis orchestra serenades Angela Brown's guests. Newport, Rhode Island, 1957.

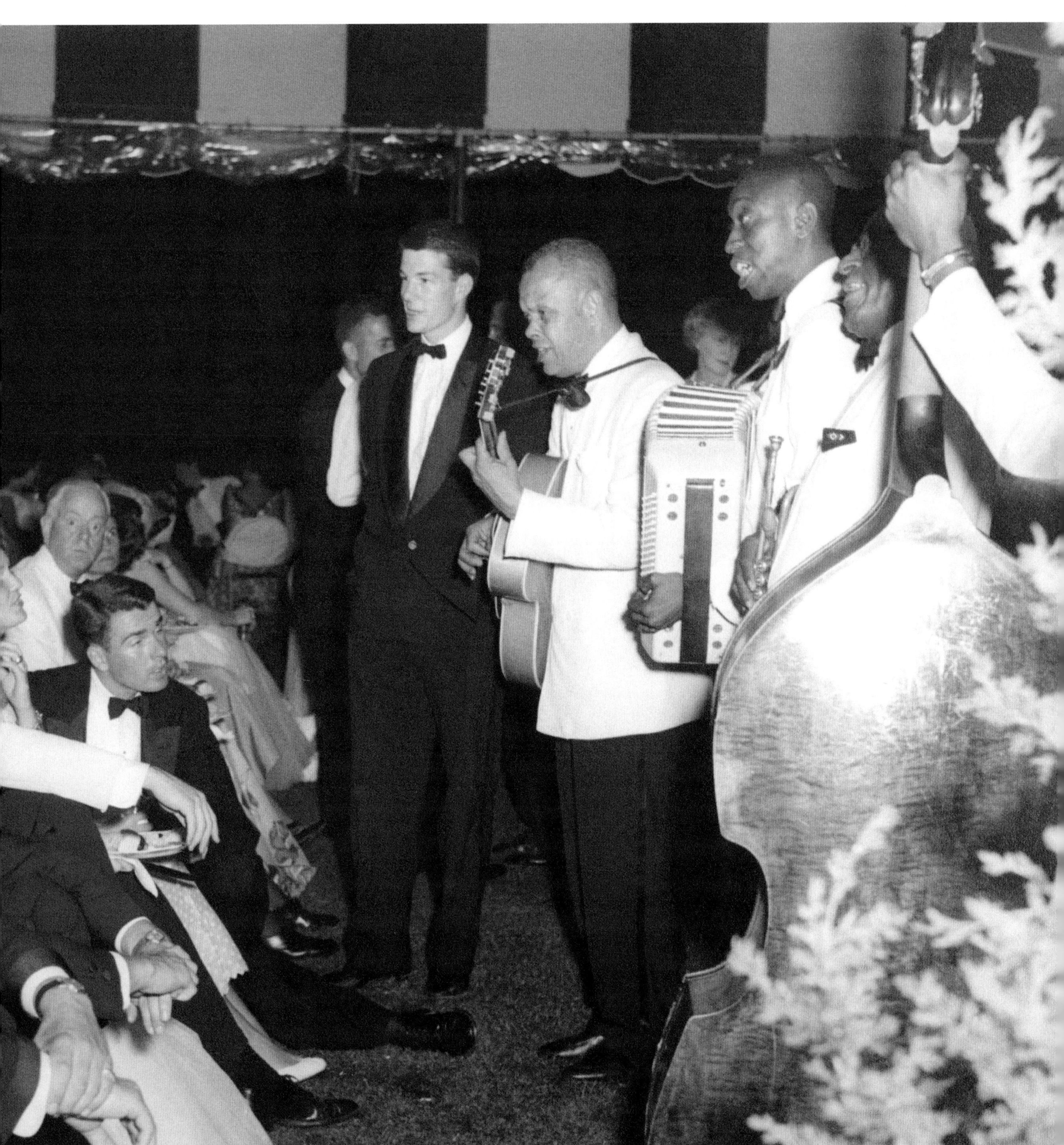

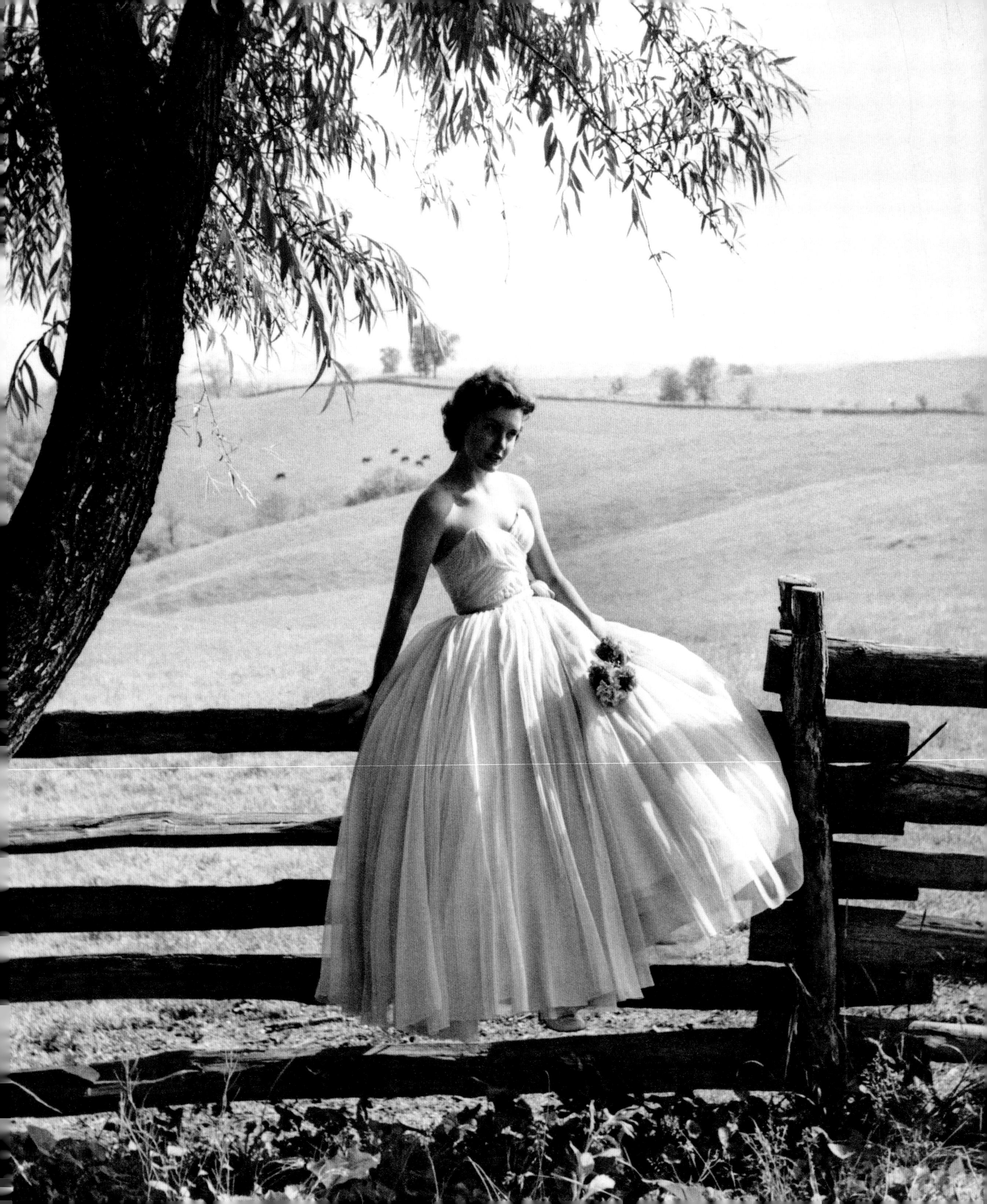

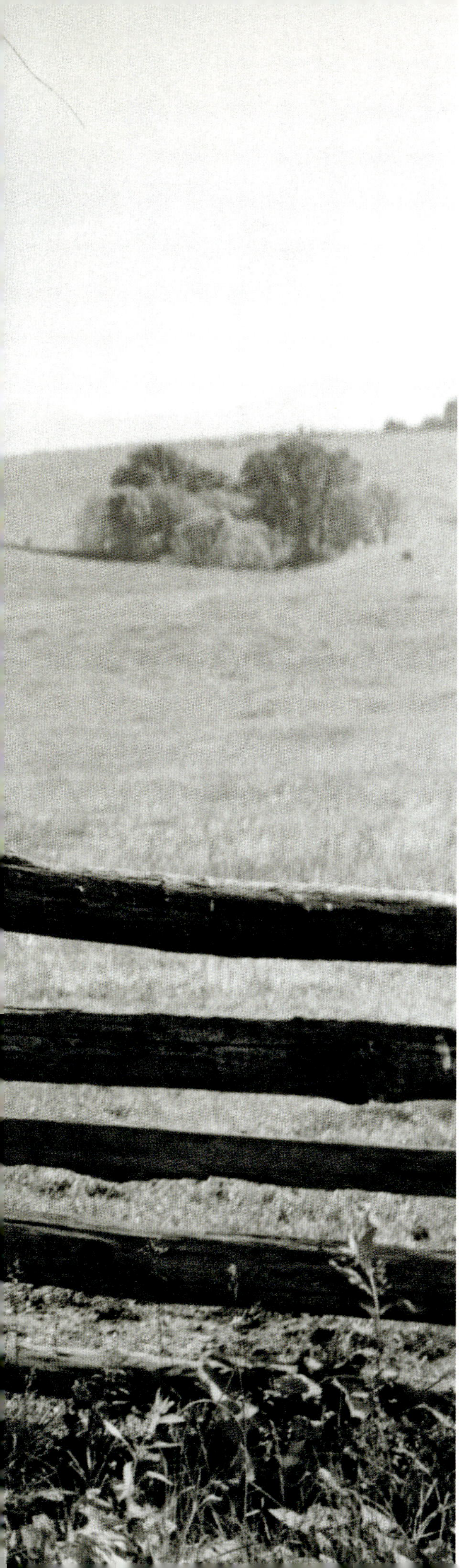

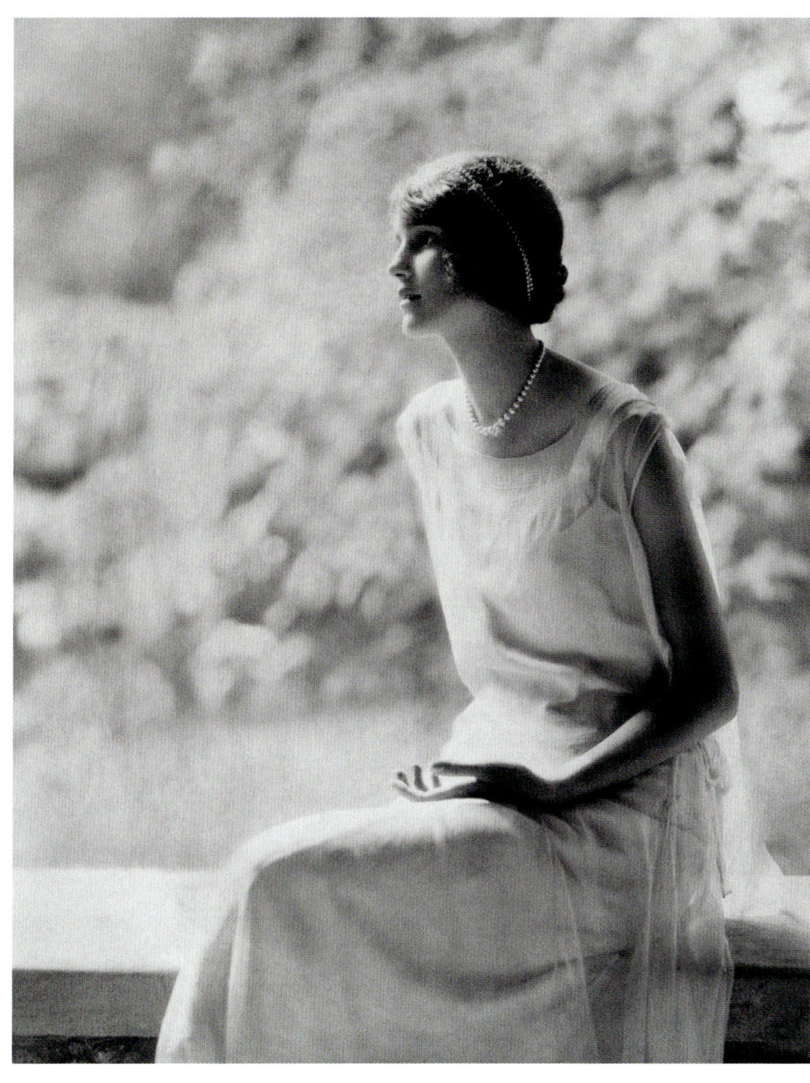

LEFT
While a debutante could make a sojourn to their designer of choice for their dress, another option included stopping at a department store to browse the couture selections. Debutante Catherine Mellon, daughter of Paul Mellon, in a strapless white dress with bouffant skirt by the Salon de Couture at Bonwit Teller. 1955. Photo by Toni Frissell.

ABOVE
Philadelphia debutante Laura Biddle wears a chiffon dress, 1924.

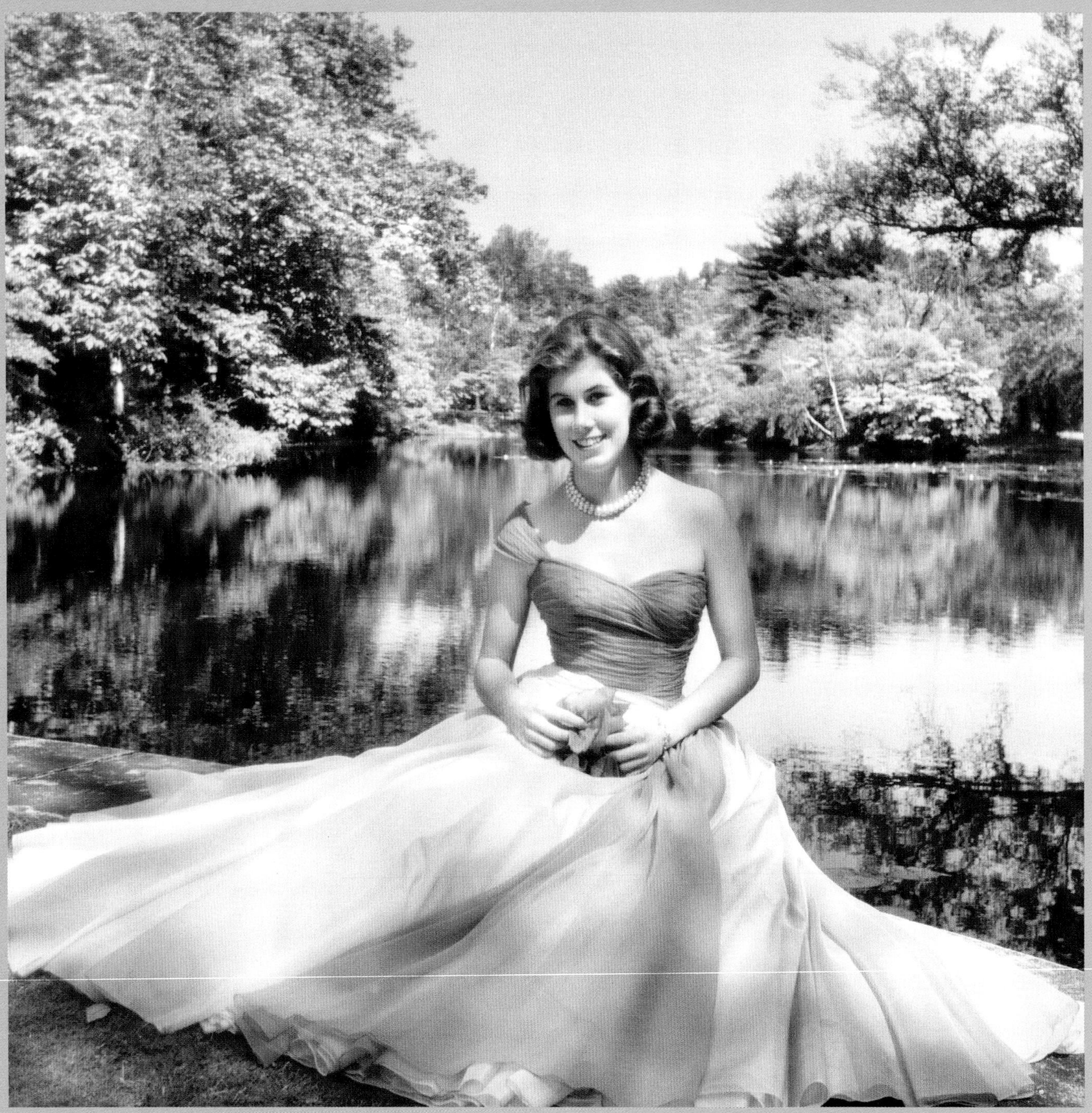

ABOVE

Debutante Elaine "Nonie" Phipps in an off the shoulder chiffon dress by Elizabeth Arden. Elizabeth Arden competed in the world of haute couture by first hiring designer Antonio Canovas del Castillo, followed by Oscar de la Renta. Westbury Long Island, 1955. Photo by Toni Frissell.

OPPOSITE

Debutante Nina Auchincloss wears a strapless tulle dress by Anne Lowe, 1955. Several years earlier, Anne Lowe had designed Nina's stepsister Jacqueline Lee Bouvier's wedding dress. Photo by Toni Frissell.

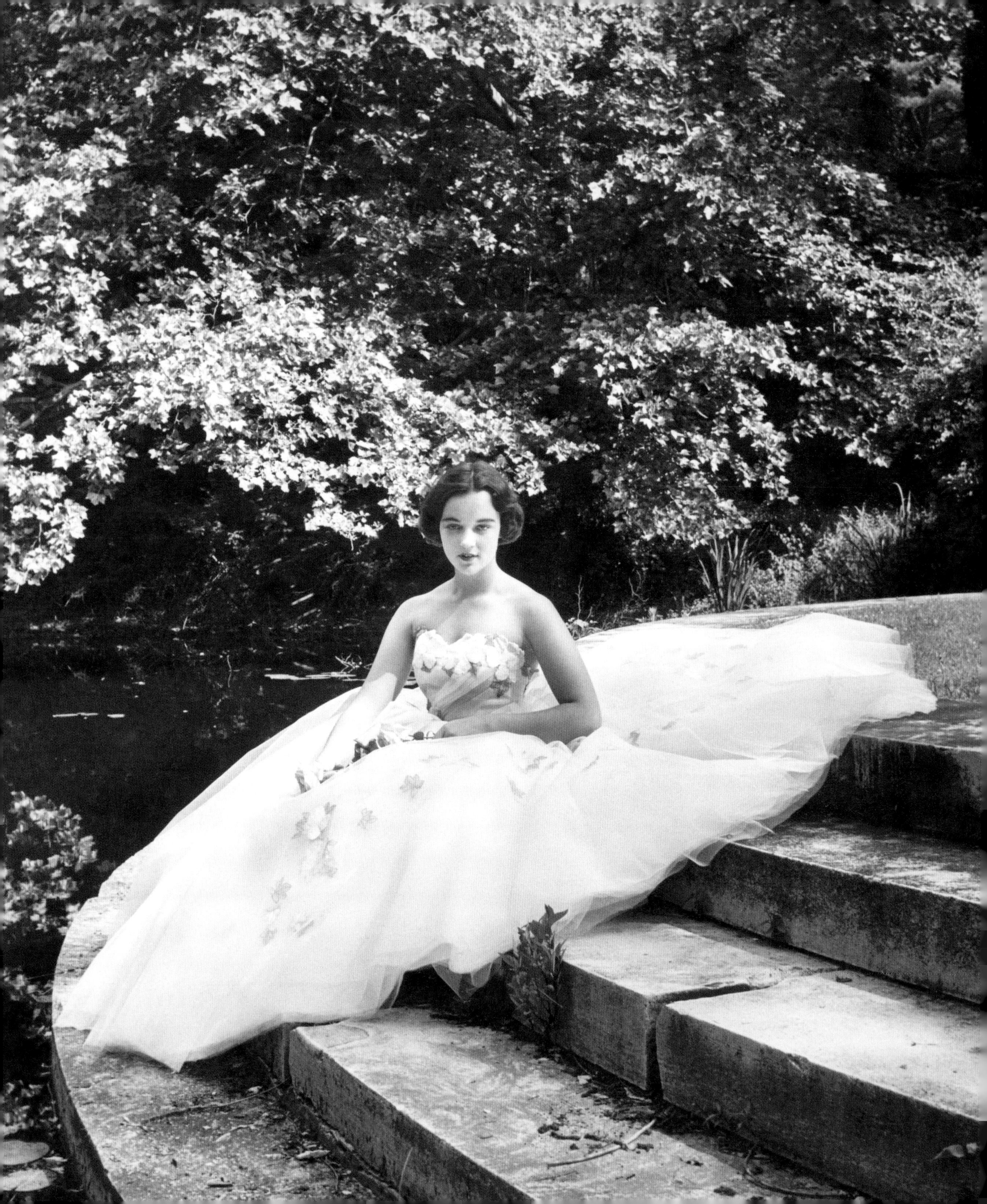

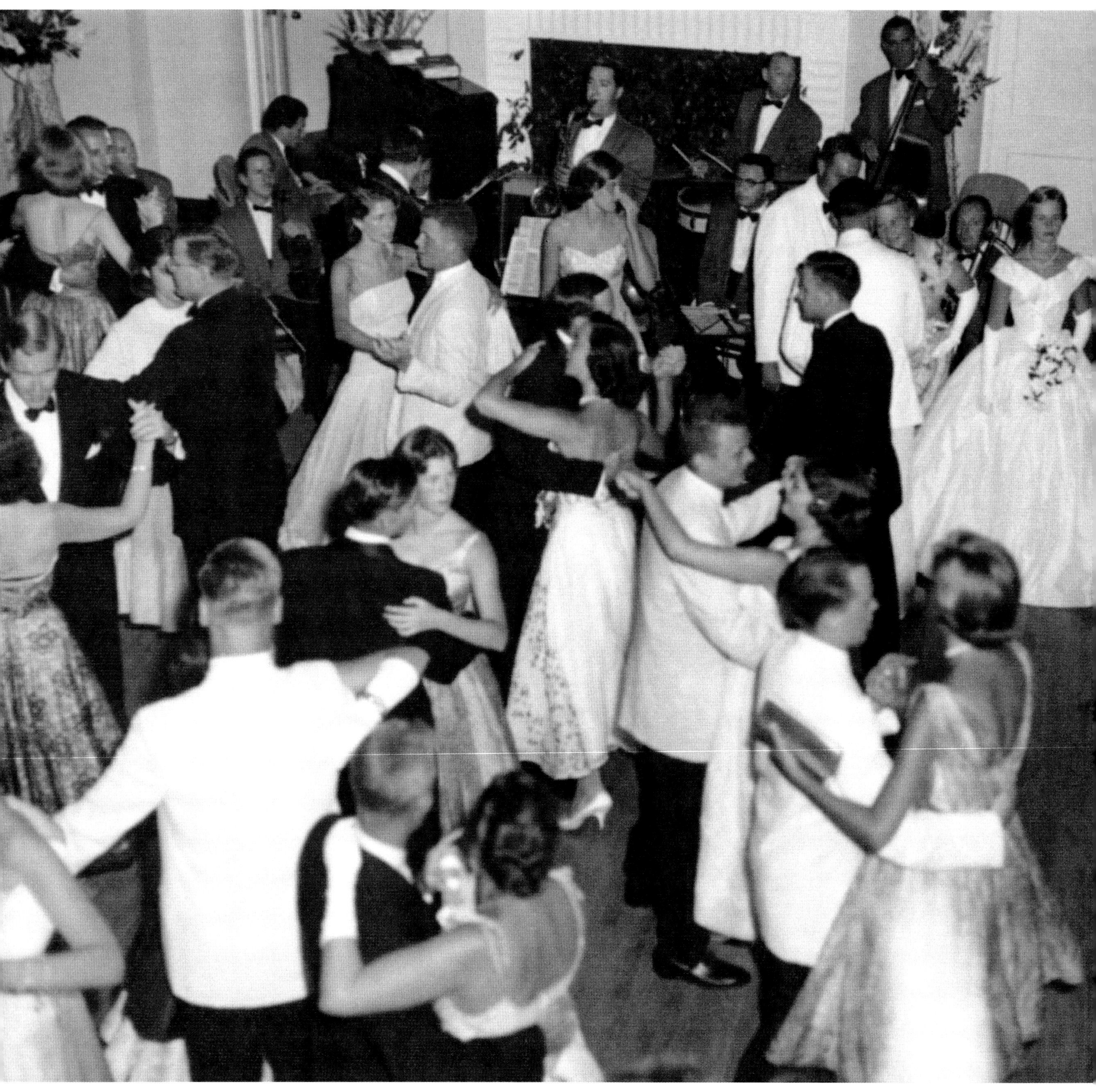

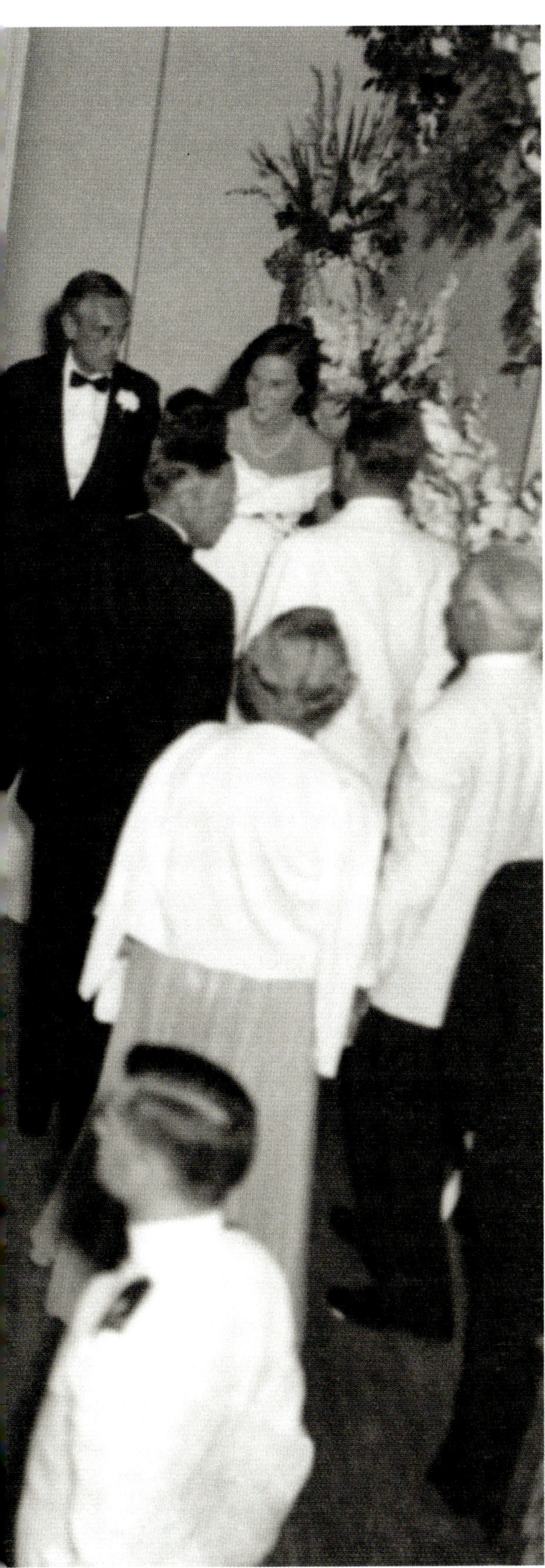

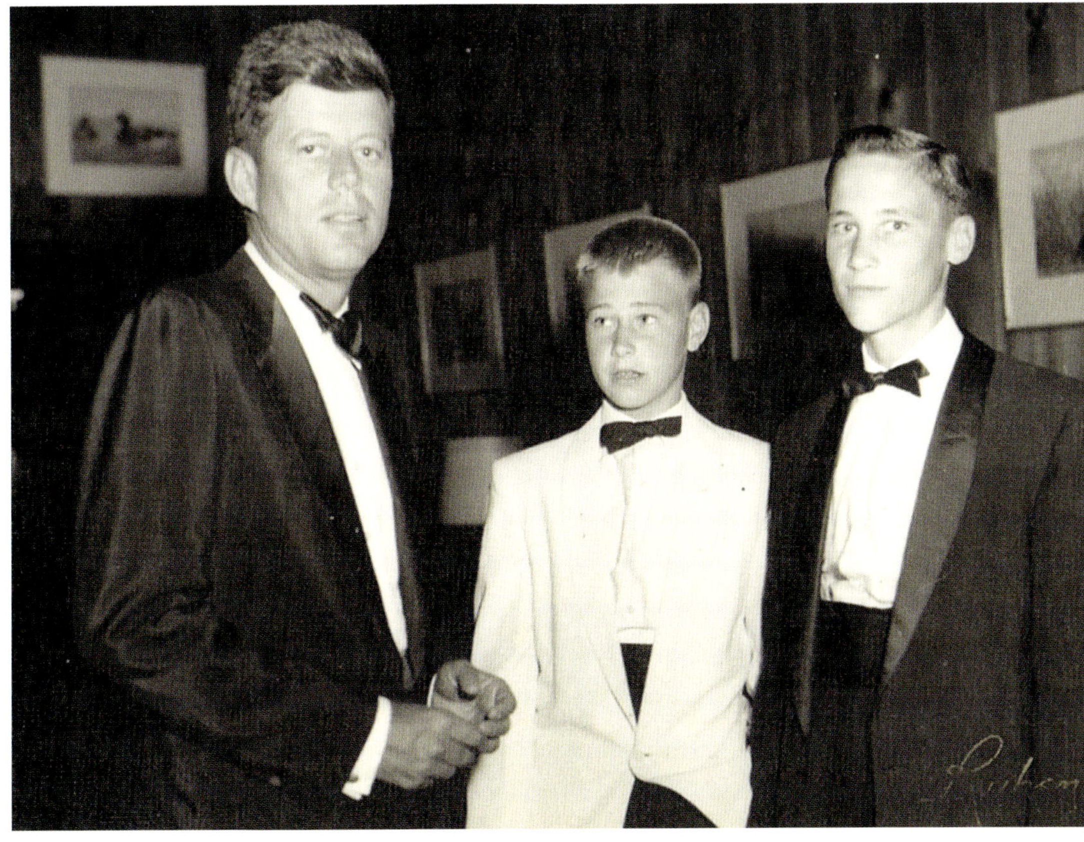

LEFT

View from the balcony at Bailey's Beach during Rosalie Sellar's coming out party. Newport, Rhode Island, 1958.

ABOVE

Then Senator Jack Kennedy talking with Hobson Brown Jr. (center) and Owen Sellar (right), the respective brothers of the evening's debutantes. Newport, Rhode Island, 1958.

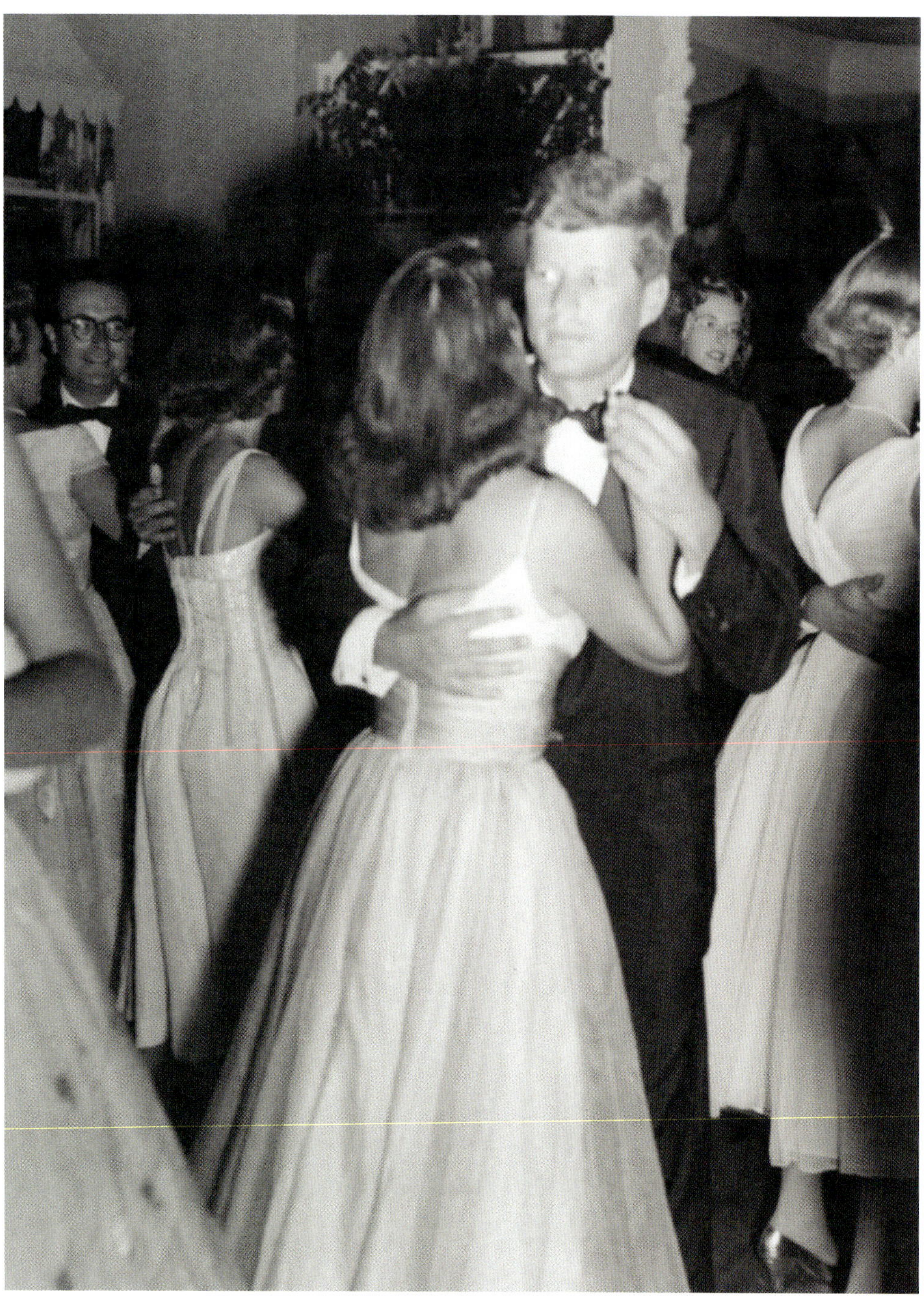

ABOVE

Then Senator Jack Kennedy dancing with Foxcroft graduate Mary McFadden at Rosalie Sellar's party. Newport, Rhode Island, 1958.

OPPOSITE

An escort gives an earnest toast at a dinner for Rosalie Sellar and her cousin Sandra Brown. Clambake Club, Newport, Rhode Island, 1958.

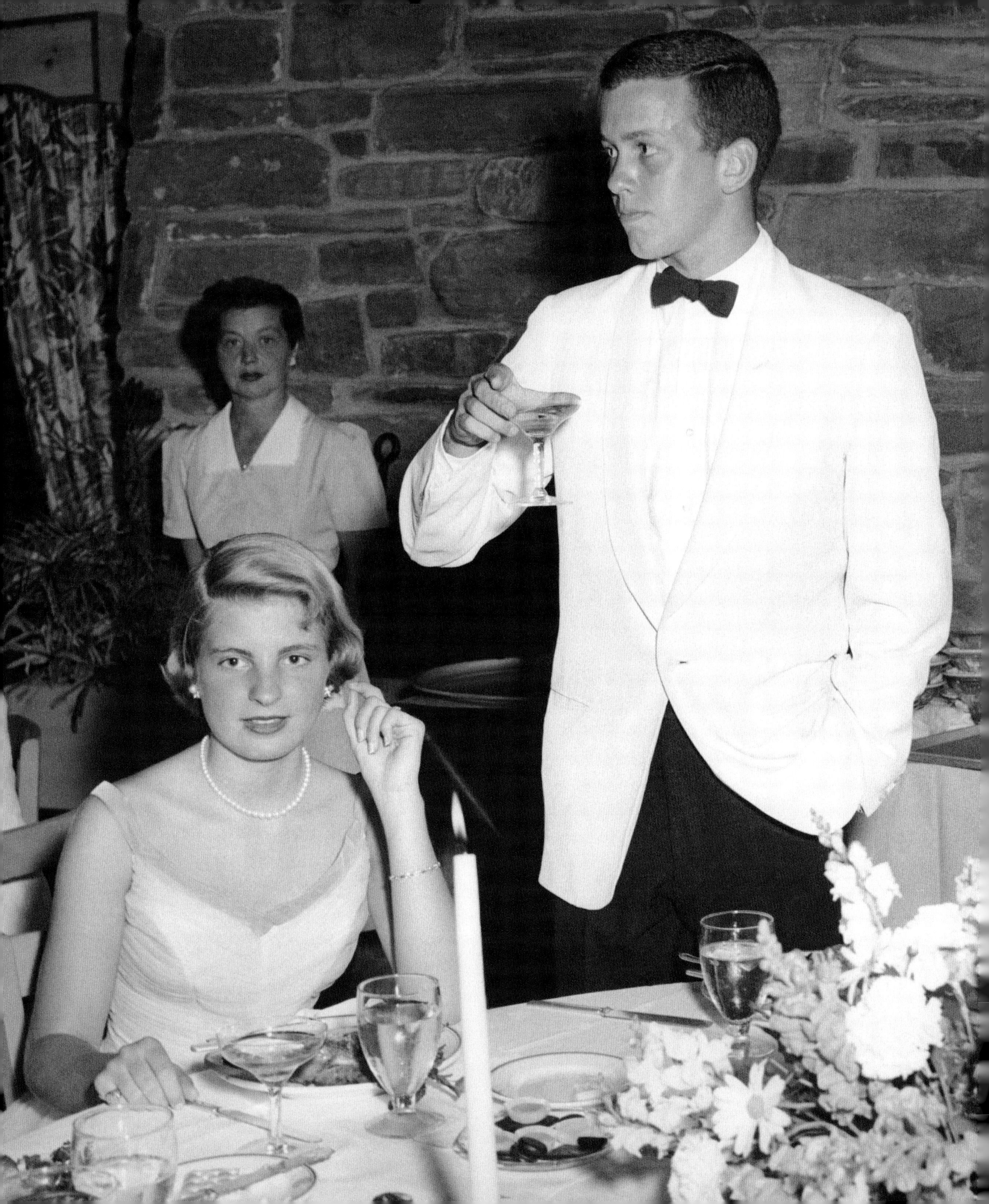

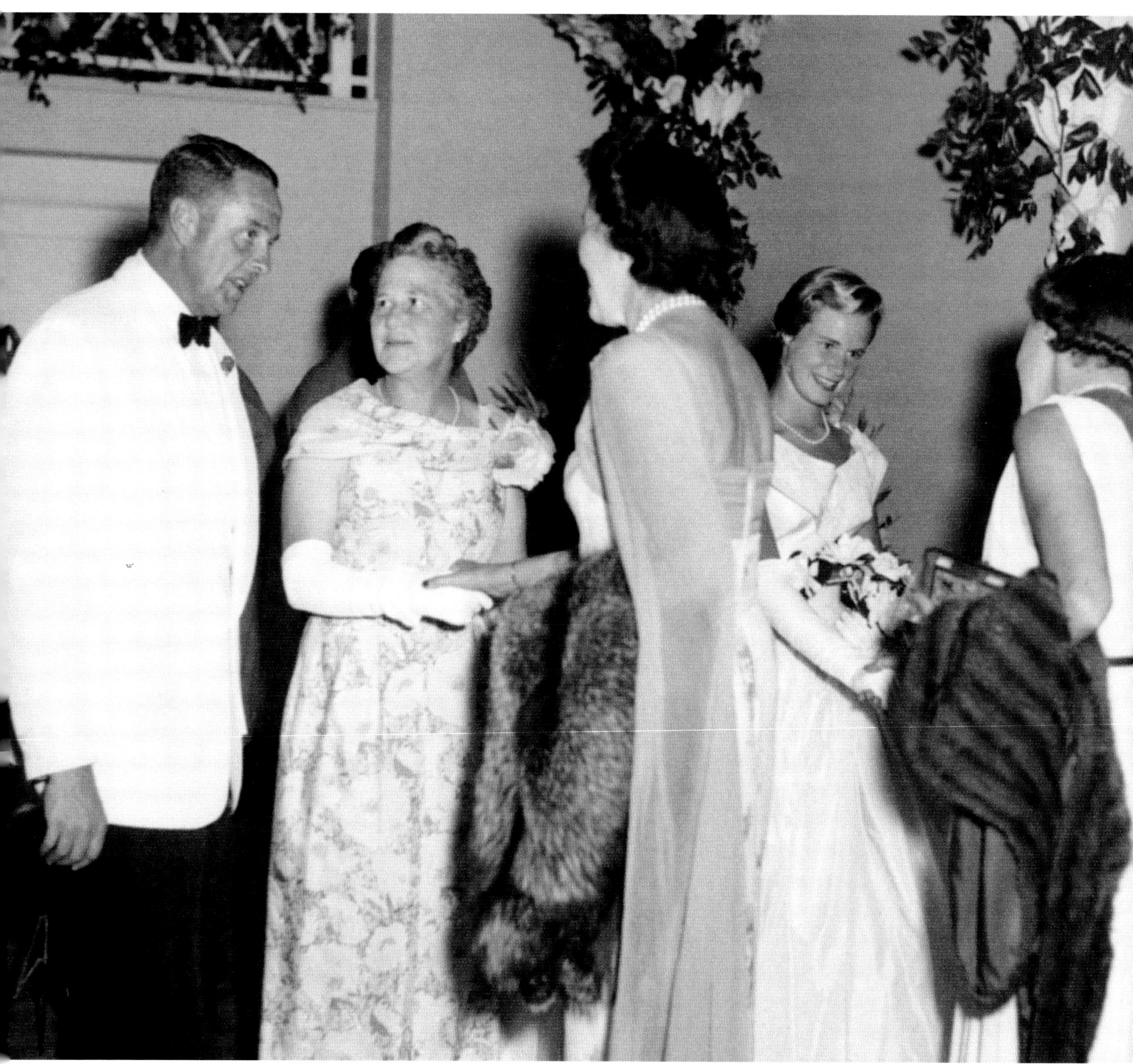

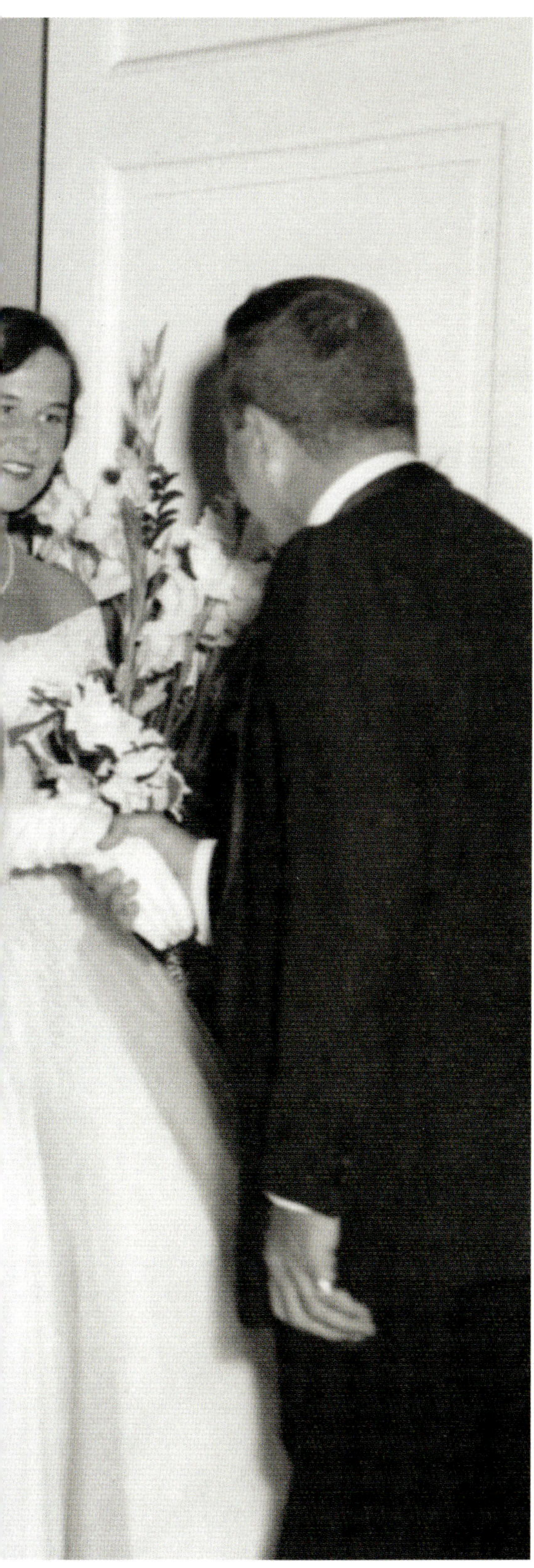

LEFT

The receiving line at Rosalie Sellar's debutante party (from right to left): Rosalie Sellar, co-deb Sandra Brown, Rita Dolan Sellar (Rosalie's mother), and Hobson Brown (Sandra Brown's father). Newport, Rhode Island, 1958.

RIGHT

The Count Patrick de Sercey (a cousin of debutante Rosile Sellar) in conversation with a kilted Ian MacKay. Newport, Rhode Island, 1958.

BELOW

Gentleman take a break from dancing to socialize at the "tennis court" bar at Bailey's Beach. Newport, Rhode Island, 1958.

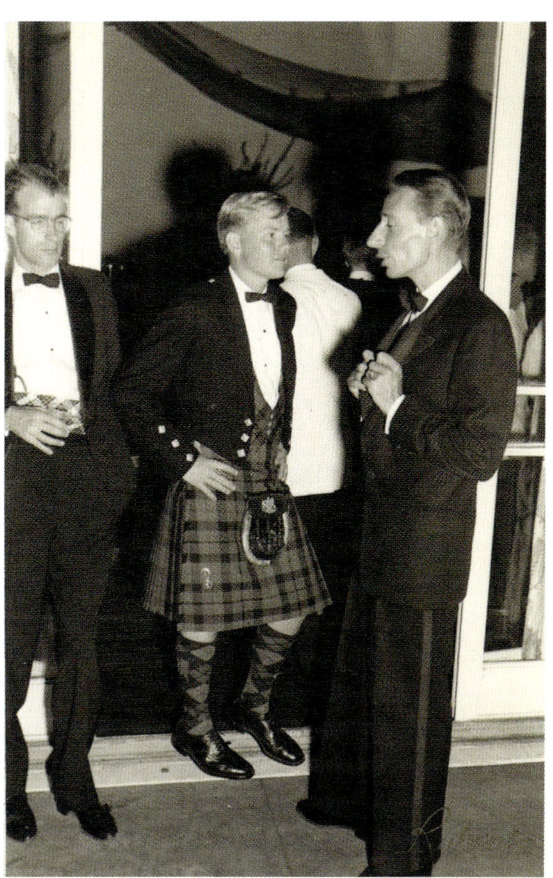

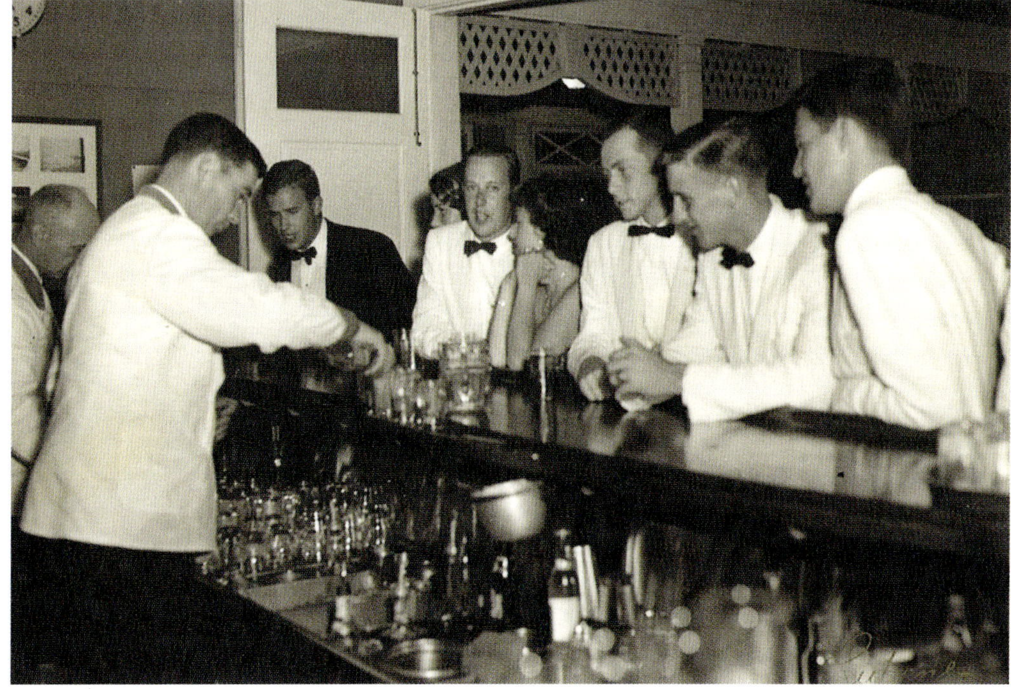

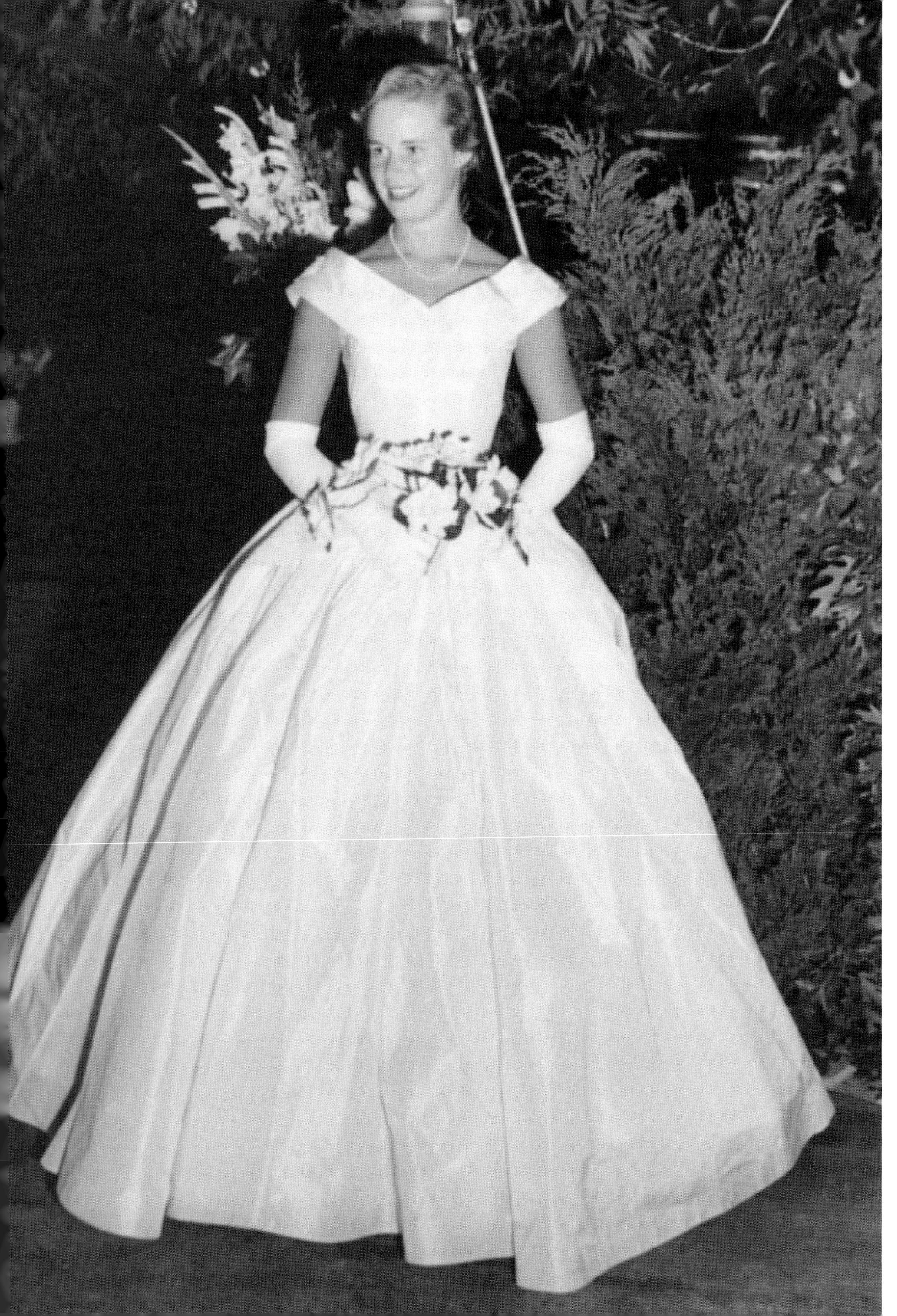

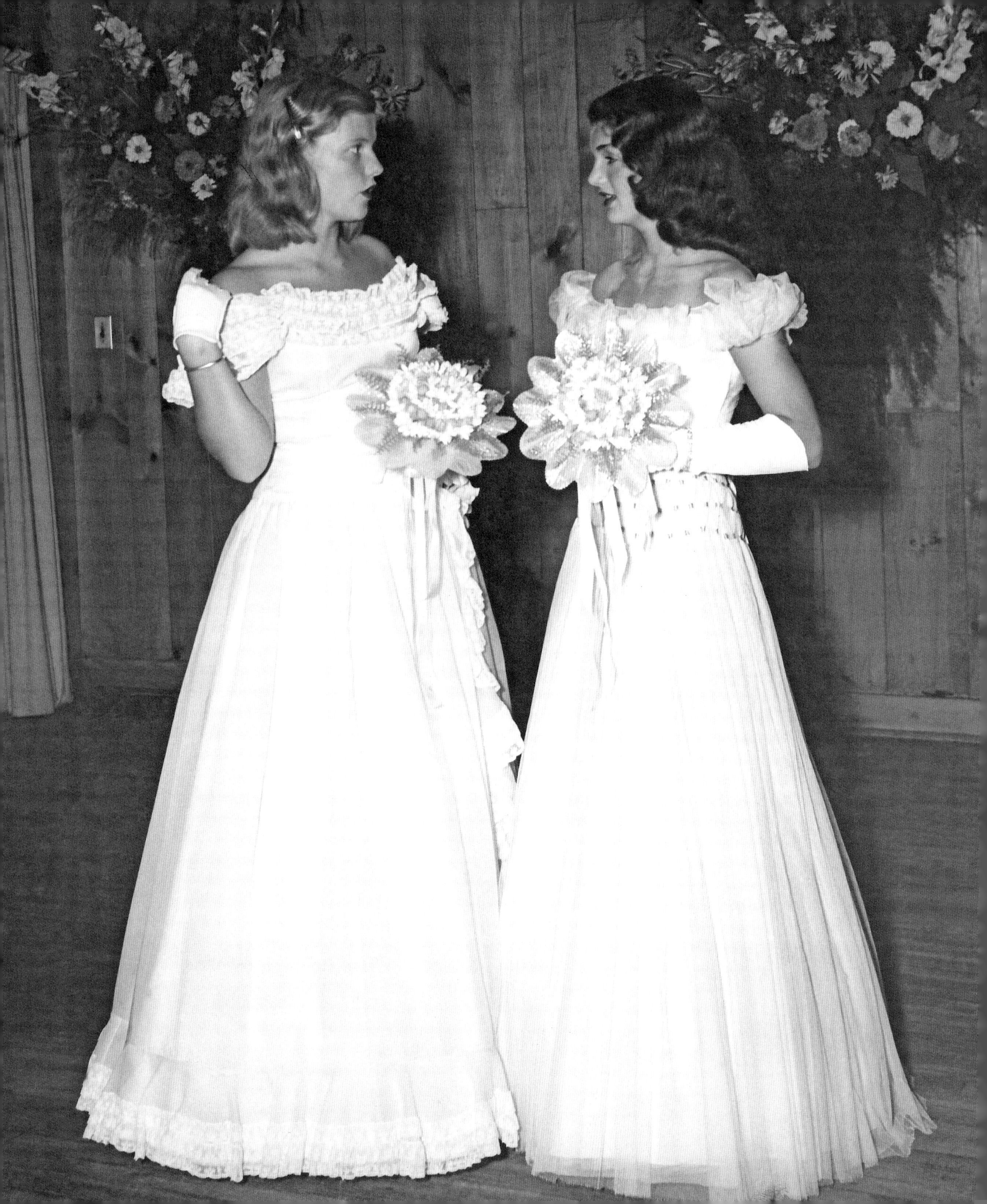

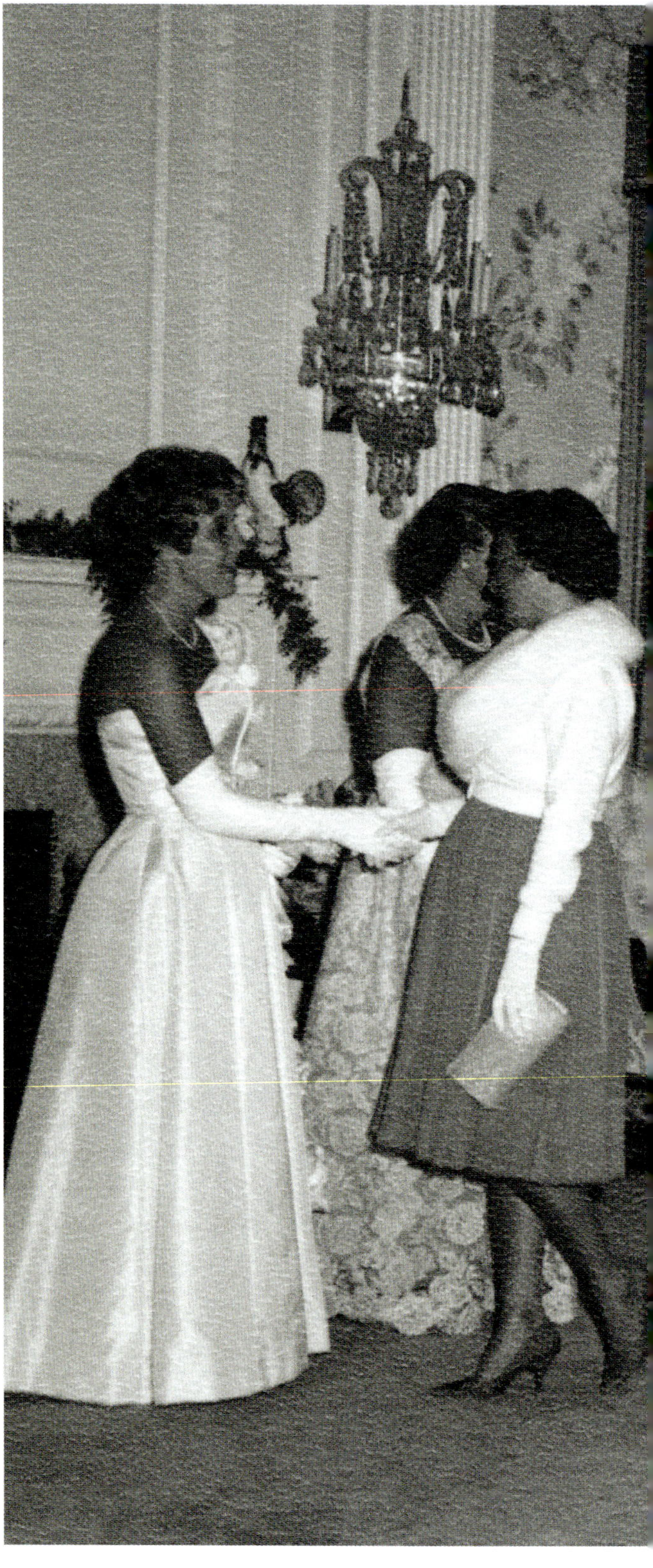

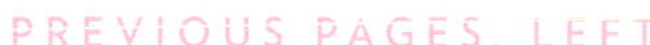

PREVIOUS PAGES, LEFT

Debutante Sandra Brown of Philadelphia at her coming out party. Newport, Rhode Island, 1958

PREVIOUS PAGES, RIGHT

Jacqueline Lee Bouvier and co-debutante Rosie Grosvenor. Newport, Rhode Island, 1947.

OPPOSITE

Guests arrive at debutante Linda Ryan's dinner dance at Vaucluse in Middletown, Rhode Island, 1961. Guests included the cream of Newport's high society, such as Mr. and Mrs. Sheldon Whitehouse and Mrs. Guy Fairfax Carey, as well as the Firestones and the visiting Hon. and Mrs. Harry Morgan-Grenville of England.

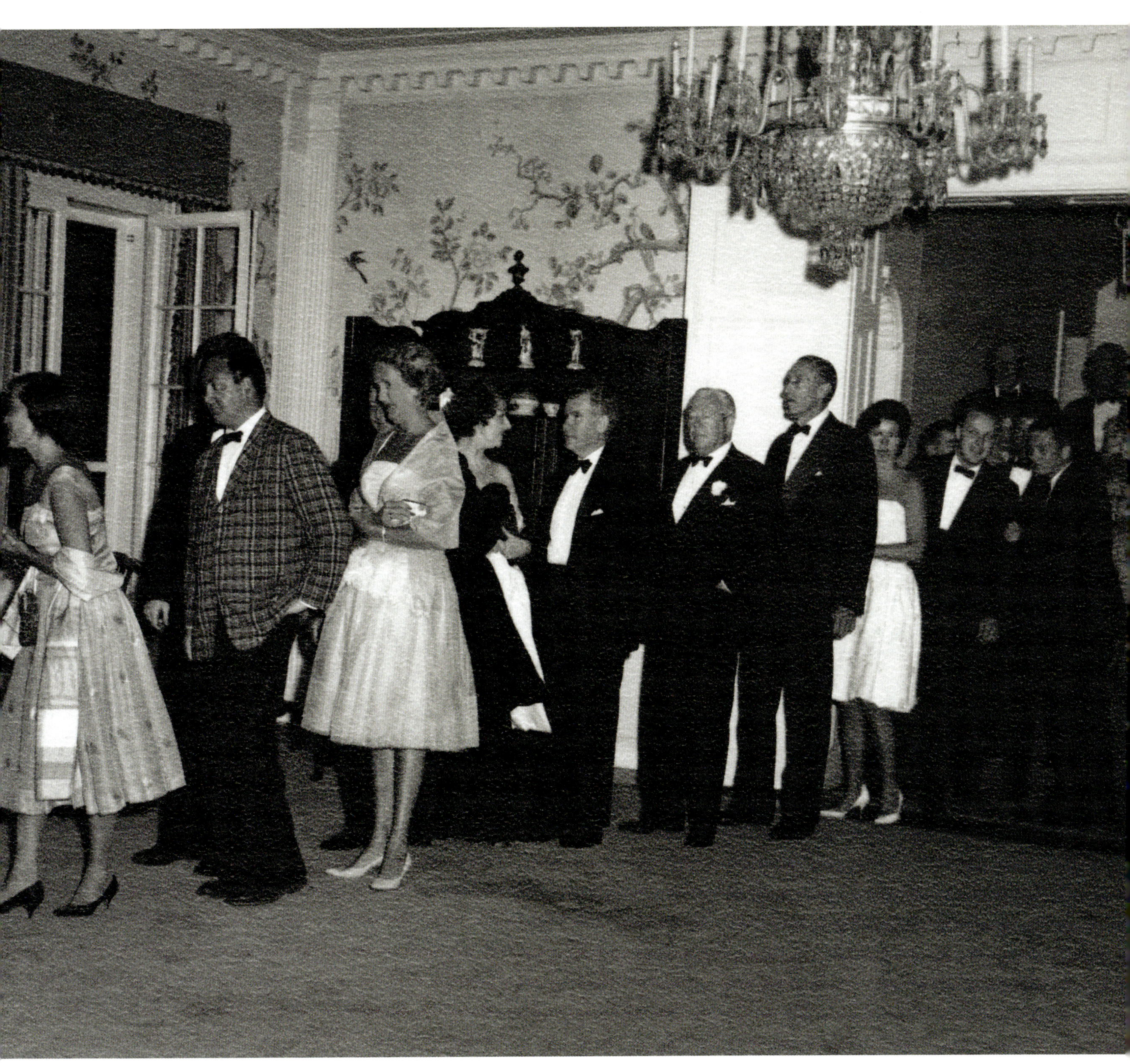

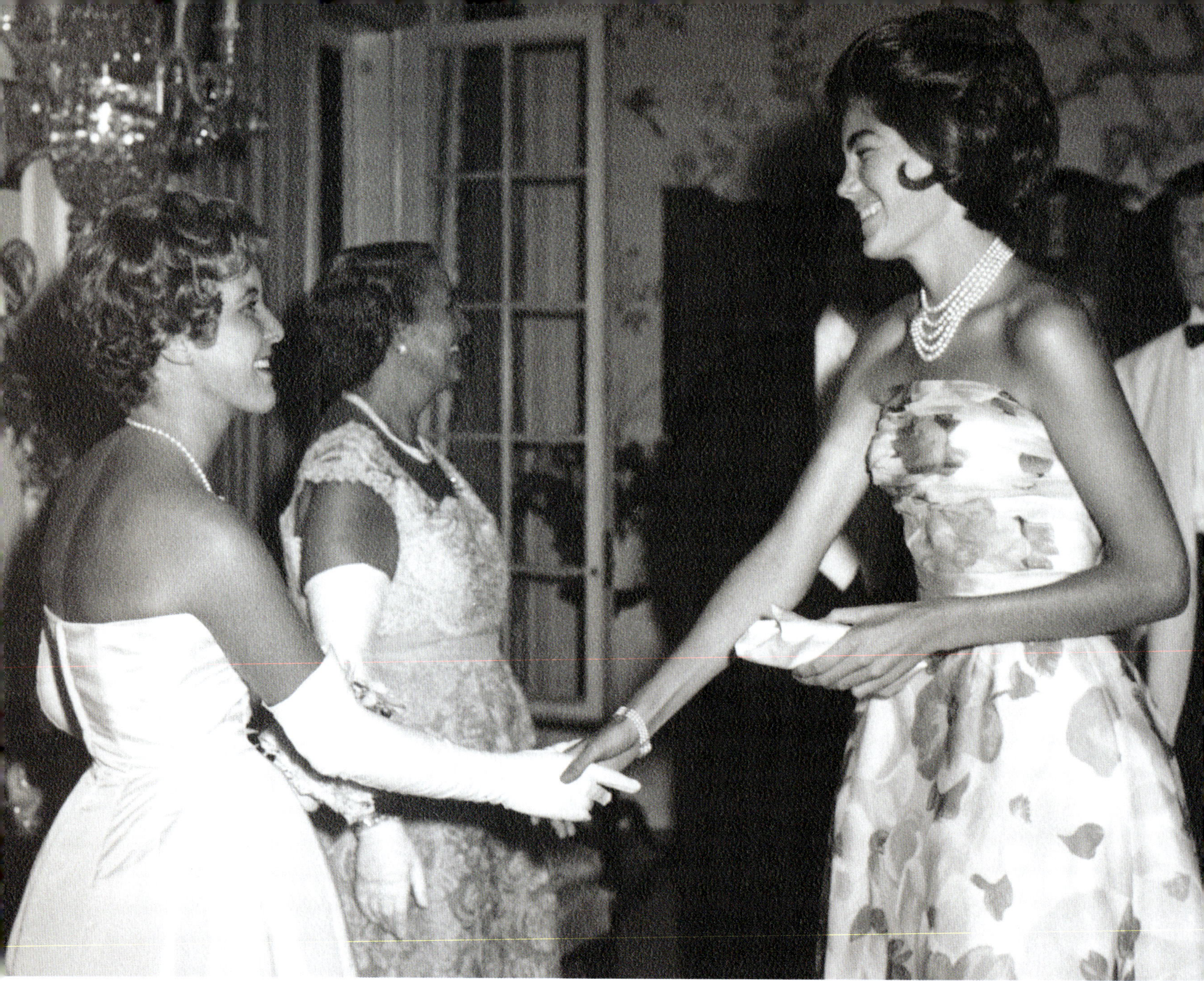

ABOVE

Linda Ryan greets guest Minnie Cushing at her coming out party. Newport, Rhode Island, 1961.

OPPOSITE

Linda Ryan enjoys one of the many dances of the evening. At midnight, Linda danced with her step-grandfather, George Widener, while fireworks boomed overhead. At Widener's insistence, the music never stopped—from eight o'clock at night until eight o'clock in the morning, he was resolute that there not be a moment of silence. The orchestra, under famed bandleader Meyer Davis, played without missing a beat, hiring stand in musicians to seamlessly take the place of tired orchestra members. Newport,Rhode Island, 1961.

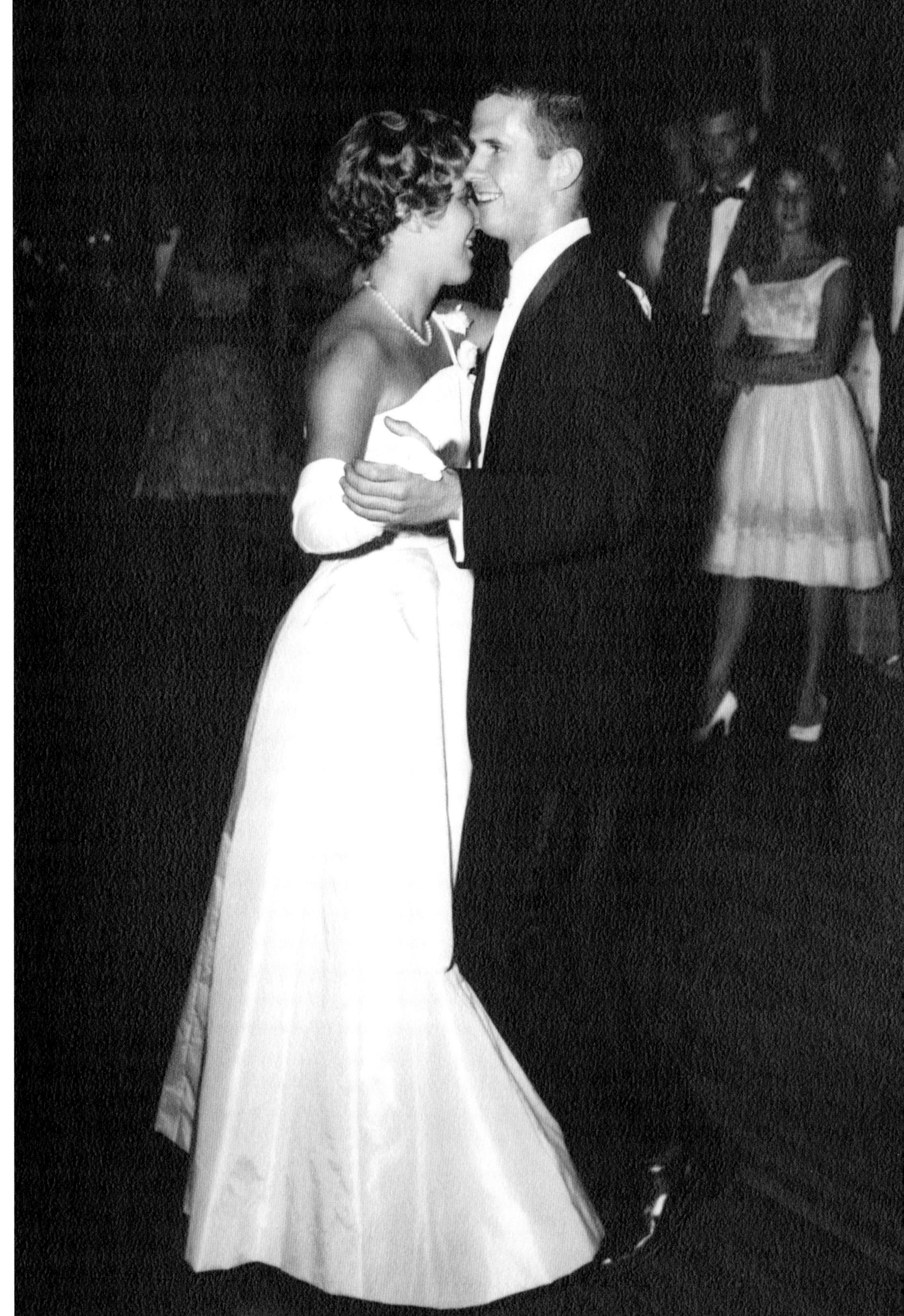

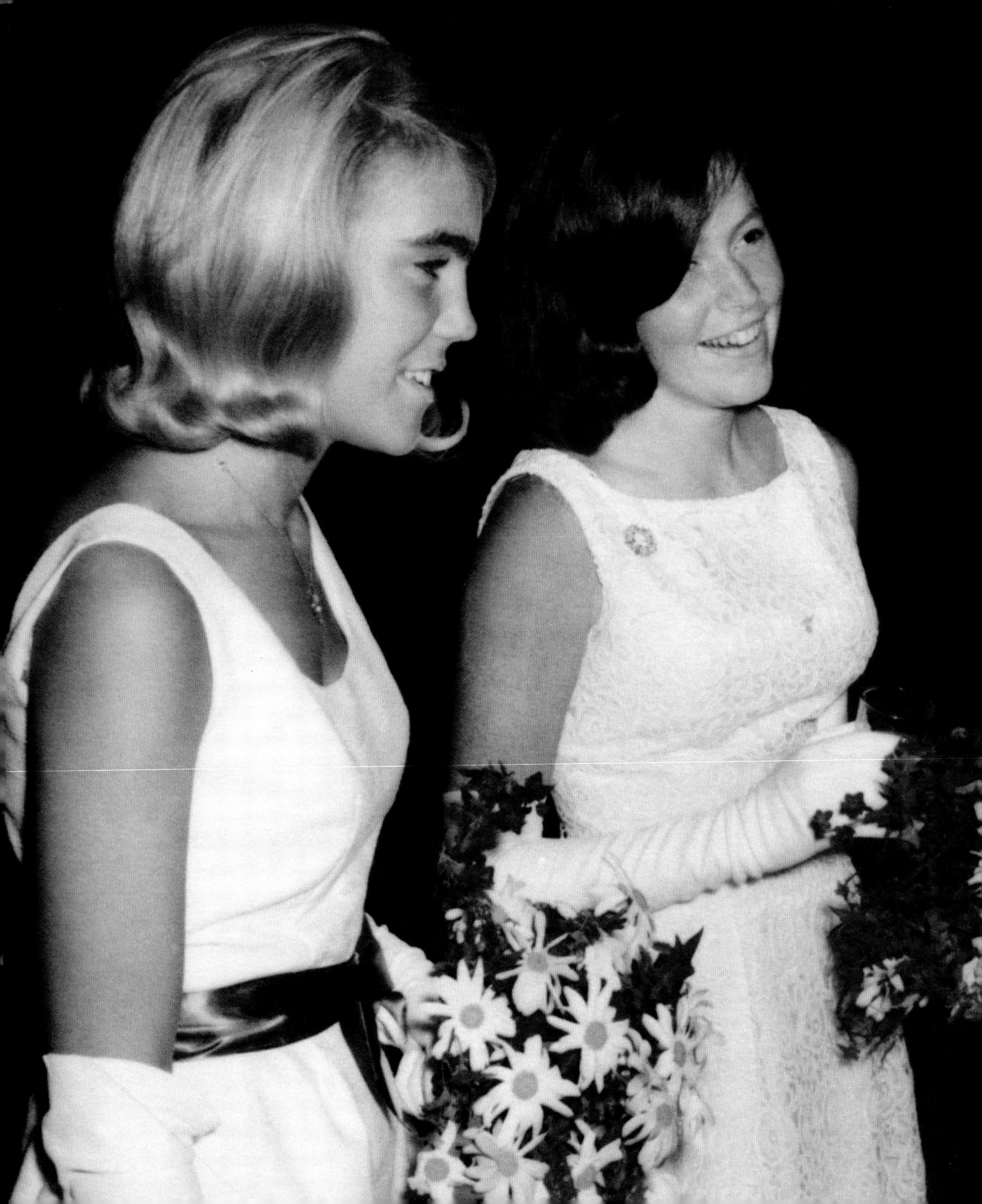

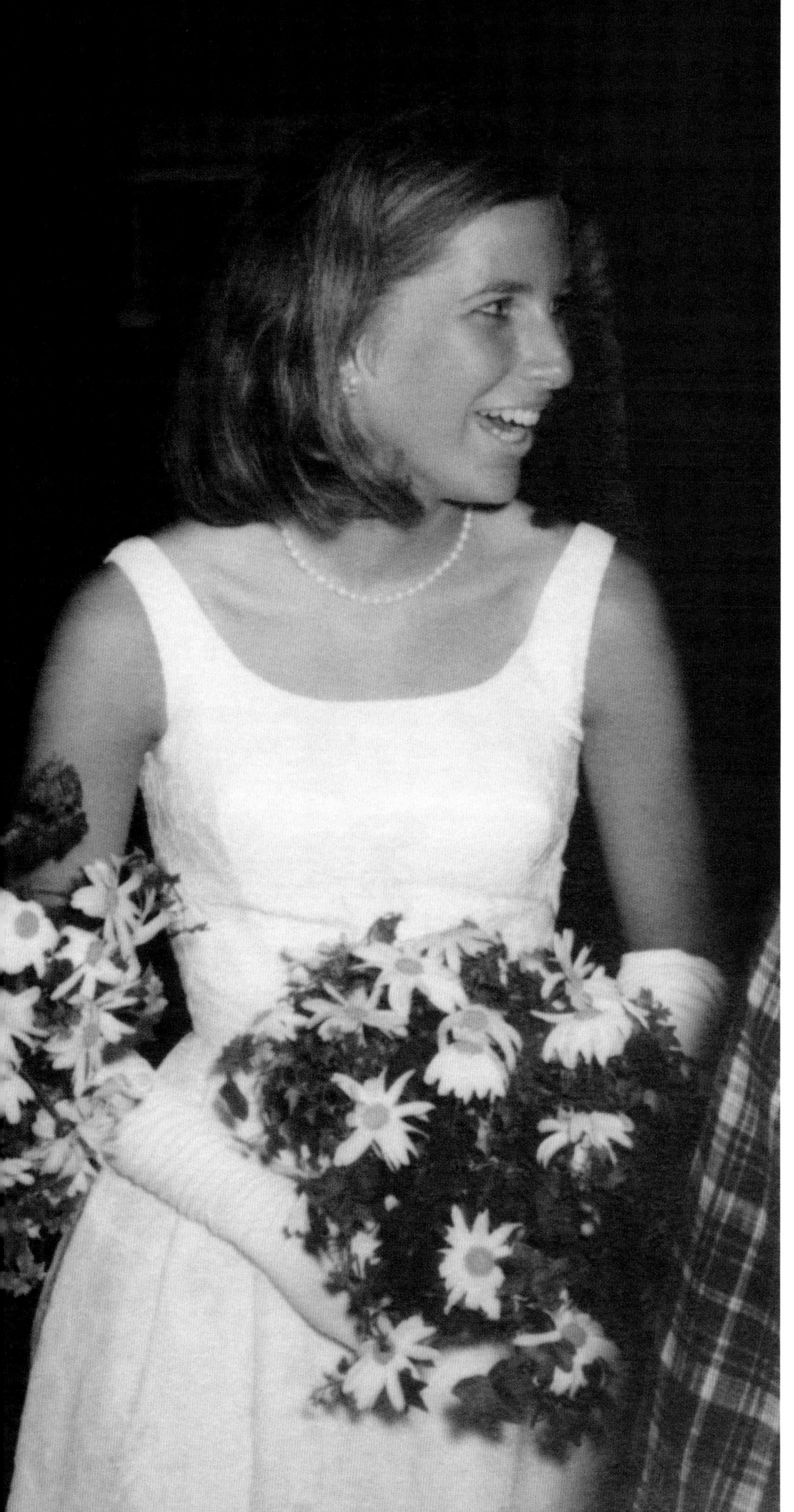

Three Philadelphia debutantes (from left to right) Miss Emily Tilghman, Miss Julia Toland, and Miss Shirley Davis enjoy a relaxed moment at a supper thrown at the home of Julia Toland's parents, Mr. and Mrs. Alexander Toland. Wynnewood, Pennsylvania, 1965.

Mr. and Mrs. Newlin Fell Davis
Mr. and Mrs. Joseph Fox Tilghman
Mr. and Mrs. Alexander Brown Toland
request the pleasure of

company at supper
in honour of
Miss Shirley Brewster Davis
Miss Emily Read Tilghman
Miss Julia Rush Toland
Sunday, the twentieth of June
at seven o'clock
334 Aubrey Road
Wynnewood, Pennsylvania

Informal
Supper will be seated
promptly at eight o'clock

R.s.v.p.

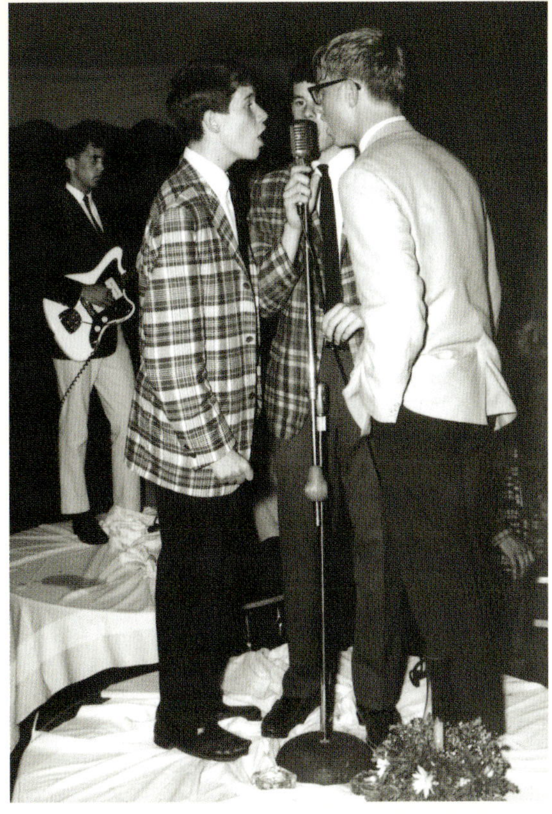

RIGHT

The dinner for the three Philadelphia debutantes is followed by an a cappella performance. Wynnewood, Pennsylvania, 1965.

BELOW

Mrs. Toland vies for a birds-eye view of the band using a taller guest as leverage. Wynnewood, Pennsylvania, 1965.

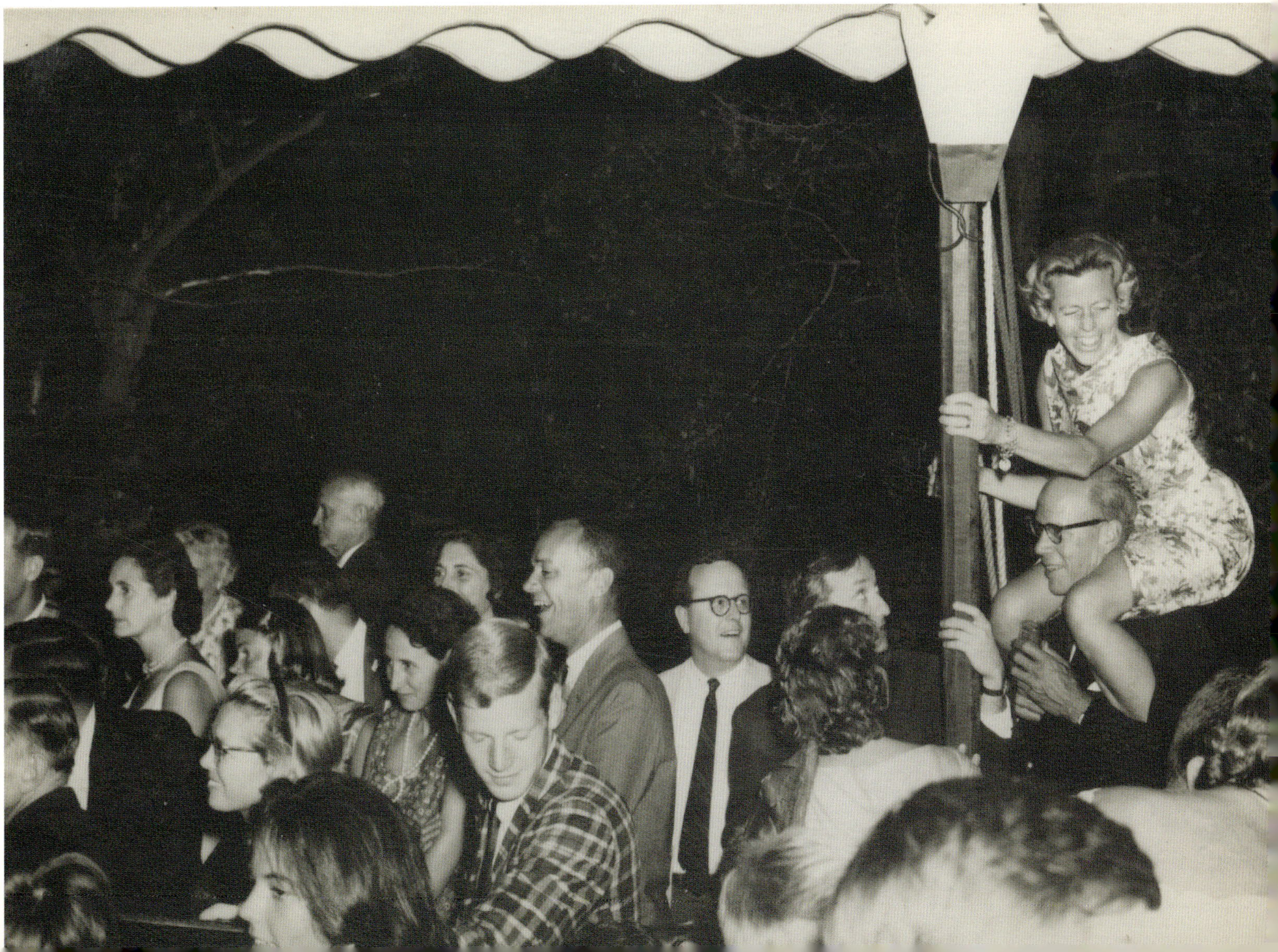

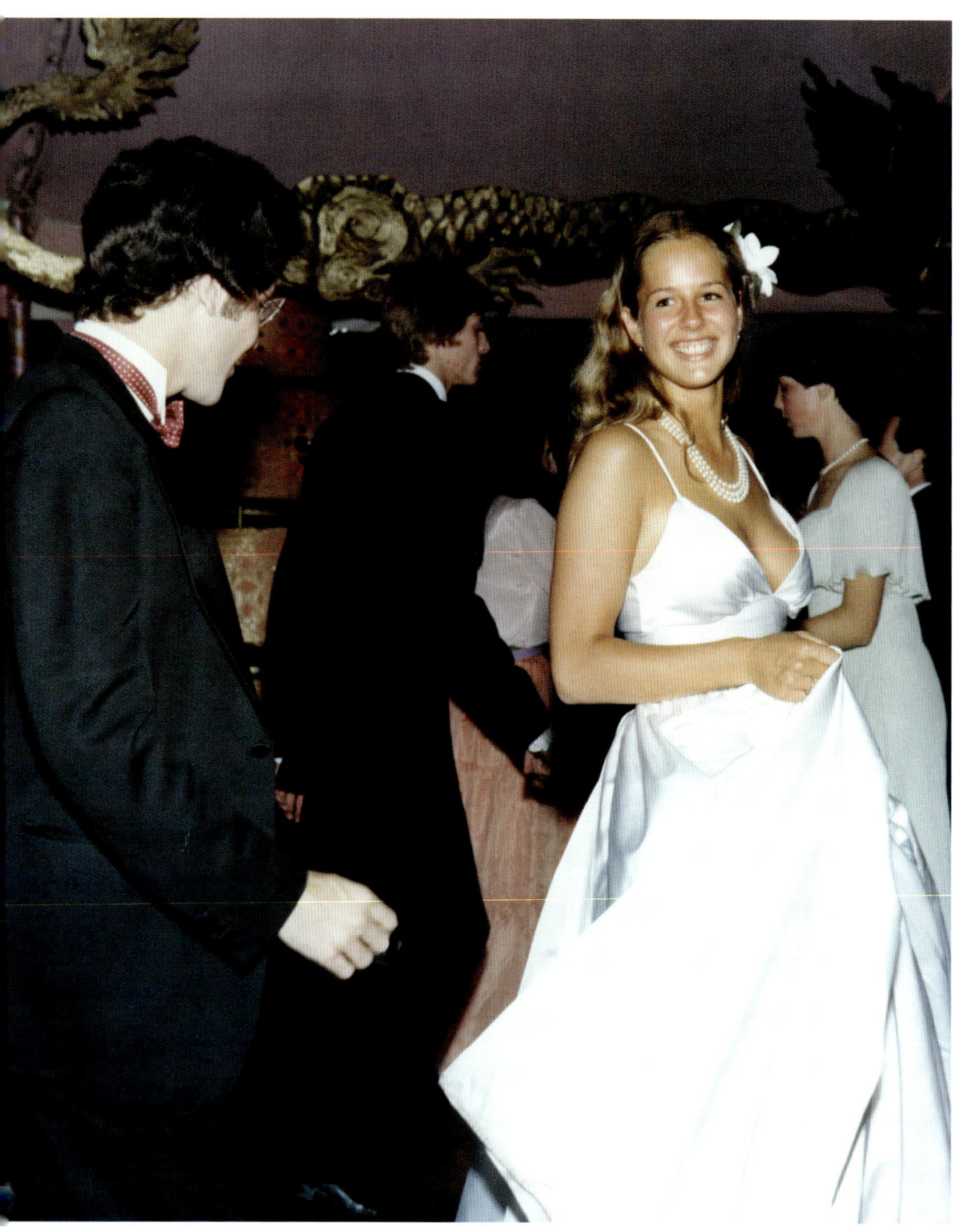

LEFT

Lavinia Baker, great granddaughter of George Fisher Baker, takes a turn on the dance floor at her coming out party. Centre Island, New York, 1977.

OPPOSITE

Debutante Lynn Willing Wanamaker dances with her escort at the home of her co-debutante Susan Bixby Andrews. The summer party was held at the home of Andrews' mother in Southampton, New York, 1958. Several years later, Lynn Willing Wanamaker's cousin, Fernanda Wanamaker Wetherill, was given a lavish coming out party in Southampton, which would rank among the most famous social scandals of the decade.

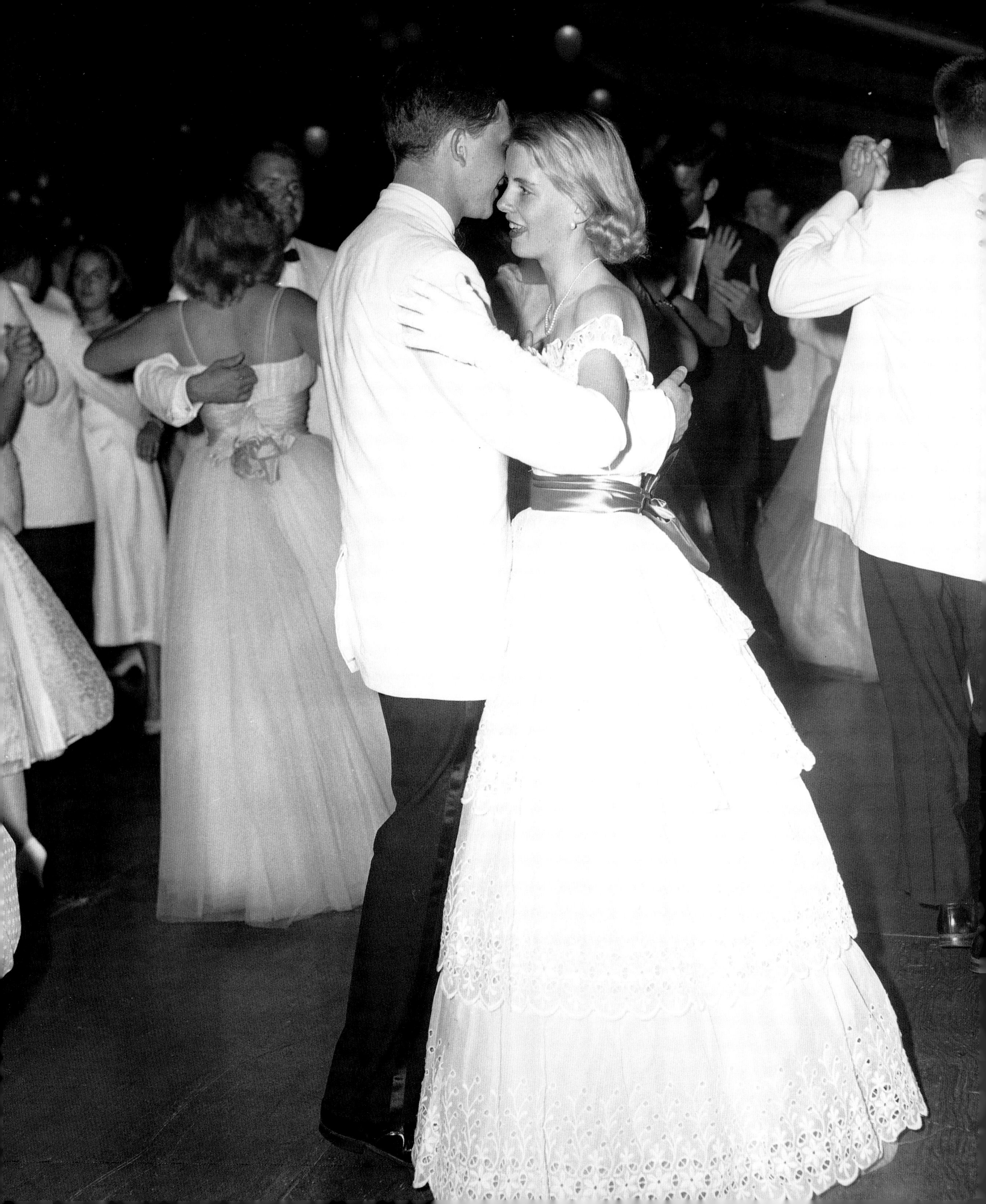

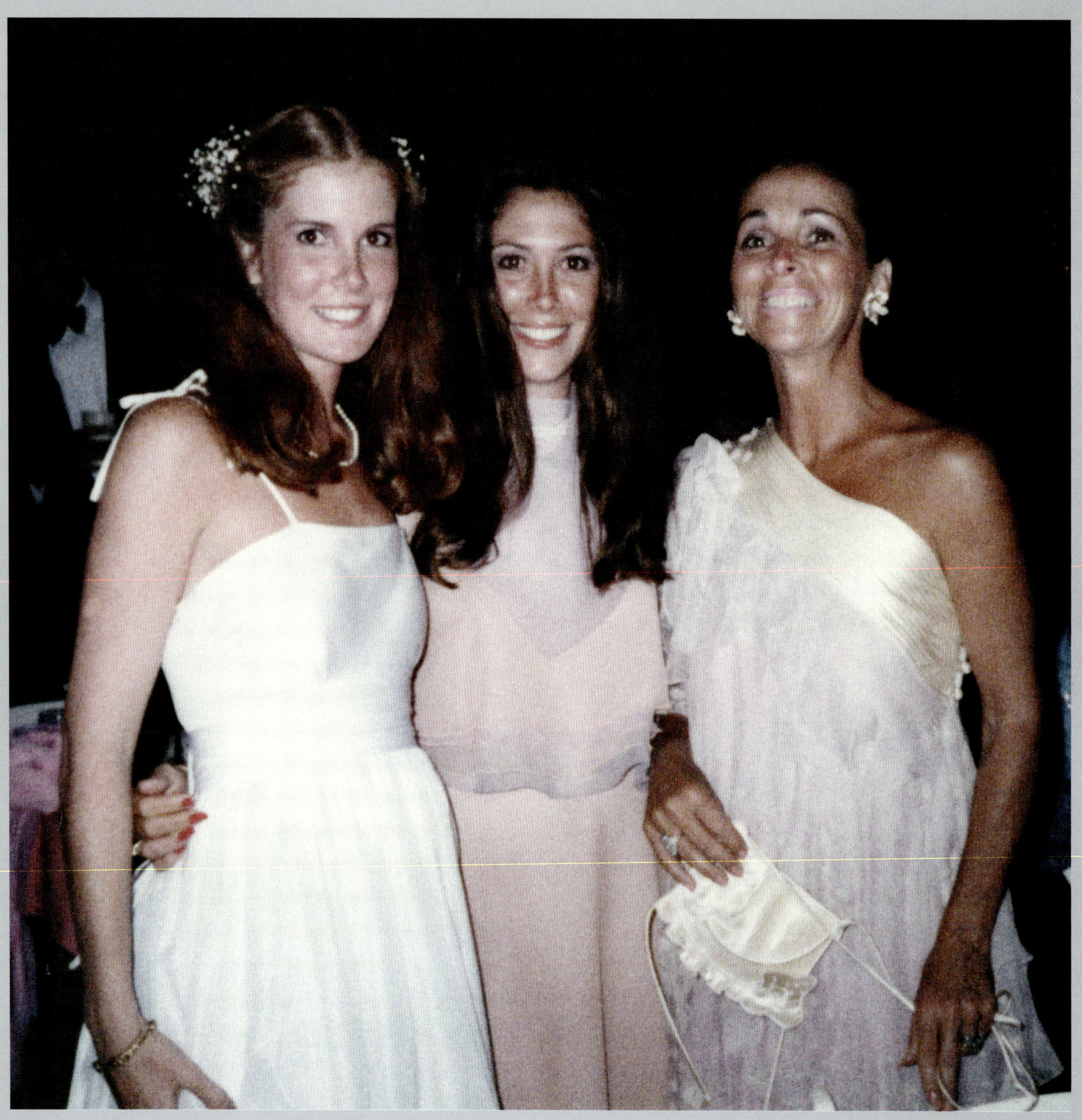

Debutante Pamela O'Conner with her sister Robin and their mother Ruth at Pamela's summer coming out party. Newport, Rhode Island, circa 1979.

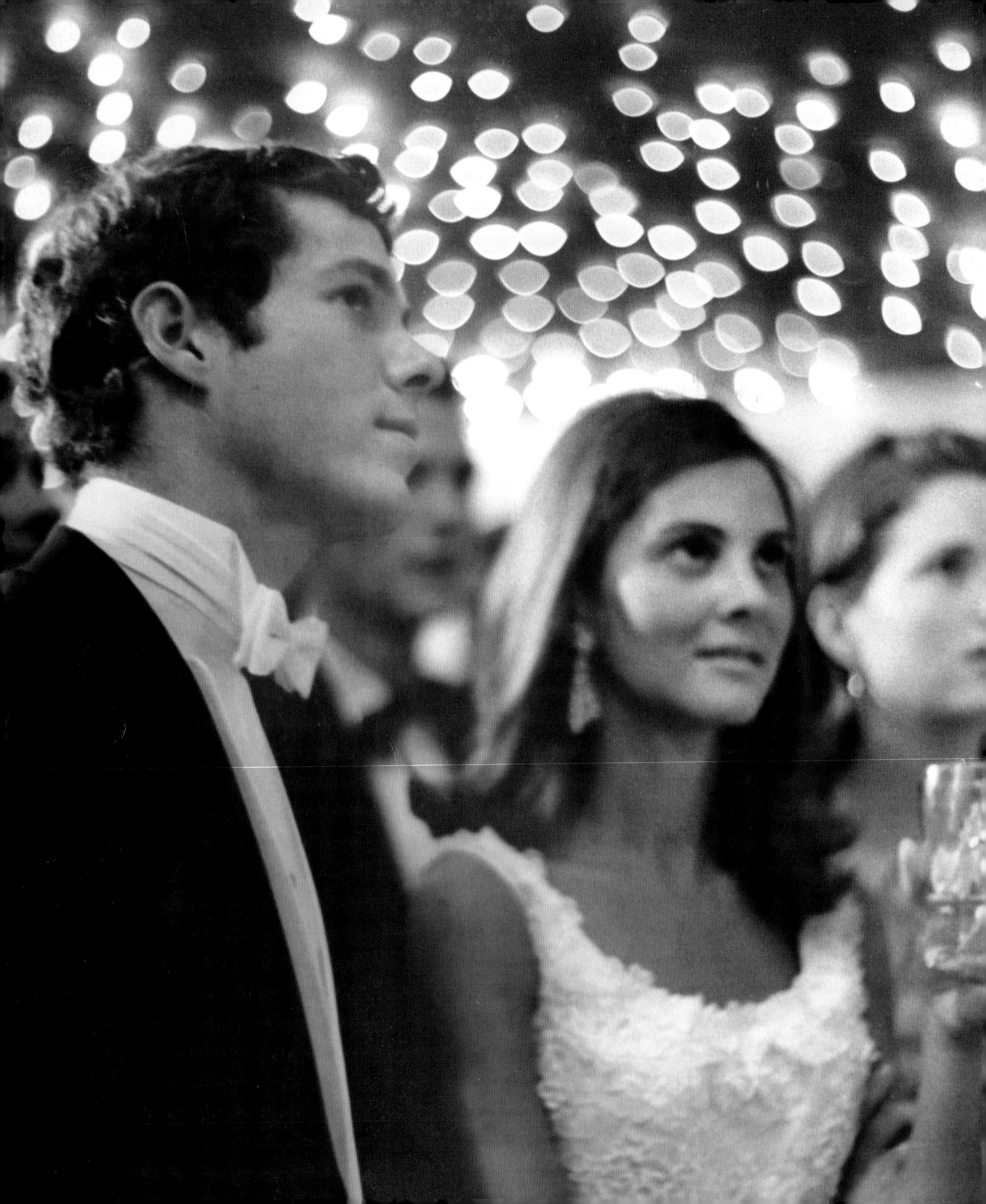

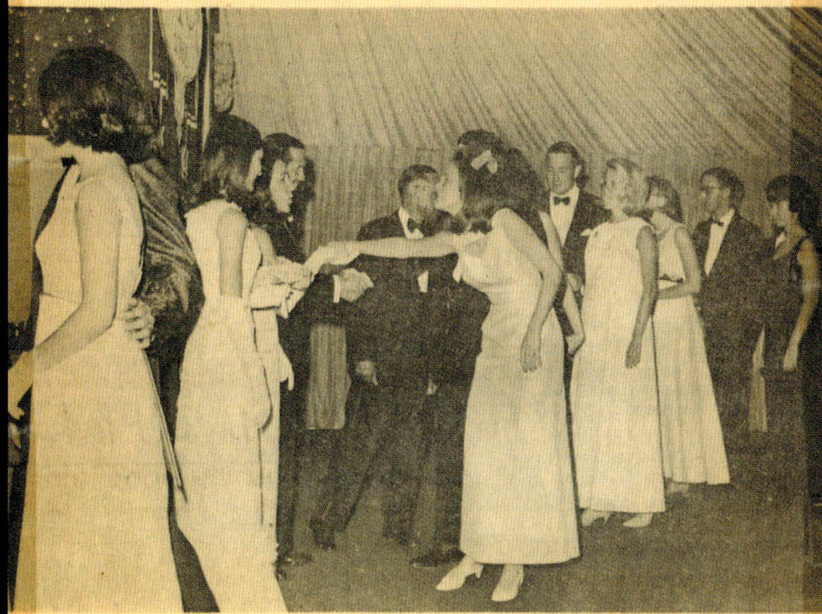

# Fairy-Tale Splendor Marks Ford Debut

*In an Arabian Nights setting, Detroit society turned out last night to honor the debut of Eleanor Clay Ford, oldest daughter of Mr. and Mrs. Walter Buhl Ford II. The gala event was held in three gaily decorated tents erected on the grounds adjoining the Little Club. In the receiving line, in the huge main tent (above), a couple pass by (left) as Miss Ford (Nonie) and her mother greet Leslie Renchard (center) and the group of young couples at right.—News Photos by Howard Shirkey.*

Debutante Nonie Ford's coming out party.
Grosse Pointe, Michigan, 1966.

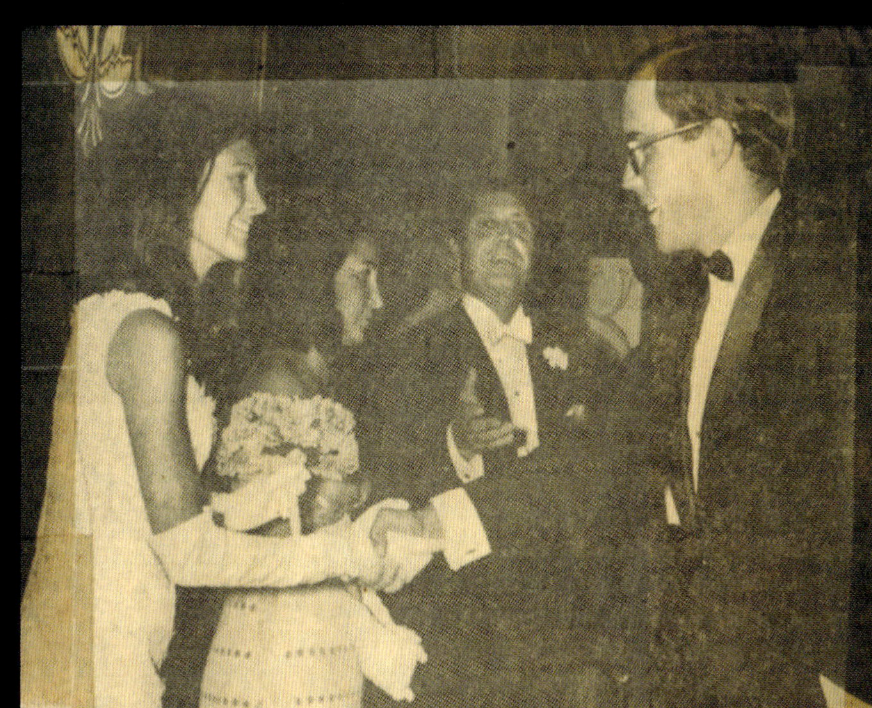

**FIRST TO BE** welcomed were three members of the stag line, including Jan Rieveschl (right). The young crowd was far more prompt in arriving than their elders who lingered over their after-dinner coffees.

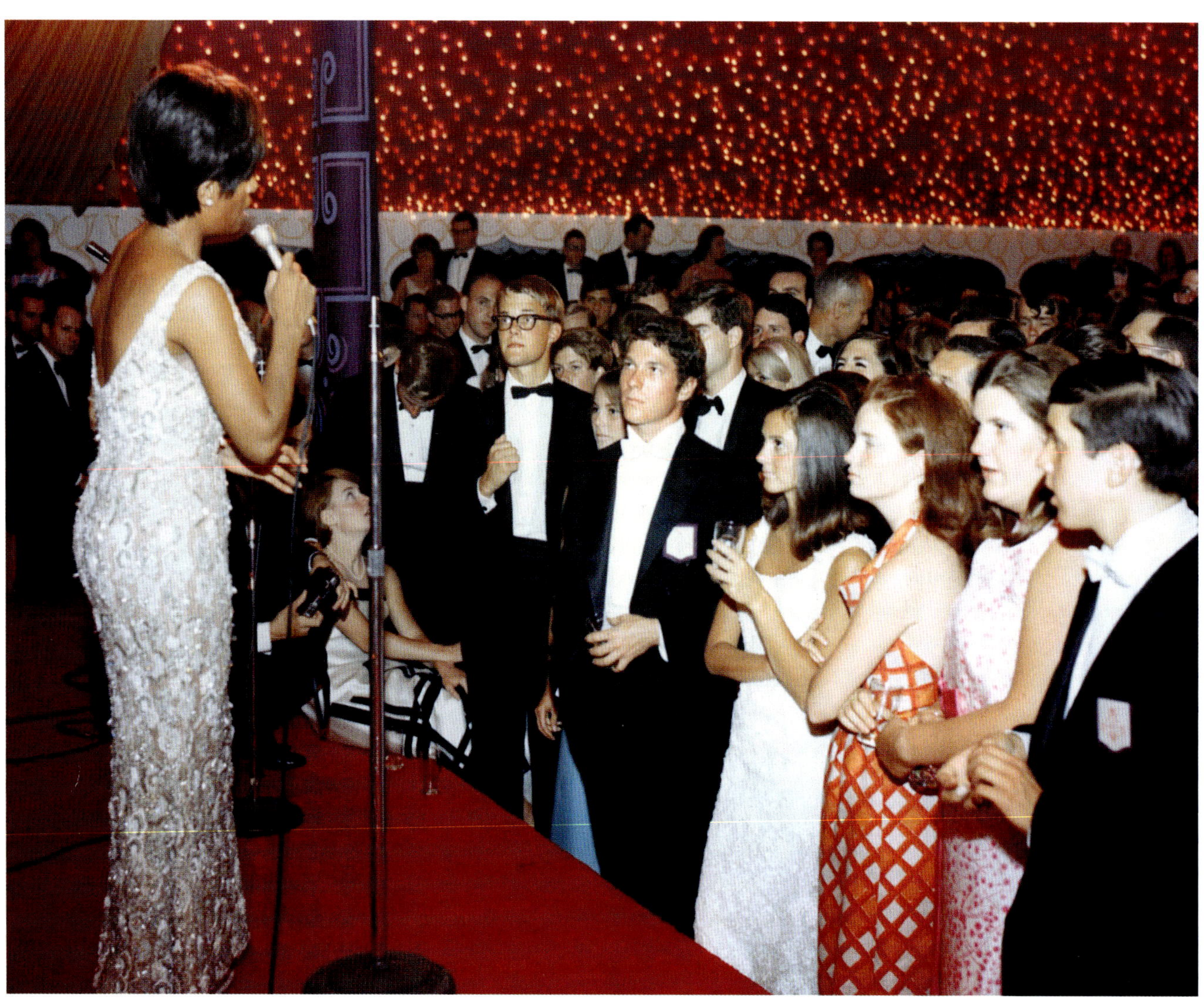

ABOVE AND OPPOSITE

As was often the case at debutante parties thrown in Grosse Pointe. MI and the surrounding suburbs, talent was handily imported from Motown Records in Detroit. Barbara McNair, a Motown star who later went on to become a television sensation, performs at Nonie Ford's party. 1966.

FOLLOWING PAGES

Nonie Ford and her guests enjoy drinks on beach. Grosse Pointe, Michigan, 1966.

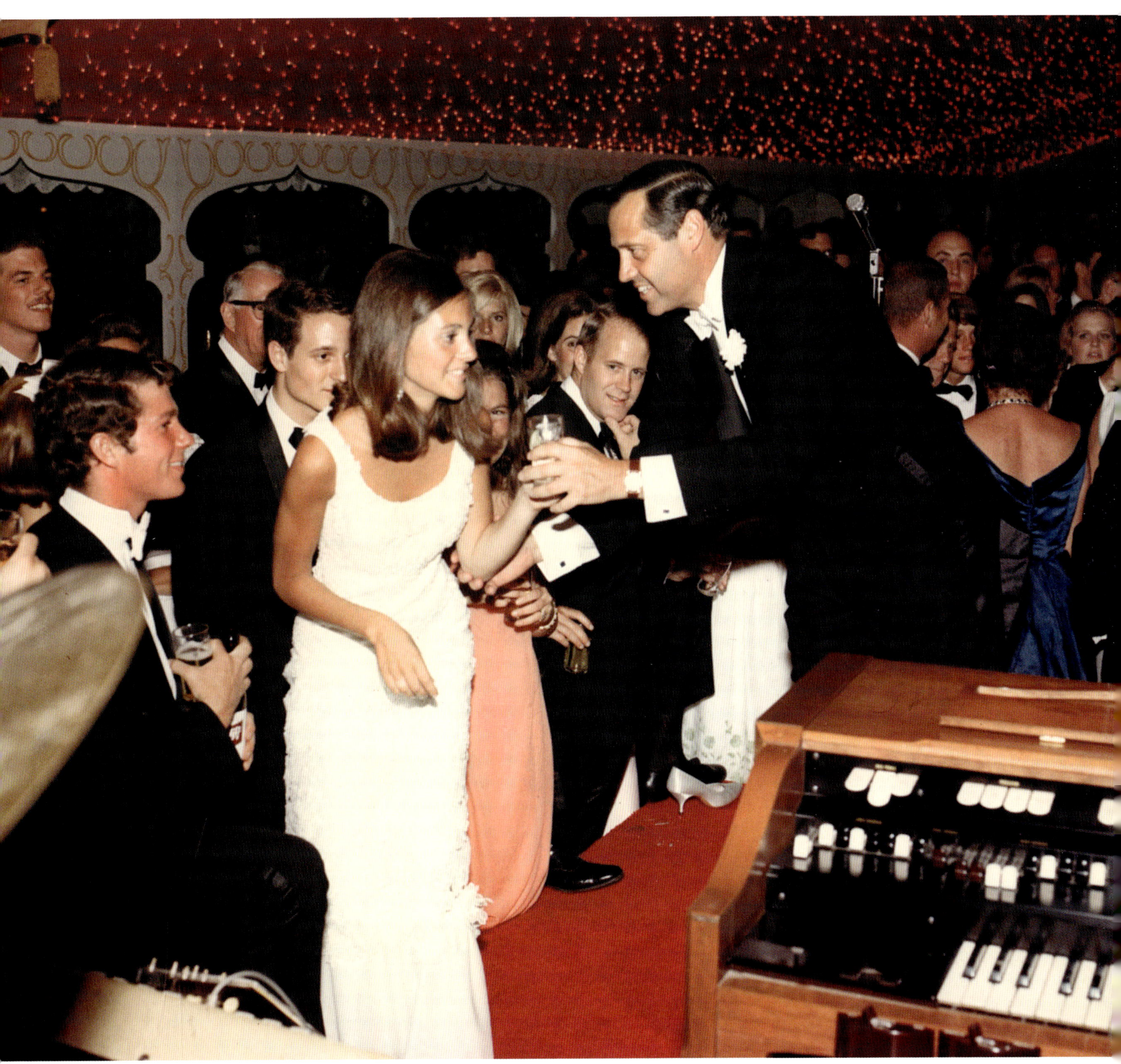

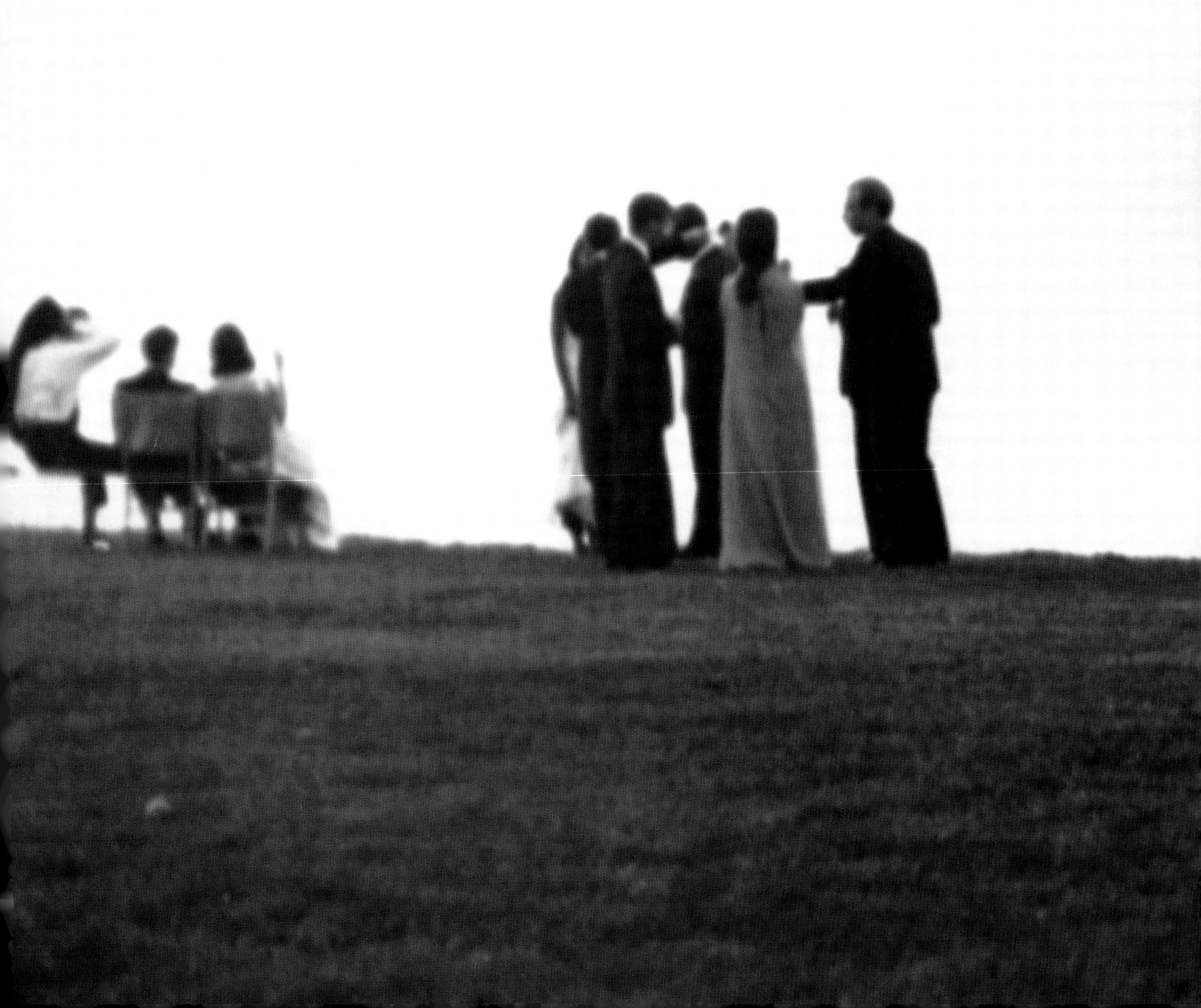

# ACKNOWLEDGEMENTS

I WANT TO FIRST THANK Marianne Strong who was a great source of help and support in the realization of this book. I also want to thank all the debutantes and/or their families that participated and included their photos in this wonderful collage of days gone by. I want to thank *Town & Country* magazine for their invaluable archive library—and for allowing me to spend hours on end looking through their leather bound volumes of past issues. I also want to thank Allison Power for her insight and tireless support, and everyone involved in helping to bring this little slice of glamour back in our lives.

# PHOTO CREDITS

Courtesy Jane Aldred: 12–13; Courtesy Hugh D. (Yusha) Auchincloss III: 19–22, 48–49, 137; Courtesy Lavinia Baker: 146; Courtesy Angela Brown: 116, 118–125; Courtesy Sharon Bush: 57, 71; Courtesy Tony Cointreau: 39; Courtesy Condé Nast images, Beaton/ *Vogue*; © Condé Nast: xiii; Courtesy Condé Nast images, Erickson/ *Vogue*; © Condé Nast: 38; Courtesy Condé Nast images, Frissell/ *Vogue*; © Condé Nast: 126, 128–129; Courtesy Condé Nast images, Gowronska/ *Vogue*; © Condé Nast: 74–75; Courtesy Condé Nast images, Horst/ *Vogue*; © Condé Nast: 36, 72, 83; Courtesy Condé Nast images, de Morgoli/ *Vogue*; © Condé Nast: 77; Courtesy Condé Nast images, Platt-Lynes/ *Vogue*; © Condé Nast: 32; Courtesy Condé Nast images, Rutledge/ *Vogue*; © Condé Nast: 35; Courtesy Condé Nast images, Steichen/ *Vogue*; © Condé Nast: 9, 127; Courtesy Maria Cooper: 54; Courtesy Wanda Corrado: x–xi; Courtesy Mazie Cox: ix, 30–31, 82, 104–107; Courtesy Alexandra Booth Cutchins: 56, 114–115; © Everett Collection: 3–5, 37, 59, 64–67, 78; Courtesy Nonie Ford: vii, 150–155; © Getty Images: pp. ii–iii, xvi, xviii, 10, 16, 26–27, 55, 63, 68–69, 76, 81, 88–89, 98–103, 110–113, 147; Courtesy Mary Henderson: 96–97; Courtesy Francine LeFrak: 24; Courtesy Victoria Leiter: v, 42–43; Courtesy Helen Michaelis: 90–91; Courtesy Tricia Nixon: 60–61; Courtesy Oates family: 79; Courtesy Pamela O'Conner: 148; Courtesy Pamela O'Connor © Bill Cunningham: 87; Courtesy the Author, Diana Oswald: 40–41; Courtesy Nicole du Pont: viii, 92–93; Courtesy Linda Ryan: 138–141; Courtesy Sheila Ryan: 84–85; Courtesy Rosalie Seller: 130–136, 158; Courtesy Julie Toland: 142–145; Courtesy *Town & Country* © Hearst Publications: 6–7, 25, 33, 44–45, 50–53, 108–109; Courtesy Sophie Trevor: 86; Courtesy Heather Whitney: 62; Courtesy Ginny Wright: 94–95.

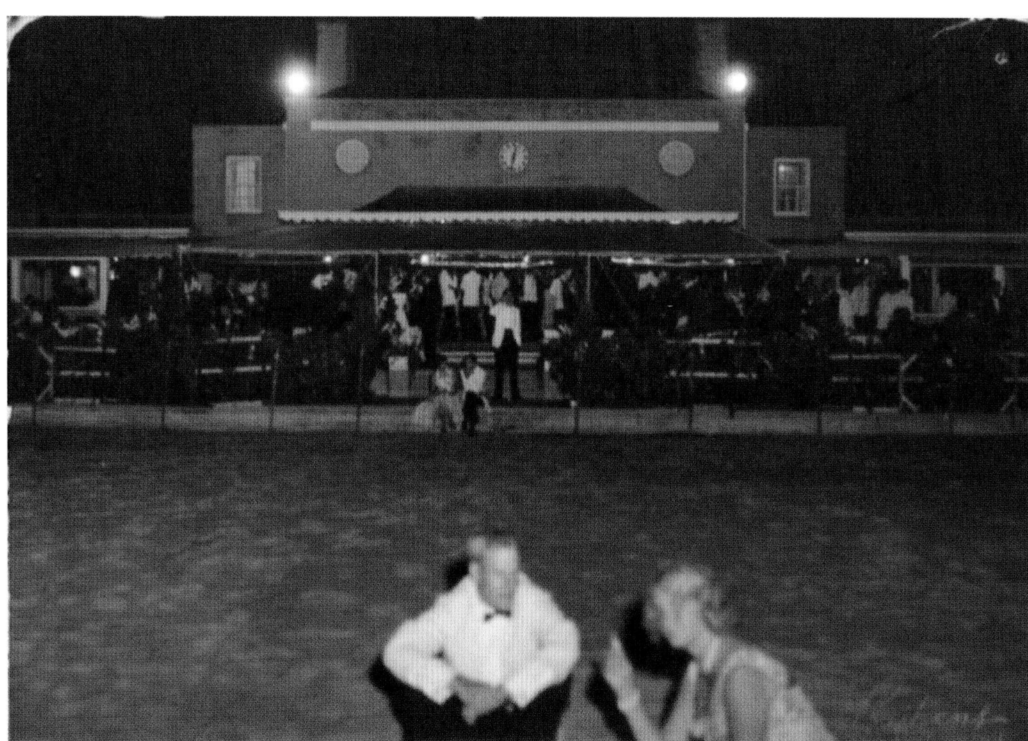

First published in the United States of America in 2013
by Rizzoli International Publications, Inc.
300 Park Avenue South
New York, NY 10010
www.rizzoliusa.com



2013 2014 2015 2016 / 10 9 8 7 6 5 4 3 2 1
Printed in China
ISBN: 978-0-8478-3787-8
Library of Congress Catalog Control Number: 2013941652

Frontispiece: Debutantes stand in a reception line at the Waldorf-Astoria Hotel. New York, 1944.

v: Final touches to debutante Victoria Leiter dress. Washington D.C., 1968.

vii: Debutante Nonie Ford, granddaughter of Edsel Ford, walks through a whimsical curtain of flowers at her party held at the Little Club. Grosse Pointe Farms, Michigan, 1966.

vii: Nicole du Pont. Wilmington Delaware, 1959.

ix: Mazie Cox with her brothers, Edward and Howard. New York, 1963.

x–xi: Wanda Corrado (7th from the right) and other debutantes of the season make their debut at the St. Regis Hotel. New York, 1951.